ORIGINS

By arrangement with BBC Books,
a division of BBC Enterprises Limited

ORIGINS

THE ROOTS OF EUROPEAN CIVILISATION

——EDITED BY——
BARRY CUNLIFFE

The Dorsey Press
Chicago, Illinois 60604

Cover photo: Minoan palace at Phaestos, Crete; Konrad Helbig/Zefa
Picture Library

Typeset in 11/13pt Sabon by Phoenix Photosetting, Chatham, Kent

Library of Congress Cataloging-in-Publication Data

Origins: the roots of European civilisation / edited by Barry
Cunliffe.
      p.   cm.
    Bibliography: p.
    Includes index.
    ISBN 0–256–07221–3 (pbk.)
    1. Europe—Civilisation. 2. Europe—History—To 476.
I. Cunliffe, Barry W.
D60.074 1988
940—dc19   88–29757
                                          CIP

Printed in the United States of America
1 2 3 4 5 6 7 8 9 0 ML 5 4 3 2 1 0 9 8

CONTENTS

ILLUSTRATIONS

COLOUR PHOTOGRAPHS (pp 85–100)

vii

PREFACE

MALCOLM BILLINGS

'The archaeologist . . . is the modern maker of ancient history and his work is the scientific technique of exploring the past from its material remains.' With those words the Cambridge archaeologist, Glyn Daniel, launched archaeology on BBC radio. On 13th October 1946 *The Archaeologist* series laid the foundation of a BBC commitment to broadcasting about archaeology that has lasted almost half-a-century.

Those early talks in the Sunday evening schedules of the Third Programme faced a formidable challenge: they had not only to describe and interpret current archaeological work, but also to dispel archaeology's image of 'a glamorous and expensive pastime for a few cranks'. Each week in the first series of eight programmes *The Archaeologist* sought to change public opinion. The scientific nature of archaeology was a constant theme in the fifteen-minute talks given by such distinguished exponents as Stuart Piggot, Grahame Clarke, Gordon Childe and, later, the ebullient Mortimer Wheeler. They introduced the radio audience to the techniques of excavation and the layers of pre-history in Western Europe that had been explored in the 1930s and early 1940s. They drew attention to new sites uncovered by wartime airfield construction: the remains of a Celtic temple at Heathrow; a rich collection of Iron Age weapons, currency bars, bridle bits and wheel tyres on Anglesey; and the floor of a Neolithic Long House at Ronaldsway on the Isle of Man. By the early 1950s those archaeological programmes produced by Gilbert Phelps had won a regular and popular place in the Third Programme and the West of England Home Service.

In 1952 the fledgling BBC television service borrowed the idea. Drawing on the success of *The Archaeologist*, Paul Johnstone launched the panel game *Animal, Vegetable or Mineral*, in which a panel of archaeologists, under the chairmanship of Glyn Daniel, had to identify unlabelled objects supplied by museums. This formula soon gathered a big following and, by 1954, Professor Sir Mortimer Wheeler had been awarded the accolade of Television Personality of the Year. Wheeler, who disarmingly introduced his broadcasting production colleagues as 'BBC scruffs', continued to appear as a radio archaeologist throughout the 1950s and 1960s; but in 1967 a new series called *Archaeologists on Site* took BBC microphones to excavations working in the field. Archaeological broadcasting had broken out of the studio.

At the time, an unprecedented number of sites was being dug by a hard-pressed corps of professional excavators. They were struggling to keep one step ahead of Britain's motorway construction; of the new high-rise concrete and glass developments that were gutting the medieval nuclei of many historic towns and cities; and of the new agricultural practices that were spreading across the landscape at an alarming rate, wiping out important archaeological sites. The broadcasters' response to this burst of activity was to introduce a new series called *The Changing Past*, a magazine programme, first broadcast in July 1968. It reflected the way in which new discoveries and improved scientific techniques were changing our perception of the past. Peter Fowler was the 'resident' archaeologist, and *The Changing Past* carefully charted the progress of the reorganisation and expansion of British archaeology as it responded to the increasing challenge of continuing development and an explosion of new archaeological sites. The story of 'Rescue' archaeology featured constantly in *The Changing Past* throughout the 1970s.

Origins succeeded 'The Changing Past' in July 1977 and marked a new BBC commitment to the broadcasting of archaeological subjects on radio. The number of programmes on Radio 4's network was doubled and the producer, Roy Hayward, was briefed to 'broaden the coverage from archaeological activity in Britain alone to world archaeology'. A welcome rebroadcast on the BBC World Service added twenty-five million to the *Origins* audience and, under the direction of Roy Hayward and, since 1983, John Knight, archaeologists digging up the past have been recorded at some of the world's most spectacular sites.

In 1978, *Origins* looked into the newly discovered and unplundered tomb of Philip of Macedon in Northern Greece (described by Richard Tomlinson in Chapter Nine) and raised the lid of the solid gold casket that contained the king's charred remains, wrapped in a purple cloth. The first feature on radio about the spectacular 'Pottery Warriors' of China's Emperor Qin Shih Huang Ti was broadcast in *Origins*. We took our microphones around the temples of Philae at the conclusion of a twenty years project to save them from the rising waters of the Nile. In its ten years, *Origins* has trekked with archaeologists in the foothills of the Himalayas, to the end of the Silk Road in China, along the Indus Valley in Pakistan, across the deserts of Jordan and Saudi Arabia to countless sites throughout the British Isles and around the classical world of the Mediterranean.

Should all those archaeological riches have been better left to the searching close-up and panoramic pictures of a television camera? I think not. Whilst television may seem to be the most likely mass medium for such tangible subjects, radio's archaeological pictures have been remarkably clear in transmission. The sounds of the locations: crawling along the galleries of a prehistoric flint mine in Poland, or the scrape of the excavator's trowel gently probing the cluster of bronze bracelets that survived with a 1000 B.C. skeleton of a child in Northern Thailand; the echoing footsteps across the marble floor of a Byzantine church; all these can evoke a picture as clear as any camera. And while a television shot ponderously pans across a subject, the radio audience can receive a dozen different ideas that give great breadth and depth to an archaeological story. Nothing could have been more graphic than the recordings John Knight and I made in a rubber dinghy, riding on a Mediterranean swell, along the coast near Syracuse: with waves crashing onto the rocky shore just fifty yards away, you could hear the anxiety in our voices and the sound of bubbles from the marine archaeologists as they dived on a third-century Roman ship. Almost two thousand years before a storm had tossed her against the cliff face and, as some of the artefacts were recovered from the sea bed and hoisted into the dinghy, the listener could surely feel the salt spray on his lips!

The collection of articles by leading archaeologists in this book celebrates *Origins* ten years of reporting from the studios of BBC Bristol on the world of archaeology. Although the scope and technique of archaeological broadcasting have changed markedly since Glyn Daniel's first encounter with a radio audience in 1946, his closing remarks almost half a century ago have not dated. 'Archaeology tells us the origins of so many of the elements of our culture, the roots of which lay buried long before history began. We are, I suppose, all interested to some extent in origins.'

INTRODUCTION

BARRY CUNLIFFE

Every minute of the day, somewhere in the world, new facts about our past are being unearthed. It is one of the great joys of being an archaeologist that the subject, and the data-base upon which it is constructed, changes so fast. But change is reflected not just in the accumulation of new pieces of information: the questions which archaeologists ask, indeed, the whole philosophy of the subject, is expanding out of all recognition.

There are many popular stereotypes of archaeology. A few years ago it would have been the ageing academic in khaki shorts directing gangs of natives as they hacked soil away from ruins, or the desiccated scholar tucked away in the corner of a dusty museum categorising the depiction of athletes' calf muscles on Greek vases. Nowadays, it is more likely to be attractive young women in rubber wetsuits diving on wrecks, or bearded men in lab coats peering through microscopes at the wings of dung beetles from Iron Age middens. Most caricatures have a grain of truth. Archaeologists do indeed have to operate at many levels. To extract a body of new data they must work on a macroscale, undertaking arduous field surveys or long-term excavations, but they must always complement this with work on the microscale – the minute analysis of the material recovered.

What is seldom depicted in these popular stereotypes, however, is what archaeology is really all about – the painstaking reconstruction of the development of human society, showing how communities evolved complex systems (political, social and economic) to enable them to establish a degree of equilibrium with their environment, including, of course, other communities. These studies lead to a recognition of the general laws controlling social behaviour – in short, they provide us with an explanation of ourselves. Seen against this perspective it becomes possible to appreciate why the work of archaeologists proves so fascinating – both to themselves and to others.

In the last ten years the BBC Radio 4 programme *Origins*, produced first by Roy Hayward and later by John Knight, has attempted to report archaeological endeavour throughout the world, and in so doing it has built up an ardent and enthusiastic following among professionals and amateurs alike. Its great strength has been its reliance on professional archaeologists to tell the stories of their own work. There is an immediacy about this which is compelling: the listener is in direct contact with the cutting edge of the subject.

This book is a celebration of *Origins*. An attempt has been made to retain the quality of the radio programmes by asking some of the archaeologists who have contributed to the broadcasts to write a chapter on their work. Inevitably in a book of this size, much has had to be left out in order to give cohesion to what remains. Geographically, we have restricted ourselves to Europe and, chronologically, to the period from the origins of food production in the seventh millennium BC to the early years of the Roman Empire. It is a colossal span, but the contributions have been selected to reflect, as fairly as possible, both the time range and the geographical spread. A motif that is threaded through the book is that of the archaeologist at work, asking questions, extracting data, examining it, and building the results into an interconnecting picture of human society. Methodological jargon and technical trivia have been left out in the belief (with Wittgenstein) that 'Everything that can be said can be said clearly.'

To generalise about something as complex as the evolution of European society is very dangerous and yet, standing back from the mass of detail, a very simple general pattern can be detected – three great cycles of development, each building upon the one before. The first began in the seventh millennium with the spread of systems of food production from the Near East, first into Anatolia and the Aegean and later, by *c.* 3000 BC, throughout most of Europe. Later, in the Aegean, precocious development led to the emergence of Minoan-Mycenaean civilisation – the first to root itself in Europe. This core of vibrant innovation influenced, in various degrees, the peripheral barbarian areas of Europe. All were interlinked by complex social and economic networks which continuously evolved until the thirteenth century BC, when the core systems collapsed and the larger social groupings disintegrated in the mêlée of migrations known as the Greek Dark Age.

Out of the detritus left by the collapse of the Mycenaean world the second cycle, Graeco-Roman civilisation, emerged. The earliest developments, in Greece and the Aegean coast of Asia Minor, quickened in the eighth century BC and reached a spectacular peak in fifth-century Athens, after which the centre of innovation passed to what had been the periphery, to Macedonia (very briefly) and to Italy, where Rome became the new core. By the end of the second century BC the Roman core had grown to include the entire Mediterranean and by the end of the second century AD what had been the European periphery, northward to the Rhine–Danube line, had also been engulfed. Two hundred years later Graeco-Roman civilisation was disintegrating in a new chaos of folk movement and migration – the Early Medieval Dark Age.

The third cycle – Western European civilisation – grew from the ruins. Apparent by the eighth century AD, it had reached great heights of achievement in the fifteenth century, when new peripheries began to develop in America and Africa. Where we have gone since then, and where we are going, is an intriguing theme but, sadly, beyond the scope of this book.

Generalisations are dangerous. History does not repeat itself – it cannot, because the scale and complexity of the situation are constantly expanding – but since our environment is circumscribed and the range of human behaviour is limited it is hardly surprising that certain regularities can be detected from time to time. Indeed, it is one of the fascinations of archaeology that its vast perspective encourages us to think on a grand scale.

Note: In this book dates are quoted in two ways, as bc and BC. The latter refers to absolute years as accurately as they can be estimated using historical evidence of various kinds. The dates quoted as bc are estimates based on radiocarbon dates. These are now known not to be absolute and before about 3000 bc may be several centuries too late. We have made no attempt here to calibrate them.

CHAPTER ONE

AEGEAN CIVILISATION AND BARBARIAN EUROPE

BARRY CUNLIFFE

The transformation from food-gathering to food production was a process of crucial significance to the development of European society. Before the threshold had been reached, communities remained comparatively small and mobile, their lives geared to the seasonal movements of animals. At some stage during the year the groups would have had to split into small hunting bands, while at other times the bands would have coalesced at seasonal camps. A rhythm of life existed, established generations before and learnt from birth by each new generation. Between the seasonal movements and the hunting there was time to sit and to be creative – the cave art of France and Spain bears ample witness to artistic ability, and even in extreme conditions, as in the Arctic fringe, groups of Eskimos have become renowned for the quality of their stone-carving.

Established hunter-gatherer economies, in the past and, in some parts of the world, until quite recently, were usually well adapted to their environments but required space and a degree of environmental stability if they were to remain in a state of equilibrium. In the distant past two principal factors could upset that equilibrium and cause rapid changes: increase in population size and climatic change affecting the natural habitat. The first could be controlled by social mechanisms but the only responses to the second were either movement away from the affected region or adaptation.

The period following the end of the Ice Age was a time of environmental readjustment for much of the world and in consequence hunter-gatherer communities were constantly having to move or to modify their behaviour to meet the changing conditions. One of the areas in which highly significant adaptation took place was the Near East. The process of change was long drawn out; at each stage it was accompanied only by slight shifts in the economic strategy and of these the grossly incomplete archaeological record allows us only brief glimpses – it is rather like having to construct a movie film from the surviving scraps of a few individual frames. Yet these tiny shifts were of vital significance to world history.

Among the earliest modification that can be recognised was the selection of certain local animals for domestication. At Nahal Oren,

Mount Carmel (Israel), in levels dating to 16,500 bc, 74 per cent of the animal bones found were gazelle while a little later, at Wadi Madamagli near Petra (Jordan), in levels dating to 11,000 bc, 82 per cent of the animal bones recovered were goat. By c. 8000 bc a number of sites in the Near East were showing similar specialisation. While it would be wrong to be too dogmatic about crude statistics such as these the most reasonable implication would seem to be that a man/animal symbiosis was beginning to emerge, with human communities exercising a degree of control and protection over flocks and herds. Further evidence that this was so comes from Zawi Chemi in Iraq, where, in about 8000 bc, large numbers of sheep were found, of which a high percentage were very young. This suggests a deliberate control over the composition of the flock by seasonal culling.

By 8000 bc there is, then, reasonable evidence to suggest that the movement towards domestication was well underway in the Near East. At about the same time, other changes can begin to be detected. The appearance of quernstones (for grinding grain) and stone sickles, glossed along the cutting edges by the silica grains in the stems of grasses, strongly suggest that emmer wheat and two-row barley, growing wild in the hills, were being selectively collected for food. It was only a matter of time before wild grain brought back to the home site and accidentally spilled was seen to germinate and grow. The next step – the deliberate sowing of grain in tended plots protected from animals – must have followed soon. Man had now become a cultivator.

Both processes, domestication and cultivation, would have involved selection. A flock of young sheep would have been manipulated by culling and castration to enable a well-balanced breeding flock to be maintained. By carefully selecting those to be killed as juveniles, weaklings could be removed and the strength of the flock improved. The analysis of skeletal remains gives evidence of physical changes of this kind gradually taking place. Similar processes were involved in the selection of cereals. Those that survived to be collected and stored, both as food and seed corn, were those in which the ear was strong and the grain firmly attached. Here selection was more accidental, but in the long term it was no less beneficial.

The movement towards a food-producing, as opposed to a food-collecting, economy brought with it other significant changes. Crops had to be maintained and guarded from predators – including other men – while the grain collected in the autumn had to be stored so that a supply of seed corn was available for the next sowing. Inevitably, then, the community moved towards a more sedentary way of life and seasonal camps gave way to permanent villages.

One of the most dramatic of these villages at present known to us is Jericho. The oasis site was already occupied in the ninth millennium bc, and by about 8000 bc or soon after it had grown large enough to be

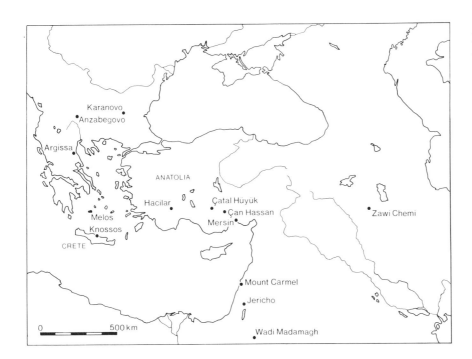

1.1 Major Neolithic and Bronze Age sites in the Eastern Mediterranean and Near East

classed as a town, reaching the remarkable size of four hectares and possessing a four-metre high stone defensive wall. Its site was a particularly favoured one, commanding an oasis surrounded by fertile land where emmer wheat, hulled two-row barley and lentils were grown to supplement the diet of hunted meat (there is no positive evidence of domestication at this stage). No doubt it gained in importance by virtue of its position as a watering place for migrant bands or hunting communities. Such people would probably account for the occurrence, at Jericho, of fine blades of obsidian – a black volcanic glass, brought ultimately from central Anatolia.

In our present state of knowledge, the size and sophistication of Jericho at such an early date makes it unique. Nevertheless, it should be seen as simply one element in an expanding pattern of food-producing communities spreading across the Near East and into Anatolia. By the seventh millennium the area was blanketed with a patchwork of small villages relying on the cultivation of emmer and barley and maintaining flocks and herds of sheep, goats, pigs and cattle. Economic strategies varied quite considerably from place to place, and by no means all of the possible cultivates or domesticates were adopted by every community, but a farming existence – the Neolithic pattern – had become firmly established.

Anatolia (modern Turkey) soon became the centre of remarkable developments of its own, unique, kind. High on the Konya Plain a large town developed at Çatal Hüyük, the total occupied area approaching 13 hectares. The earliest levels have not yet been examined but by *c.* 6300 bc the settlement comprised a close-packed mass of rectangular-roomed houses accessible only from their roofs. Shrines containing mounted bulls' horns and ornamented with painted and moulded plaster abound. The economy was based on fully dom-esticated cattle as well as cereals, including a hybrid bread-wheat. More impressive still is the evidence for long-distance trade which brought to the site a range of imported stone, including obsidian from a source 200 kilometres away. Indeed, it is even possible that Çatal Hüyük owed its evident prosperity to its ability to control the movement of this rare and much sought-after volcanic glass. The community was also productive in its own right, creating a range of wool and linen textiles.

On present evidence, Çatal Hüyük lies at the beginning of an urban system which continued to develop in Anatolia in the fifth millennium at sites like Hacilar, Çan Hassan (both inland) and Mersin on the coast. But the precocious quality of Çatal Hüyük about 6000 bc strongly suggests that this stage came as the culmination of a long period of local Neolithic development, the details of which at present remain obscure.

It was probably from Anatolia that knowledge of food production spread to the Aegean and to the European mainland. On Crete, deep beneath the courtyard of the palace of Knossos, early occupation levels dating to 6100 bc have been found, representing an early food-producing economy: cattle, sheep and pigs were raised, while barley and bread-wheat were the main staples. The inhabitants lived in small rectangular mud-built houses. Where they came from, and in what numbers, it is not yet possible to say, but in all probability what we are seeing here is an early stage in a movement not only of people but also of their breeding stock and seed corn, emanating from the coastal regions of Anatolia. They sailed through the Aegean, settling on many of its islands and around the Aegean coasts of Greece wherever suitable land was to be found.

Stating it in this way is, of course, a great oversimplification. The movements must have spread over 1500 to 2000 years. Some communi-ties, possibly many, would have foundered, while others would have interbred with already well-established communities, thus losing their original identity. The more successful enclaves quite probably main-tained links with the homeland over many generations and these would have become formalised into regular trading connections. In this way rare commodities, such as the obsidian from the island of Melos passed into the hands of the villagers at Morali, 80 kilometres inland from the Aegean coast of Turkey.

Further hints of these maintained contacts come from Greek settlements of the Plain of Thessaly. At Argissa, a stratified sequence of deposits showed that the earliest community here was without pottery. Later, a crude, possibly local, pottery was developed and only in the higher levels are more sophisticated wares found with red-on-white painted designs. These are similar to vessels from the Anatolian site of Hacilar dating to the end of the fifth millennium. While it would be wrong to argue too closely from data of this kind, one interpretation would seem to be that the early settlers arrived with their knowledge of agriculture and established a farming system, their successors remaining in contact with Anatolia for many hundreds of years. Perhaps the simplest way to understand these early Aegean Neolithic settlements is to see them simply as a geographical extension of Anatolia linked by complex networks of social and economic obligation.

From the Aegean the practice of food production spread throughout Europe. Two principal routes can be traced: one by sea around the coasts of the central and western Mediterranean, and the other across the Balkans to the river systems of the Danube and Rhine.

The spread of food-producing economies to the western Mediterranean presents some fascinating problems. A recent batch of radiocarbon dates from Italy, Corsica and southern France shows that animal-herding communities using pottery stamped with the impressions of cardial shells were living in the coastal regions as early as 6200–5600 bc but only later, in the fifth millennium, are barley, wheat, sheep and goats to be found. If this evidence is sustained by further work the implication would seem to be that the knowledge of pottery-making and herding (of indigenous animals) preceded the importation of seed corn and breeding stock of Asiatic origin by some hundreds of years. Once more the process would seem to be one of progressive acculturation, lasting over many tens of generations.

The penetration of temperate Europe is no less complex. From the Plain of Thessaly and Greek Macedonia food-producing economies were transported through the Rhodope and Balkan mountains to the plains and undulating hills of the lower Danube basin. The spread, from a Mediterranean to a temperate climate, brought with it necessary changes to the economic strategies. At the site of Anzabegovo in the watershed of the Vardar River in Yugoslavia the earliest levels, dating to 5200 bc, showed many cultural links with the Aegean – the same house types and the presence of imported spondylus shells from which ornaments were made – but most of the stone used was from local sources. The subsistence economy relied on a wide range of cultivates – emmer wheat together with two other types of wheat, einkorn and club wheat, as well as hulled six-row barley, peas and lentils. Most of the domesticated animals represented in the midden were sheep and goats but cattle and pigs were also quite common. The overall impression given by all this evidence is of a community well established and exploiting its local environment to the full.

By about 5000 bc much of eastern Europe – Bulgaria, Romania and parts of Hungary and Yugoslavia – had developed a broadly similar Neolithic economy in equilibrium with the local environment. In many areas a stability had been established which allowed the development of one settlement on another – each phase of rebuilding, on the detritus of its predecessor, giving rise to massive tells (mounds built up from successive habitation debris) like that at Karanovo in Bulgaria, which eventually reached a height of 13 metres. These great mounds symbolise the victory of the early farmers over their environment.

From the lower and middle Danube valley food-producing communities spread rapidly across temperate Europe, for the most part exploiting the light, easily worked loess soils of the Danube and Rhine basins. What motivated the move is difficult to say but population pressure may well have been a significant factor. Once more, men were moving into a new ecological zone requiring different economic strategies. Much of the region was heavily forested: undergrowth was cut and burnt, leaving many of the larger trees standing, and the soil between them, newly fertilized with the ash, was broken for the first time to allow the crops to be sown. Trees of the appropriate size were cut and set aside for the construction of the massively built long houses which characterised the settlements – houses suitable for an extended family and its stock. The pottery of their colonial settlements, decorated with simple inscribed lines, provides the archaeological name of the culture – *linearbandkeramic* – or Linear Pottery culture.

What is perhaps most remarkable about this culture is the speed of its advance. In barely 700 years it had spread from Romania to northern France and from Poland to the Alps. By 4000 bc much of Holland was already colonised. The socio-economic systems which motivated so rapid a movement are, in detail, beyond recovery, but the evidence which is becoming available from a number of excavations and studies suggests that in the first instance the settlements advanced after a few years because of decreasing fertility; only after a period of regeneration was the vegetation in the wake of the advance cut again and old homesteads reoccupied. This is much what would be expected as communities came to terms with the new environment in which they found themselves and learnt to modify their strategies so as not to exhaust the soil too drastically.

By 4000 bc, then, the Mediterranean fringes and a vast territory in central and western Europe had come under the sway of communities able to produce their own food. Within these core areas settled communities began to develop a great diversity, reflected in both their economies and their decorative styles – particularly the ornamentation of their pottery. Stability brought with it specialisation and a sense of ethnic identity.

Alongside this there was further advance into central and northern Iberia, central France and Switzerland and northwards across Britain, and into southern Scandinavia and European Russia. By about 3200 bc the whole of Europe, except for northern Scandinavia (that is up to the latitude of about 62°N), was occupied by communities practising a Neolithic food-producing economy. In the following centuries their diversity became enormous – the seashore dwellers of Denmark, the 'lake villagers' of France and Switzerland, the creators of the great passage graves of the Boyne valley in Ireland – the picture is as varied as it is fascinating.

Each region, and indeed each site, that is examined on a large enough scale has an immense amount to tell. It is for this reason that the beginnings of settled agriculture in Europe have been the subject of considerable archaeological activity, particularly in the last 30 years or so. The development of the radiocarbon dating technique has freed archaeologists from the need to establish relative sequences and synchronisms by means of studying changes in different types of artefact. The time and energy previously spent in this pursuit is now being used to examine the social and economic systems which bound and linked these early communities together: the example examined by John Howell in 'Neolithic Lake Villages of France' shows what can be achieved.

While food-producing communities were spreading across the face of temperate and northern Europe the next major advance – the emergence of the first European civilisation – was well underway in the Aegean. Of the many factors that were no doubt involved in this remarkable process one of prime significance was the intensification of trade. The towns that were already long-established in Anatolia, and especially in the Troad (northwestern Turkey), were centres of production vying with each other for power. The best known example of this is Troy – a small town, early fortified, that may have been the base of a powerful local chieftain. In such a society, control of rare raw materials was a way of controlling power. Gold, silver, copper, tin and lapis lazuli were all much in demand, along with a range of other commodities. To supply them a complex network of reciprocal exchange developed, drawing in the Aegean sphere and land beyond – Egypt and the North African coast for example. The Aegean islands were particularly productive: Melos yielded the much-revered obsidian which, as we have seen, was exploited at an early date; silver came from Siphnos; high-grade white marble from Paros. The significance of the islands is explored further by John Cherry in the next chapter.

Crete played an increasingly important role in these developing exchange networks. This was a large, comparatively fertile island with well-established farming communities. Even more important was its central position on the major sea routes linking the Near East with Europe and North Africa with Asia Minor. Gradually, as the brilliant Neolithic culture of the Aegean islands waned, Crete began to rise in importance.

Some 4000 years after the first Neolithic farmers had established themselves on Crete there emerged a flamboyant 'palace-centred' society with all the characteristics of a civilisation – complex socio-political organisation, monumental architecture, distinctive art styles and writing. The island seems to have been divided into a number of territories in each of which there was a 'palace' – a large ornate building serving as an administrative and economic centre for its region. Massive storage capacity, mainly for olive oil, complex record-keeping and skilled craft production, are all attested, showing that one of the prime functions of these palaces was to serve as centres of redistribution for locally produced and imported products.

Much has been written about the Minoan society of Crete since Sir Arthur Evans made his first investigations at Knossos at the turn of the century. Data accumulates in quantity, studies of artefact forms refine the chronologies, theories about the nature of the society come and go, but most agree that the Minoan world, seen through its art and architecture, was vibrantly energetic, and a love of the natural world – light, space, vistas, plants and animals – is everywhere to be seen. Against this background some of the recent discoveries made at Minoan shrines, suggesting human sacrifice, come as something of a surprise: here is an aspect of society that few would have suspected. Peter Warren surveys the new evidence in 'Crete: The Minoans and Their Gods'. It is a reminder that archaeological research, even the study of a culture as well known as that of Crete, is very much in its infancy, and that there is still much to be learnt.

The high peak of Minoan culture, the Palatial period, lasted for a brief 500 years (from 1900 BC to 1375 BC). It was during this time that there emerged on the Greek mainland a brilliant barbaric culture known to archaeologists as Mycenaean, after the great citadel at Mycenae. The two principal foci of Mycenaean power were Messinia in western Greece, dominated by the palace at Pylos, and the Plain of Argos, where the citadels of Mycenae and Tiryns were located.

Mycenaean culture owed much to Minoan civilisation, particularly as regards craftsmanship and painting, yet it was distinct in its own right, emerging from the indigenous Middle Helladic culture of the Greek Bronze Age. The architecture of its palaces, for example, grew not from the palaces of Crete but from a type of house, known as a *megeron*, which can be traced back to the Greek Neolithic. Moreover, Mycenaean culture was decidedly warlike. In paintings and relief carvings, the armed warrior and the war chariot are much in evidence, and excavations have brought to light a formidable array of weapons and armour. All this is in dramatic contrast to our conception of Minoan culture on Crete.

By about 1600 BC the inhabitants of Mycenae were burying their elite in shaft graves furnished with a rich array of grave goods including gold face masks. Two groups have been found, the most spectacular of which are the six burials found in Grave Circle A by Heinrich Schliemann in 1876. So convinced was he, on uncovering one of the gold masks, that he had found the tombs of Homer's heroes, that he is said to have telegraphed to the King of Greece, 'Today I have looked upon the face of Agamemnon.' As is now well-known, his enthusiasm was misplaced: even supposing the Agamemnon of Homer's epic to have been an historical figure, the mask Schliemann had found can be dated 300 or 400 years earlier.

The power of the Mycenaean dynasts continued to grow and in the fourteenth century BC we find them enclosing the citadel at Mycenae with a massive defensive wall, built in Cyclopean masonry and entered through the famous Lion Gate: the way that visitors enter today. Just outside lay the contemporary tombs – high beehive structures built of corbelled masonry finely dressed to an even curve and approached by a long passageway or *dromos*. The architecture for the living and the dead is redolent of power.

While the Mycenaean leaders of the Greek mainland were developing their distinctive chiefdoms, the Minoans on Crete were suffering various setbacks. Massive earthquakes in *c.* 1750 BC and 1500 BC, followed by the cataclysmic eruption of the volcano of Thera on the island of Santorini a few decades later, caused extensive damage and destruction which some archaeologists believe greatly weakened the Minoan economy. At any event soon after this Knossos rose again, although this time apparently under the domination of a Mycenaean authority, for this is the implication of the sudden increase in Mycenaean pottery, the appearance of weapon burials and the introduction of the Greek language for accounting purposes preserved now in the famous Linear B tablets which replaced the non-Greek Linear A script. A hundred years later, *c.* 1375 BC, Knossos fell, quite probably as the result of enemy attack, and Minoan civilisation was at an end.

This story, so briefly outlined here, has been built up by the painstaking research of archaeologists and linguists over the last hundred years or so, and we can now begin to see the development of individual sites like Mycenae and Knossos as part of a much broader pattern of social and economic change in the Aegean world. The Palatial culture of Crete was the culmination of a number of developments going back into the Neolithic period. Favoured by her natural resources and central position, Crete became a focus for production and distribution in the second millennium. Crete was the core, and around the periphery, particularly on the Greek mainland, local communities serving as middlemen in the acquisition and transport of commodities grew rich. The most spectacular were the Mycenaean enclaves of Greece. The war-lords of the Plain of Argos controlled the routes northwards into central and eastern Europe where rich supplies of metals were to be had, while those who dominated Messinia on the western edge of the Peloponnese were able to oversee trade northwards along the Adriatic and westwards to the central Mediterranean and beyond. To begin with, the Mycenaeans constituted a peripheral zone to the Minoan core, and beyond them, deep into barbarian Europe, their influence was felt by indigenous communities who straddled trade routes or commanded resources. A new interpretation of these fascinating relationships is given by Andrew Sherratt in 'Warriors and Traders: Bronze Age Chiefdoms in Central Europe'.

It may have been the successive natural disasters suffered by Crete that so weakened the Minoan core, or it may have been the growing power of the Mycenaean periphery. In any event, by the middle of the fifteenth century BC, the centre of power now lay with the Mycenaeans – in other words, the innovative core had now shifted northwards to mainland Greece.

The succeeding centuries saw the further spread of Mycenaean influence to a new, far-flung periphery. Mycenaean pottery has been found in the east at Miletus on the Anatolian coast, at the court of Akhenaten at Tell el-Amarna in Egypt, northwards at Iolkos in Thessaly and in the west at several sites on Sicily and in Italy as far north as the island of Ischia in the Bay of Naples. Some of these sites may even have been colonial settlements of Mycenaean traders – the point is debatable – but what they do represent at the very least is the interface between Mycenaean trading systems and the world beyond.

In the middle of the thirteenth century BC the old order began to crumble. The full reasons will never be known, nor will we ever be able to reconstruct even the principal events in any detail, but in a brief period of less than a century Europe's first civilisation – the Minoan-Mycenaean civilisation – collapsed and disappeared. In the same series of interlinked events the Hittite Empire of Anatolia disintegrated, while Egypt, also under attack, managed to survive.

The archaeological evidence for this collapse is dramatic. On mainland Greece most of the Mycenaean cities came to an end some time about 1200 BC and in a number of cases there is evidence that they had been sacked. At the same time the population seems to have declined rapidly. Similar wholesale destruction and abandonment can be traced among the coastal cities of the Levantine coast (Syria, Lebanon and Israel), and at sites on the Aegean coast of Anatolia, at Troy and Miletus. Inland, the Hittite cities suffered in the same way.

Contemporary Egyptian texts fill out the picture. In 1230 BC, and again in 1190 BC, miscellaneous bands of people in loose confederacy swept down on the Delta in a series of raids. These Sea Peoples, as they were called, were beaten off by Ramesses III, and Egypt survived. Among those listed were the Akawasha. These were the same as the Ahhiyawa, listed by the Hittites and the Achaioi – the name Homer uses for the Mycenaean Greeks. Thus, among the marauders in the eastern Mediterranean were boatloads of Mycenaeans. On Cyprus several

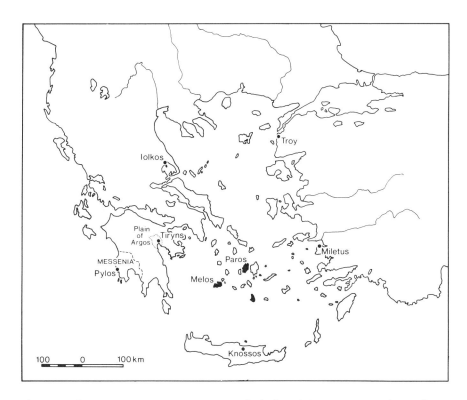

1.2 Bronze Age sites in the Aegean

destroyed native sites were resettled by Mycenaeans, but these settlements too ended in destruction.

There have been many theories about the cause of the thirteenth-century collapse. Many writers favour the view that the migrations of northern peoples down into Greece and into Hittite territory so disrupted the already unstable socio-economic structure that there was a total collapse of all systems. The Hittite Empire and the Mycenaean world disintegrated into a mêlée of warring, mobile factions who rampaged through the length and breadth of the eastern Mediterranean for two or three generations, destroying, looting and sometimes settling. It is a reflection of these times, or a prelude to them, that Homer records in the stories of the *Odyssey* and the *Iliad*.

At the end of it all the world was a very different place. Admittedly, Egypt remained, but it was now an isolated kingdom in a state of decline. Elsewhere, the vacuum caused by the disappearance of the centralised systems of the Mycenaean and Hittite worlds was gradually filled by small isolated communities, sometimes in limited confeder-ation. The old trade networks had gone and isolation had set in. The first great cycle in the development of Europe which had begun in the seventh millennium BC was over by about 1150 BC but as we shall see in 'Lefkandi and the Greek Dark Age', the detritus left in Greece was to provide a fertile seed bed in which the next cycle could begin to germinate.

CHAPTER TWO

ISLAND ORIGINS: THE EARLY PREHISTORIC CYCLADES

J.F. CHERRY

It is a very odd thought that visitors to the Greek islands, were they able to travel back in time as little as 8000 years or so, would find them free not only of holidaymakers in search of sea, sand, sun and fun, but of *all* human beings. On Delos, Naxos, Rhodes, Crete and elsewhere, they would not see people, but a bizarre collection of animals found only on the Mediterranean islands: pygmy elephants no taller than a man, pig-sized hippos, dwarf deer and antelope, and – equally strange – mice and other rodents of gigantic proportions. Simply because getting there is difficult, small islands, such as those of the Cyclades, represent unusual environments, supporting a far less varied range of plant and animal species than does an equivalent area on the mainland. With less competition for limited food resources, and particularly without carnivores, hippos could afford to abandon their aquatic environment and live safely on land, deer had less need of speed to escape, and rodents too large to escape detection by hiding in crevices could survive perfectly well. In the absence of predators, evolution allowed some remarkable morphological changes.

Although some of these animals no doubt arrived later by swimming across from the mainland or by clinging to rafts of drifting vegetation,

2.1 Pleistocene pygmy elephants from the Mediterranean islands: no taller than a man

the ancestral endemics probably reached the islands between six and seven million years ago, during times when the straits of Gibraltar were closed and the whole Mediterranean dried up to become a salty desert. Man, of course, was not around then, or even much later, to make the crossing: southern Europe and the lands around the Mediterranean were not permanently colonised until some time in the period between 500,000 and 200,000 years ago. Yet, on this timescale, the *islands* did not acquire humans until very much more recently. On present evidence, the earliest occupations, on Crete and Cyprus, belong to the Neolithic period some 8000 or 9000 years ago, and they are characterised from the beginning by the presence of non-native domesticated animals and the practice of agriculture. In the Cyclades, on which I focus in this chapter, the pattern is still more striking, since it has become clear, as a result of nearly a century of exploration, that the earliest finds on most of these islands are no older than the Early Bronze Age (roughly, the late fourth to late third millennium BC). Once the first farmers were established, however, they were remarkably successful, quickly spreading to virtually all the islands, no matter how small and unpromising, engaging in widespread maritime trade and exchange, and producing memorable objects such as the vessels and figurines of white marble which today grace the shelves of museums throughout much of the Western world. In a few cases, they developed as small centres, arguably the first towns in the Mediterranean, and similarly modest settlements in Crete laid the foundations of the Minoan Palatial civilisation shortly after 2000 BC.

The archaeologist, then, faces a double puzzle. Firstly, why did man reach the islands so very much later than other animals, and why, by comparison with adjacent mainland areas, was settlement delayed for so long in what to us appear attractive environments? Secondly, why did such rapid cultural developments take place in the islands, rather than in parts of the Greek mainland where permanent settlements had flourished for many thousands of years longer?

At first sight, a plausible answer to the first question might be lack of suitable transport: without adequate boats, people simply could not get to the islands, even though many of them are clearly visible from the mainland on clear days. Unfortunately, our earliest information about prehistoric seacraft in the Aegean – apparently dug-out, oared longboats – dates from the Early Cycladic period, *after* the settlement of the islands; it consists of simple models of lead or clay, and crude sketches scratched on pottery vessels or pecked on stone. But it is simply a form of temporal chauvinism on our part to suppose that early people in the Aegean were incapable of constructing boats able to make the relatively modest crossings involved. After all, prehistoric settlers successfully navigated 80–100 kilometres of open sea to reach Australia some 40,000–50,000 years ago.

2.2 Marble figure of the Folded-Arm type, Syros Group: Early Cycladic period

2.3 Representations of early Cycladic longships: (above) incised on Early Bronze Age clay 'frying pans' from Syros; (below) pecked on a stone slab from Naxos, apparently showing a man driving an animal on board an early Cycladic boat

In fact, there is new archaeological evidence, of an indirect sort, to show that man *did* have the ability to travel amongst the Greek islands many thousands of years before they were actually settled. American archaeologists excavating in the southern Argolid peninsula of Greece at the Franchthi cave, a site with a remarkable sequence of levels spanning the period from 25,000 to 5000 years ago, have recently reported small quantities of obsidian in layers dated by carbon-14 as early as the 11th millennium BC. This seemingly insignificant discovery is of real importance, for obsidian – a highly valued volcanic glass used for making tools – has only one major source in the Aegean, on the Cycladic island of Melos, some 130 kilometres to the southeast across open water. Chemical and trace-element analyses of the obsidian from Franchthi, conducted by Professor Colin Renfrew and various colleagues, have shown that it did, indeed, come from Melos, presumably by boat.

We should not rush to the conclusion that long-distance overseas travel was normal, already in the Palaeolithic period: then, as later, navigators probably preferred to travel by landmarks, hopping from island to island and avoiding the traverse of expanses of open water. Nor was the geography of land and sea then the same as today, for there have been substantial changes of shoreline as a result of sea-level rise since the height of the last Ice Age about 20,000 years ago. The latest reconstructions reveal a very strange-looking Greece, with many of the islands joined to each other or to the mainland by landbridges. Melos, nonetheless, was an island even in late Pleistocene times, and the prehistoric hunters and gatherers of the Franchthi cave would probably have got there by travelling overland to Attica or Euboea and thence by sea along the 'western string' of Cycladic islands. It seems probable that the first visitors to Melos can scarcely have known in advance that an abundant, easily worked source of obsidian existed on this island alone, among so many scattered over the Aegean. Does this not force us to assume that it was merely a chance by-product of a much more widespread pattern of movement and exploration among the islands of which the archaeological record, so far, gives no obvious hint? And does it not also imply that many, if not all, of the Mediterranean islands could have been reached and settled many millennia before the majority were, in fact, first inhabited?

That conclusion is perhaps not surprising. Palaeolithic hunters would have found the dwarf elephants, deer and hippos easy prey – too easy, in fact, for these animals have a low reproductive rate and would quickly have been hunted to extermination. Continuous human settlement was thus not possible on the islands before the advent of animal husbandry and agriculture. The domestic livestock introduced by Neolithic people eventually replaced most of the earlier mammal fauna, but whether man caused their extinction is hotly debated. At sites like the Gerani cave on the north coast of Crete, discovered recently during road-building operations, early Neolithic pottery and other artefacts were found together with antlers and bones of the now-extinct dwarf deer *Megaloceros cretensis*, but it cannot be shown that they were killed by man, or even that man and deer were present at the same time. Similarly, a pygmy hippo's footbone from Cape Andreas Kastros on Cyprus, one of the earliest sites yet known on that island (*c.* 6000 BC), might just as well be a curiosity picked up by some Neolithic palaeontologist, as an indication of live hippo-hunting!

The first clear evidence of permanent settlement in an island setting came, oddly enough, from a site whose later significance for the whole of the southern Aegean was momentous. In his excavations at Knossos in Crete early this century, Sir Arthur Evans discovered that the Bronze Age palace was built upon an artificial mound of accumulated occupation débris seven metres high, the remains of continuous demolition and rebuilding of the mud-brick houses of a Neolithic village. These levels, in the area below the West Court of the later palace, were explored a few years ago by Professor John Evans, who detected ten successive buildings levels, the earliest of which (Level 10) produced a carbon-14 date in the late seventh millennium bc. This first settlement was not much more than a simple camp: its inhabitants lived in wooden huts (whose post-holes have survived) and they either did not know how, or did not care, to make pottery. But they must have been able to build adequate boats to reach Crete from Anatolia or mainland Greece, bringing with them not only enough people to found a reproductively successful community, but also emmer and bread wheat (originally from the Near East) and breeding populations of sheep, goats, cattle, pigs, dogs, and even – so it seems – badgers![1]

Island sites as early as the one at Knossos, or nearly so, remain extremely rare; despite very careful searching by archaeologists over many years, only a handful are known on Crete and Cyprus, the two largest islands in the East Mediterranean. They must have been isolated and precarious specks of life in a large ocean. Until a few years ago, it seemed that the smaller islands of the Cyclades had no settlement at all before the start of the Bronze Age around 3000 BC. The picture is no longer quite so bleak, yet scarcely any of the dozen or so Cycladic Neolithic sites that have now been recognised seem to represent permanent occupations, and all are small. It seems strange that the introduction to Greece of farming, which allows man greater control over his environment and permits survival in less hospitable areas, did not result in the rapid expansion of settlement throughout the Greek islands. A puzzle still remains.

As always, the archaeologist must ask whether the pattern he sees is real or merely the accidental product of the survival of sites, of chance discoveries, or even of where other archaeologists have chosen to work

2.4 Map of the southern Aegean, showing places mentioned in the text

in the past. The only way to find out is by means of intensive archaeological survey – the systematic search for *all* traces of past human activity scattered on the surface of the ground, usually through gruelling, and sometimes tedious, fieldwalking by large teams who criss-cross the landscape on foot at close-spaced intervals. Such highly organised prospection is a relatively novel approach in archaeology and it has been applied in Greece only within the last 10 to 15 years.[2] The *Origins* radio team visited one such group, from the University of Southampton, in action on the island of Melos in 1976. That work, and the results of still more recent fieldwork on Keos four years ago, allow us to suggest with conviction that the apparent lack of evidence for early prehistoric settlement in the Cyclades is *not* an accident of haphazard research: it seems there really are very few Neolithic sites in the Cyclades. Their excavation would probably add little to what we already know. Those on Melos (where eight are now known) are not only much later in date than the first farming villages on Crete and Cyprus, but are also much smaller, and lack architecture, pottery, and indeed any other indications of settled life. They may have served special purposes, perhaps as fishing camps, as some of the stone tools might suggest, or as seasonally occupied settlements of farmers normally living on the mainland who visited the islands in the summer months to pasture flocks, fish, and gather raw materials such as obsidian (which, as early as the sixth millennium, was distributed by exchange over an area stretching from Macedonia to Crete).

Two sites have been excavated, both in the 1960s. The earlier, of the fifth millennium, is on Saliagos, now a tiny islet scarcely 100 metres across, but at the time of its occupation a promontory extending northwards into a sheltered bay formed by the islands of Paros and Antiparos which were then joined together as a single landmass. The inhabitants, living in rectangular stone houses within an enclosing wall and served by a nearby fresh-water spring, evidently comprised a very small, self-sufficient village. They grew wheat and barley, and kept the same domestic animals as did their counterparts on the Greek mainland at this time; not surprisingly, shellfish and fish – particularly the tunny, whose size makes it the equivalent of a floating pig – also played a part in their diet. Saliagos probably lasted about 500 years before its abandonment, apparently with no successor.

A similar picture has emerged from excavations by the University of Cincinnati at the later fourth millennium BC site at Kephala, a somewhat unpromising location for settlement on an exposed promontory headland on the north coast of the island of Keos. The scattered foundations of small stone houses have been excavated on the steep, but more sheltered, southern slope, and the most recent investigations at the site – a detailed surface survey in 1983–4 – have suggested a population for the entire settlement of between 45 and 80 individuals. A cemetery on the neck of the peninsula, though badly eroded, supports that conclusion: it contains individual and multiple contracted inhumation burials in circular and rectangular graves, sometimes with stone platforms built over the top. Neither the quality nor variations in the quantity of grave goods give any reason to see important differences in the social status of those buried, and perhaps none should be expected in a community so small. The very establishment of a formal place of burial for those who died on the island does, however, presumably reflect the permanence of the settlement and the attachment to the land of its occupants, much like a country churchyard today.

These and a few other similar sites still awaiting excavation scarcely constitute a coherent pattern of island settlement. In any case, they seem to have been occupied for just a few centuries and then abandoned

2.5 The rocky promontory of Kephala in Keos. The Neolithic settlement was spread over the protected southern slopes of the promontory, with its cemetery at the base, next to the sandy beach

permanently, leaving no obvious successors. Only one or two aspects of material culture – for instance, the manufacture of marble vessels and crude stone or terracotta figurines, or (in the case of Kephala) the working of copper – provide any links with later sites. The spectacular expansion in settlement that occurred during the third millennium thus appears all the more striking. For while Neolithic finds of any sort have been found on less than 10 per cent of the Cycladic islands, more than 90 per cent of them were settled during the Early Bronze Age. Though often very small – perhaps representing the homesteads of individual families – dozens of new sites now appear throughout the Cyclades for the first time, and not only in the larger islands such as Naxos, Paros or Andros, but also on tiny, barren, waterless islets which are today completely uninhabited.

One reason why so many Early Cycladic sites are known is that many of them are small cemeteries, whose shallow, stone-lined graves frequently contain the remarkable marble figurines and vessels which are highly prized by museums and private collectors and which now command astronomically high prices on the antiquities market: a single piece of prehistoric Cycladic sculpture recently fetched over one million dollars at auction.[3] Sadly, but not surprisingly, illicit excavation and looting have become a livelihood on many islands, despite the vigilance of the authorities. Consequently, far more is known about the art of the early prehistoric inhabitants of the Cyclades and about their way of death, than about their way of life and settlements.

The results of intensive surveys, once again, are proving important in correcting this imbalance, helping to locate the settlements which obviously must have accompanied every Early Cycladic cemetery and to demonstrate the true scale of the transformation of the settled landscape that occurred in the third millennium. For instance, the Melos project, mentioned earlier, has raised the total number of Early Bronze Age sites on that island from a handful to nearly three dozen; and, since only a representative sample of one fifth of the island was covered by fieldwork, a good many more almost certainly await discovery. On the other hand, not all of these sites were concurrently occupied. And those Cycladic cemeteries that have been fully exca-vated, such as the one at Ayioi Anargyroi in Naxos, usually contain a mere 10 or 20 graves (only half a dozen exceed 50), perhaps repre-senting the dead of a settlement occupied by a single family over the course of a century or less. Panermos on Naxos, one of the few completely explored Early Cycladic settlements, is but 15 metres across! In short, it is the ubiquitous presence of small farming societies throughout the islands, not the scale of individual communities, that is such a novel feature of the archaeological record at this time.

So we must return to the puzzle noted at the outset. Why did this occur only some 3000 to 4000 years after the first farmers arrived to settle in Crete, and fully 8000 years after the earliest known visits to the islands by man? Some hints are forthcoming from the distinctive chronological pattern of island colonisation in the eastern Mediter-ranean as a whole. We have already seen that the earliest settlements, in the late seventh and sixth millennia BC on Crete and Cyprus, were not on the most easily accessible, but, rather, on the largest, of the islands; it was not the development of suitable boats, but the advent of agriculture as a mode of subsistence, that made this possible. Later, in the fifth and fourth millennia, farmers began to settle on other islands, all of them relatively large and easily visible from the mainland, such as Lefkas, Euboea, Rhodes, Kos or Chios. The expansion of the late fourth and third millennia represents the colonisation of most of the remaining islands, irrespective of their size and distance from the mainland. This is a genuine pattern that has only recently been recognised, and it reveals something much more selective than simply a steady spread of farming from one side of the Aegean to the other.

Now insularity presents special problems and opportunities which all species, including man, must face in reaching and adapting to islands. Ecologists and geographers who study island populations emphasise the risks of living on small islands which, by their very nature, are able

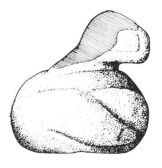

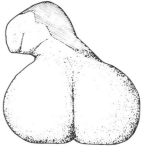

2.6 The 'Fat Lady': a crude marble seated figurine from Saliagos

Neolithic

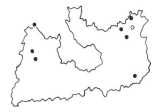

Early Bronze Age

Middle Bronze Age

Late Bronze Age

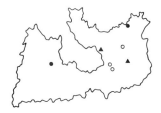

• definite site
○ probable site
▲ cemetery

2.7 Prehistoric sites on the island of Melos, showing the dramatic expansion of settlement in the Early Bronze Age and its nucleation in Middle and Late Bronze Age times

to support fewer types and smaller numbers of plants and animals.[4] The small islands of the Cyclades and the Aegean, moreover, are fragile environments, with poor soils and a pattern of low, seasonal and very unpredictable rainfall which makes disastrous crop failure sooner or later a virtual certainty. According to the Greek historian Herodotus, it was traditionally just such a problem – seven consecutive drought years which killed every tree on the island except one – which led the people of Thera in 631 BC to consult the Delphic oracle and eventually to reduce the population of their island by founding a new colony at Cyrene in North Africa. In large mainland regions, bad conditions for farming in one area are often balanced by normal, or even beneficial, conditions elsewhere, and catastrophe can be averted by moving food or people from one area to another. This is not so easy on islands, where a disaster can wipe out an entire population. Small isolated groups would have a low probability of being able to maintain themselves indefinitely without recourse to food and mates from beyond the island. It is easy to imagine how an especially bad harvest, or even a run of indifferent ones, would spur pioneer settlers to return to the relative safety of the mainland, or to move on to other possibly more advantageous islands, leaving behind little for the archaeologist. So perhaps we should not be surprised to see in the archaeological record the effects of inexorable selective pressure favouring the larger islands and those closer to the mainland.

One possible illustration of the risks of island life for small scattered settlements is to be seen in early prehistoric Cyprus. Over a dozen sites of the Khirokitia Culture have been dated by carbon-14 to the late seventh or sixth millennia bc, and most have been excavated at least to some extent. Yet of the following millennium virtually nothing is known and only a single (suspect) radiocarbon date has been reported. It may, of course, simply be that no fifth-millennium sites have chanced to be discovered, although years of survey work on the island make that a remote possibility. More likely, the initial colonisation was not successful in the long run. The sites are few, small and widely scattered; the first small boatloads of farmers may not even have been aware of each other's existence. Starvation or accidents of small-group demography – for instance, a complete lack of female babies to ensure the reproduction of the group into the next generation – could simply have snuffed out this first attempt to settle the island, so that Cyprus had to be colonised anew during the fourth millennium (when more than 100 sites belonging to the so-called Painted Pottery Neolithic phase are known). If the settlement of a large island like Cyprus proved so precarious, how was it that so many far less promising islands in the Aegean came to be settled with apparent ease after 3000 BC?

The answer is perhaps summed up in the words of the great French historian Fernand Braudel, writing of the Mediterranean as a whole in a

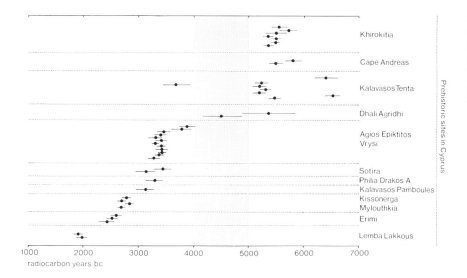

2.8 Carbon-14 dates from early prehistoric Cyprus; the shaded area indicates the 5th millenium bc, a period at which there may have been no human settlement on the island

very different age, that of Philip II of Spain:

> None of the islands was assured of the future. The great problem for all of them, never or only partly solved, was how to live off their own resources, off the soil, the orchards, the flocks, and if that was not possible, to look outwards.[5]

The Neolithic island settlements, whether on Crete, Cyprus or the smaller Aegean islands, *never* looked outwards. Their styles of making pottery and other sorts of artefact, and even the layout of their settlements, are insular in the full sense of that word, bearing little resemblance to contemporary cultures on the mainland of Greece and Anatolia; in some way, this must reflect prolonged isolation, with little exchange and interaction in the centuries following colonisation. In the Early Bronze Age, by contrast, the Cycladic islands have a prominent place in what Professor Colin Renfew has fittingly termed 'the international spirit' of the third millennium BC, a homogeneity of style that not only unites most of the Cyclades as a distinctive cultural zone, but links them with most other parts of the Aegean.

The widespread distribution of certain types of finds, such as the various forms of marble figurines of the Grotta-Pelos and Keros-Syros cultures, are a tangible remnant of prehistoric social and economic relationships between individual island communities, and sometimes also with those on adjacent mainlands. The maintenance of such close ties, whether through intermarriage or trading partnerships, would have given access to food and other resources in times of acute shortage, and can thus be regarded as a sort of adaptation to the inherent risks of island life, one that must have contributed very considerably to the success of colonisation at this time. It was from the amalgam of insular

25

independence and regular maritime contact that there developed the traditions and values that governed the uniquely distinctive development of Early Cycladic art and culture.

Yet some of the islands actively involved from the outset in these emergent regional networks – for instance, the Erimonisia which lie between Naxos and Amorgos (the 'deserted isles' of Keros, Schinousa and the two Kouphonisia) – are among the smallest and most infertile. Was it their role in trading that allowed them to be settled at all, rather than *vice versa*? Archaeologists and anthropologists working in other parts of the world, such as Polynesia, have noted that specialised traders are often based in areas poor in resources, and suggested that exchange is a specialised adaptation which allows populations to exploit regions which, from a basic subsistence perspective, have only marginal value. This may also be true of the Cyclades, for some of the most characteristic aspects of Cycladic material culture seem to have been the products of specialist craftsmen and required the procurement of resources and the distribution of goods on a regional scale. One real advantage enjoyed by archaeologists working in island contexts is the opportunity to distinguish local products from imports, and thus to trace trade, much more clearly than is often possible elsewhere. Recent research has capitalised on that advantage.

For instance, the fine white marble, whose brilliance and purity had such a determining influence on Early Cycladic sculpture, is found chiefly in the central Cyclades, though stone of lower quality also occurs quite widely. Attribution of archaeological specimens to their marble source by scientific means is not yet wholly satisfactory; museum curators, in any case, are understandably reluctant to surrender priceless objects for analysis! But where marble figurines occur on islands with no natural marble of their own (e.g. Melos), exchange of some sort must have taken place – exchange carrying with it associated concepts and values at which we can only guess. A widespread unity of ideas is certainly implied not merely by the recurrence of complicated and distinctive types, such as the seated harpist, but also by Dr Pat Preziosi's recent discovery that canons of proportion were used to set out the figurines before they were carved from the marble.[6] She has also demonstrated that examples from different islands can be attributed to individual hands or workshops, though where these were located is not clear. Very many of the looted objects of marble came originally from the tiny island of Keros, including, perhaps, a newly acquired near life-size statue put on display only last year in the Goulandris Museum in Athens.[7] If this was a cult-image, as seems possible, then perhaps Keros had some central religious significance for the Cyclades as a whole. One is reminded, certainly, of another equally 'useless' island – Delos – and of the unifying role its religious cults played in later historical times. A collaborative Greek–British project on Keros is to start in the summer of 1987 and it may well shed fresh light on the question.

The importance of specialised production and regional exchange in the islands is also becoming very much clearer as a result of work, by Drs N. Gale and Z. Stos-Gale of Oxford University, on the sources of the metals used in the prehistoric Aegean. They have used a mass spectrometer to measure the proportion of the four isotopes of lead present in naturally occurring metal ores and in finished metal artefacts; because the chemical processes of smelting, refining and corrosion leave the original isotope composition unaltered, artefacts can be compared directly with ores from ancient mines. The analysis of numerous Early Cycladic objects of silver and lead – for instance, the lead boat models mentioned earlier – showed, to everyone's surprise, that they were almost all made of ores coming either from the island of Siphnos or from the Lavrion, on the east coast of Attica opposite Keos.[8] Investigation of ancient mine galleries at Ayios Sostis on Siphnos has confirmed their conclusion, for pottery found amongst the surface scatter of slag and litharge, together with carbon-14 and thermoluminescence dates, all point to their use early in the third millennium BC.

Yet more recently, the same technique, applied to Early Cycladic copper sources, has revealed that Kythnos, two islands to the north of Siphnos, was (once again with Lavrion) a dominant supplier of the copper used for the manufacture of tin- or arsenic-alloyed bronze objects over much of the southern Aegean at this time.[9] Fragments of pottery of Early Cycladic II date associated with slag heaps and ores provide direct evidence of the early use of the source: indeed, this site is now the earliest proven copper-smelting site yet known in Greece, and it provided the material for metal objects found as far afield as Ayia Photia on the north coast of eastern Crete. The mining of metal ores, together with their smelting, refining and alloying, would have required detailed knowledge of the source itself, as well as of the technology involved, together with very considerable inputs of time and labour, for instance in collecting fuel. Such considerations imply that specialised production for exchange must have been involved, unlike the 'serve yourself' approach that new studies have suggested was the case with the acquisition of Melian obsidian.

The finding of objects of Cycladic copper at Ayia Photia is of particular interest, for at that site there was excavated a few years ago a very large cemetery of graves which reflect burial customs so similar to those typical in the Cyclades that they have been supposed by some scholars to be burials of actual Cycladic colonists. The idea of a colony, in the sense of a planned venture by a mother-city as in the Archaic Greek world, is obviously anachronistic at this time; but there certainly exists a scatter of evidence, which scientific provenance studies are now beginning to confirm, for sporadic exchanges of pottery and other goods between Crete and the Cyclades. Links with the Greek mainland are rather more abundant, and there too there exist Cycladic-type cemeteries (near Marathon and at Ayios Kosmas in eastern and southern Attica); similar finds have been made at Iasos in southwestern Turkey. The middle of the third millennium, in fact, is a time when craft items distinctive of particular regions in the Aegean are found in adjacent areas either as objects of exchange or as local copies – West Anatolian cups in the Cyclades and on the mainland; the odd pottery shape known as the 'sauceboat' in the Cyclades, Crete, the mainland and Anatolia; Cycladic marble figurines on the mainland and in Crete. This is the very sort of evidence used by Renfrew to propose the 'international spirit' of the age. Yet it is notable that many of those artefact types involved are most at home in the Cyclades, clear testimony of the strong orientation of the Cycladic islanders toward trade and interchange with the world beyond their own islands. How very different from the introverted isolation of Neolithic times.

Yet though unified in a cultural and artistic sense, and bound together by ties of kinship and by interactions of other kinds, the individual small communities dotted throughout the Cyclades were not united politically, either in the third millennium or later. The same geographical factors which made these islands difficult to settle in the first place also militated against their amalgamation. To be sure, hierarchies of leadership do seem to have developed in some places, at larger well-planned centres whose rise went hand-in-hand with the abandonment of the former, small rural settlements. Melos provides the clearest instance of the process of nucleation, since the establishment of the large Middle and Late Bronze Age site at Phylakopi on the north coast (excavated by British teams in 1896–9 and again in 1974–7) can be understood in the context of the results of the recent intensive survey in its territory.[10] Nucleated patterns of settlement of this kind are known on others – possibly most – of the islands in the second millennium, and the most important centres (important, perhaps, because they are also the most fully excavated) at Ayia Irini on Keos, Phylakopi on Melos, and Akrotiri on Thera lie at convenient intervals along a major maritime route connecting Crete and the Greek mainland.[11]

The great palace territories of Minoan Crete developed shortly after 2000 BC, and trade and contact between Crete and certain of the islands intensified from that time on, to reach a point where it becomes questionable whether it is possible to speak any longer of a distinctively Cycladic culture, so strongly pervasive were the prestige and influence of Minoan economy and society. That is a story which cannot be pursued here. But we may note that the Cyclades were no longer central, but merely peripheral, small-scale entities in a world of larger powers embracing most of the southern Aegean; their survival depended not on links with each other, but with the Minoan and Mycenaean states.

Much the same was true later. In the early days of state formation in Archaic Greece, island states like Naxos, Paros and Thera were important independent centres, famous for the work of their artists and sculptors. But the inexorable growth of bigger powers made them backwaters in the world of Classical Athens or Sparta, and the vitality and originality of Cycladic culture was once again eclipsed. History does, sometimes, repeat itself.

1   J.D. Evans, 'Neolithic Knossos: the growth of a settlement,' *Proceedings of the Prehistoric Society* 37:2 (1968) 95–117.
2   D. Keller and D. Rupp (eds.), *Archaeological Survey in the Mediterranean Area* (Oxford, 1983).
3   J. Thimme and P. Getz-Preziosi (eds.), *Art and Culture of the Cyclades* (Karlsruhe, 1977); C. Doumas (ed.), *Cycladic Art: Ancient Sculpture and Pottery from the N.P. Goulandris Collection* (London, 1983); J.L. Fitton (ed.), *Cycladica* (London, 1984).
4   R.H. MacArthur and E.O. Wilson, *The Theory of Island Biogeography* (Princeton, 1967).
5   F. Braudel, *The Mediterranean and the Mediterranean World in the Age of Philip II* (London, 1972) 152.
6   P. Getz-Preziosi, 'Cycladic sculptors and their methods,' in *Art and Culture of the Cyclades* (n. 3) 71–91.
7   C. Renfrew, 'A new Cycladic sculpture,' *Antiquity* 60 (1986) 132–4.
8   N.H. Gale and Z. Stos-Gale, 'Lead and silver in the ancient Aegean,' *Scientific American* 244.6 (1981) 176–92.
9   N.H. Gale and Z. Stos-Gale, 'Bronze Age copper sources in the Mediterranean: a new approach,' *Science* 4541 (1982) 11–19.
10 C. Renfrew and M. Wagstaff (eds.), *An Island Polity: The Archaeology of Exploitation in Melos* (Cambridge, 1982).
11 E. Schofield, 'The western Cyclades and Crete: a "special relationship",' *Oxford Journal of Archaeology* 1 (1982) 9–25.

CHAPTER THREE

CRETE: THE MINOANS AND THEIR GODS
PETER WARREN

When Arthur Evans made his first archaeological tour of Crete in 1894, no one could have predicted that within a few years he and others would begin to uncover a brilliant, pre-Greek civilisation on the island. But from 1900 to the present day an astonishing range of towns, 'palaces' (or urban megastructures, for those who prefer current, 'value-free' terminology), country mansions and estates, religious sites and rich tombs continues to be brought back to view. All these sites contain an abundance of objects which excite our contemporary aesthetic and artistic interests, stimulate our curiosity about their technology and demand exploration of their meaning and function. It is hardly surprising, then, that Minoan Crete attracts new archaeological approaches and thinking as much as it pours forth new discoveries.

The island's comparatively large size, about 240 kilometres east–west and 58 kilometres north–south, its geographical position in the South Aegean Sea, distant but not too distant (we shall return to this) from Anatolia, the Near East, Egypt, the Greek islands and mainland, and the potential of its climate, soils, rocks and other resources, are three clues towards understanding the success of its people in the Bronze Age. Of course, other Mediterranean islands are large and well endowed with resources. In the case of Crete it was its geographical position in combination with these other factors that was significant.

The term 'civilisation' is usually applied to the Minoan Cretans' achievement during the 2000 years (roughly 3000–1100 BC) which followed some 3500 years of Neolithic farming and herding. The centuries from about 1900 BC to 1450 BC were the time of highest achievement, when there were several large territories with a hierarchy of sites ranging down from palace capitals, an inferred centralised economy based on redistribution of foodstuffs and raw materials, and inferred social ranking. The three broad historical periods, then, are the Prepalatial (later fourth millennium BC to about 1900 BC), the Palatial (1900–1375 BC), and the Postpalatial (about 1375 BC to about 1100 BC).

But, for any sophisticated understanding of the historical development, of periods of equilibrium and episodes of change, a much more sensitive measure is needed than these broad periods. Evans had already devised his chronological system based on the life of pottery styles – Early, Middle and Late Minoan – each divisible into many shorter phases. (Early Minoan covers the Prepalatial third millennium, Middle and early Late Minoan the Palatial period and later Late Minoan the Postpalatial.) There is no more sensitive indicator of the passage of time available than these pottery phases, since together with objects imported from Egypt, when found in clear, short-period contexts, they provide absolute dates based on the Egyptian historical calendar. The current state of radiocarbon dating and its tree-ring (dendrochronological) calibration gives dates with unhelpfully wide margins for Minoan history, at least from 2000 BC onwards, when the time-links with Egypt become quite closely defined.

Current research in archaeology is concerned to probe beyond essentially descriptive accounts (which is what fill most general archaeological books) and to formulate methods of explaining why changes in cultures occur or periods of apparent equilibrium are maintained. The methods may be theoretical, with hypotheses suitable for testing against the existing evidence or through excavation to recover and record data appropriate for testing the hypotheses; or they may be inductive – drawing arguably the best inferences from the evidence within a framework of knowledge of the culture as a whole. One very useful approach towards explanation has been the application of systems analysis, whereby a culture, a geographical area or an individual site is analysed as a system in operation, by means of the interrelations between its perceived subsystems. Together with the components which make up the total system, the parameters – the external variables which affect it – must also be defined. Climate, population size, resources, and external constraints like disease, war or natural agencies, are examples of such variables. At this detailed level, then, growth or decline, slow or sudden, can be at least partly explained. In the Minoan case, the emergence of palaces, the 500 years of a brilliantly successful, high age of civilisation, and the collapse of that civilisation around 1450 BC are three critical stages for analysis and explanation.

Much of the above refers largely to life at the material level. It is equally true that material remains are the visible expression not only of social organisation (e.g. site hierarchies mirroring a structure of social rankings), but of belief systems. Indeed a culture may be defined, non-materially, as a cohesive set, or sets, of meanings expressed through symbols. This is particularly true with what we call religion, that aspect of the total system concerned, through ritual actions, to articulate and communicate hopes and fears for all aspects of the natural world to powers or forces believed to exist beyond the purely human sphere. Whether these hopes and fears owed their origin to biological factors inherent in the human make-up, or were a human response to perceived needs, like sun, rain, food and offspring, are current matters for debate in ethology. For the Minoan people it has been

3.1 Statuette of goddess from Myrtos, holding a jug to signify the protection of liquids. 2200 BC

obvious since Arthur Evans' still seminal work of 1901, *The Mycenaean Tree and Pillar Cult*, that religious belief and expression formed a major part of their lives; indeed, very many of what we recognise as the finest products of Minoan civilisation, like the so-called faience snake-goddesses, the stone bull's head, the brilliant and arresting wall-painting of a woman, all from Knossos, were created to serve a religious function. It must be said that religion cannot be regarded as a separate subsystem in Minoan society. There appears, rather, to have been no conceptual division into 'sacred' and 'secular' – hopes for the continued fertility of ancestral soil and food supplies, both dependent on wind, weather or other believed powers beyond human control, not admitting of such division. Although many religious sites and objects have been discovered, it seems clear that 'religious' beliefs were an indivisible element of living and working in the Cretan environment, as is still the case today in Cretan and Greek rural society, as in many others. In secularised, intellectually compartmentalised, capitalist societies or in desanctified socialist regimes the point is perhaps worth stressing.

In 1950 our understanding of the religion of the Minoans was much advanced with the publication (second edition) of the great Swedish scholar, Martin P. Nilsson's book, *The Minoan-Mycenaean Religion and its Survival in Greek Religion*. Excavations up to then had revealed three main types of sacred site. One type consisted of sanctuaries on mountain summits, as at Mount Juktas south of Knossos and at Petsophas above Palaikastro. Ash levels investigated on these summits were found to contain the remains of terracotta figurines of wild and domestic animals and human beings, whole or in individually made parts such as legs and arms. The prevailing cults were concerned with healing and the protection of crops and herds, with bonfires lit to the divinity and, later, with offering and rituals in buildings. A second type of site was the sacred cave, where, in great natural cathedrals of stone, offerings were placed in revered stalagmites and pools. In the cave of Eileithyia (in later Greek times goddess of childbirth) at Amnisos the stalagmite was given particular reverence by having a low wall or *temenos* built round it. The third type of site was the sanctuary room, or its adjacent treasury of ritual vessels, in palaces, towns and houses. In the palace of Minos at Knossos the 'Temple Repositories' held in store an astonishing collection of rich materials: the 'snake goddesses' mentioned above; plaques of a cow suckling its calf, an antelope, models of votive robes, of fishes and shells, of fruit and flowers (all these objects in faience), true shells, a marble cross, small stone offering tables, many storage jars for wine or oil, and deer bones suggestive of sacrifice. In short, the whole natural world of human beings, animals, plants and fish seemed to be represented, indicating a unified structure of belief.

Another treasury contained exquisite vessels of stone, including

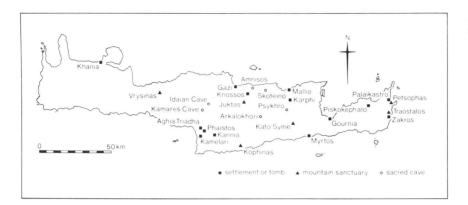

3.2 Crete in the Bronze Age: sites with important religious remains

conical rhytons of Egyptian alabaster for pouring liquid offerings and other rhytons in the shape of a lion and a lioness head. A late type of shrine within the palace, paralleled by similar ones in settlements at Gazi, Gournia and Karphi, consisted of a bench in a small room, with figurines of a goddess and worshippers or attendants set on the bench with a small double-axe, and many vessels for offerings on the floor before the bench. (The double-axe, often of decorated sheet bronze and set up on a pole, and a pair of stylised bull's horns were the two chief symbols of Minoan religion.)

Recent discoveries have both richly supplemented this picture and added wholly new and unsuspected dimensions. To discern the earliest stages of Minoan religion we now have the evidence of an area within the Early Minoan village on a low hill near Myrtos on the south coast. This community, of perhaps no more than 50 people, lived in about six houses, conjoined with each other in a communal, cellular structure, and surrounded by a defence wall. The southwestern part of the site was occupied by the village's cult area, with the shrine room containing a small stone bench or altar, on which had stood a terracotta statuette of a female divinity holding a miniature jug – symbolising her protection of liquids, oil, wine and water. Before her on the floor were vessels for food and liquid offerings. A tiny room opening off the shrine room was full of pottery, presumably the shrine store for offering vessels and cult equipment. The statuette dated about 2200 BC, takes back the Minoan domestic cult into the Prepalatial period. Together with other statuettes she shows that already, at this early date, divinity was perceived in some sort of anthropomorphic sense.

In 1979 an extraordinary discovery was made at Anemospelia on the northern slopes of Mount Juktas, overlooking the Knossos valley. Here stood a three-roomed building with a passage across the front like the narthex of a Byzantine church. The building was a temple with a special focus for offerings at the inner end of the eastern and central rooms. The offerings consisted of foodstuffs and liquids in a wide range of containers, from large store jars (*pithoi*) to small bowls and cups. In the central room was a pair of life-size terracotta feet, very possibly fitted to perishable parts to make a cult statue. In the western room stood a very low rectangular structure, near the doorway from the passage. What gave this unique shrine its special interest was the presence of four human skeletons. One lay at the entrance to the central room and held a bucket decorated with a white bull in relief, very possibly a container for a sacrificed bull's blood. The other three were in the western room. At the inner end was a woman, lying on her front with legs apart. Beside the low table, on his back, was a tall, powerful man of status; he wore an iron ring (a precious metal in Crete then) and an agate sealstone engraved with a muscular figure, perhaps a god, punting a boat. On the low table was a younger man, feet seemingly bound, and on his body was a large bronze blade engraved with a boar's head. These unique finds have been interpreted as an act of human sacrifice at the time of, and presumably to avert, a powerful earthquake. The date was perhaps about 1600 BC and the temple was destroyed, never to be used again.

On the summit of Juktas, up above the Anemospelia temple, new excavations in the peak sanctuary have produced finds of the greatest importance for linking cult apparatus and symbols, and thus presumably the cult itself, to those of other types of shrine. On the very summit is a stone-built altar with which were associated human figurines and a stone offering table, or *kernos*, with many compartments for fruits, seeds, grains or other offerings. Immediately adjacent was a collection of sheet bronze double-axes, like those of shrines in palaces, caves and the open air. Human figurines include some apparently of women giving birth. Twelve offering tables of stone have inscriptions in Minoan Linear A, again as in caves and other sanctuaries, and very possibly invocatory formulae for a divinity.

Another exceptionally rich mountain shrine is Kato Syme, high on the slopes forming the south side of the Lasithi mountains. It is not a peak sanctuary, and was built to mark an abundant, life-giving water source that sprang out there. This shrine has yielded thousands of objects of the Greek and Roman periods, when it was dedicated to Hermes and Aphrodite; but excavations in recent years have revealed, under these layers and altars, a complex of at least 11 Minoan cult rooms dating to about 1600–1400 BC. Bowls on tall stands for offerings, clay and stone 'communion' chalices, low stone offering tables (some with Linear A inscriptions), clay and bronze human and animal figurines made up much of the Minoan ritual equipment, together with a fine sword perhaps dating from a moment when Mycenaeans controlled Knossos around 1400 BC. This lay near the water source. Kato Syme was clearly a major sanctuary for this region of southern Crete, perhaps for one or more annual festivals honouring the divinity as a mountain goddess of nature and perhaps hunting. In Greek times the name Sacred Mountain was given to a location in these parts, very possibly the shrine now being revealed.

In 1963, a completely different expression of Minoan religion was discovered: the shrine and shrine treasury within the cult rooms of the palace of Zakros. The treasury was unplundered, covered over by the destruction which enclosed the palace and devastated the Minoan civilisation around 1450 BC. It contained an astonishing collection of rhytons for pouring liquid offerings and other vessels, all in beautiful stones (Cretan limestone and serpentine, Peloponnesian red marble and green porphyritic rock (*lapis Lacedaemonius*), Egyptian alabaster and Dodecanesian white-spotted obsidian), together with Egyptian Old Kingdom stone bowls adapted and refitted by Minoan lapidaries. There were also double-axes of sheet bronze engraved with the sacred papyrus-lily pattern, to be set on poles, a nautilus and animal heads of faience, ivory butterflies and double-axes and stone hammers.

3.3 Miniature terracotta amphora decorated with figure-eight shields: one of a collection of ritual vases from a building west of the palace of Knossos. 1450 BC

Other rooms in this west wing of the Zakros palace produced a beautifully carved bull's head of green chlorite and a rhyton of the same stone carved with a scene in relief showing a mountain peak sanctuary and its buildings adorned with Cretan wild goats and an apparent sacred stone, an aniconic image of the divinity. The Zakros shrine treasury is not a new type of religious assemblage, being paralleled by the old finds of the Central Shrine Treasury in the palace of Knossos and a similar, but much more limited, collection of fine stone rhytons at Aghia Triadha. But it is at least equal to the Knossian collection in quality, and provides a richer range of objects.

During the same eventful weeks of 1979 that the excavations were taking place at Anemospelia, an equally unusual discovery was made at Knossos. In a building about 350 metres west of the palace, on a main road and still within the Minoan city, was found a collection of pottery vessels for cult use, several being pairs of miniatures of large forms and all having a hole in the base for use as rhytons. There were a pair of baskets and several pairs of cups. One singleton cup was decorated with a wild gorgoneion – a probable Minoan forerunner of the Greek gorgon face and symbolic of a great Minoan goddess of nature, as earlier researchers had argued. All these cult vessels had been in store in a *pithos* on the ground floor when the building was destroyed in the island-wide catastrophe of about 1450 BC, and had collapsed into the basement below, thus preserved for us to find them.

In an adjacent basement cell was something very different, the scattered bones of parts of four children, aged from 8 to 12. The skulls, mandibles and postcranial bones were unburnt and at least 20 per cent of them bore repeated knife-cut marks, indicating that flesh had been cut off before the bones were thrown into the tiny basement. With them were some sheep vertebrae, still articulated, and on one of these was a knife-cut in a position that suggested its throat had been cut. The two preserved skulls and a selection of other bones were X-rayed and no pathological abnormalities were revealed. As far as bone and cell structure are concerned, it seems the children were in normal health at the moment of death. What had happened? The find context provided no grounds for postulating preparation and cleaning of bones for secondary burial, nor for a siege suggesting starvation and survival cannibalism. Psychopathic murder would be equally unlikely in such a public building in the Minoan city. The children were apparently healthy – that is, they did not die naturally – and the bones of at least one slaughtered sheep were with them. It would seem that the children (and the sheep) had been sacrificed.

But only that? Plain sacrifice is explicable in terms of averting a disaster, human sacrifice for a major disaster (such as, in fact, befell). The removal of flesh, however, would appear to be something more than a 'plain' sacrifice. In the adjacent room, together with the cult vessels there were a few more children's bones, one with a knife-cut, as well as quite a lot of edible snails. The flesh, therefore, may well have been cooked, and so perhaps consumed. The sacrificed children may be explained as one part of a set of ritual actions to gain communion with the divinity. Analogies with Christian belief and practice come readily to mind.

From the closing, Postpalatial stages of Minoan civilisation there has been discovered the group of shrine rooms within the ruins of the older estate centre at Kannia. Today this site lies amid olives in the heart of Crete's largest plain, the Mesara, which runs east from the hills of Phaistos. The shrine rooms and stores, probably belonging to the thirteenth century BC, have finds recalling the half life-size cult statues of Gazi, Gournia and twelfth century BC Karphi. The Kannia idols are smaller, but more numerous and richer in attached snake and other symbols, and in accompanying cult apparatus such as a relief plaque with animals heraldically placed beside a palm tree.

This array of cult places enables us to understand well enough the locations for cult, and their contents indicate both a wide range of apparatus used and accompanying symbols (such as the double-axe and stylised horns), forms of divinity (both anthropomorphic and aniconic, natural stones) and votive offerings thought appropriate to the divinity (such as human and animal figurines, miniature double-axes, real bronze double-axes and swords, food and liquids, sacrificial animals and, occasionally, human beings). From all this evidence inferences can be drawn about the physical form and general purpose of Minoan religion. But the picture is a static one, a sort of frozen moment – shrines and objects. What is missing, for any deeper understanding, is perception of ritual action – the sequences of ritual performances which express the beliefs we should really be most interested to recover. A further body of material may therefore come into play.

For his initial work of inquiry into Minoan religion in 1901, Evans used the evidence of a series of gold rings and stone seals engraved with

3.4 Terracotta statue of goddess from Gazi. 13th century BC

cult scenes, many of them from Mycenae and elsewhere on the Greek mainland. Recent discoveries at Arkhanes, Khania, Knossos and Zakros, as well as many discoveries after 1901, have greatly increased the evidence. The tiny engraved scenes, usually less than two centimetres across, are like cinematographic silent stills, but they are displaying action. Sometimes there are scenes of naked or half-naked men or women pulling down branches of a tree in a shrine, or clasping a boulder, or leaning on a small shrine; sometimes dancing figures, invocations to divinities who are seen arriving or having arrived; sometimes abbreviated processions to offer something to a seated female who is presumed to be a goddess. Shrine buildings or façades, altars, a mountain peak, the sacrificing of an animal on a table are also shown. This evidence, in combination with the evidence of actual sites, buildings and other constructions can now be used to reconstruct likely sequences of ritual action. Some examples may be looked at in more detail.

The first concerns the invocation of the goddess or god. Several scenes show women in dance movements, sometimes circular, sometimes ecstatic. The dance would have been preceded by a procession carrying offerings such as flowers. The object of the dance was to invoke the presence of the divinity, perhaps at the climax with an ecstatic gesture. At this stage of the sequence a small figure of a divinity, male or female, can be seen arriving from on high. Once arrived, the god or goddess is seen to be worshipped with saluting gestures. Circular terracotta models of dancers are known from Kamelari and Palaikastro, but recent excavation at Knossos has produced the exciting discovery of stone-built, circular platforms, the largest over eight metres in diameter. These may be understood as dancing platforms, and they immediately bring to mind Homer's famous description of a dancing place built by Daedalus for Ariadne at Knossos (*Iliad*, Book 18, 590–606).

Another ritual involves a sacred stone or *baetyl*. Here the sequence is that a male or female participant, often naked, approaches the stone, having perhaps already deposited a female's robe as a votive offering elsewhere in the cult area; then the participant kneels and touches the stone and summons the divinity by gestures. The arrival of the divinity is not shown by an anthropomorphic figure, but by a symbolic bird or butterfly. Then, finally, the participant embraces and kisses the boulder in communion with it and the divinity.

Several scenes are concerned with the offering of a robe, as referred to above. Four stages of ritual sequence can be reconstructed. First the robe or elaborate skirt is made, dyed (with saffron, for example) and embroidered. Then comes a procession to convey it to the shrine, as in Classical Athens the *peplos* was conveyed to the Parthenon. (Scenes from Aghia Triadha, Knossos and Zakros show this stage.) Then the robe is presented, and is either left as a vehicle for possession by the goddess (like the figure-of-eight shield) or clothes the goddess in the person of her priestess. (A possible further stage is shown on a seal from Mallia, the adoration of the robe.) The decoration on the Early Minoan cult statuettes from Myrtos and elsewhere also suggests the robing of the goddess.

A final example, which far from exhausts the total of ritual sequences, is sacrifice. Minoan blood sacrifice of a bull or goat is well known from scenes on seal-stones and the painted sarcophagus from Aghia Triadha. First the animal would have been selected and prepared, then brought to the place of sacrifice with accompanying music and set on the sacrificial table; the scenes show this. Then its throat was cut, the blood collected in a container and finally offered to the divinity by pouring into a further container or into the earth. Dismembered parts of the animal were probably cooked and eaten, as the burnt levels with animal bones at the Kato Syme shrine suggest.

Apparent evidence of human sacrifice has already been noted, and the ritual sequence would have been the same: selection, preparation, bringing (this is probably the stage indicated on a clay seal impression from Khania, where a young girl with a sword above her stands before a seated goddess), sacrifice (the Anemospelia table), collection and offering of blood (perhaps the Anemospelia bucket), and, possibly a further stage, the removal of flesh from the bones, cooking and possible consumption (the grim Knossian remains of children).

In all the scenes of ritual where a divine figure is part of the action complex problems arise of how such a represented figure was understood or perceived by the Minoans in the actual rituals. Nevertheless, in

3.5 Scene engraved on sealstone from Knossos, with naked woman embracing a sacred stone. 16th–15th century BC

3.6 Scene engraved on sealstone from Khania, with seated female, probably a goddess; and a girl before her. The sword above the girl suggests she is to be sacrificed. 1450 BC

reconstructing these sequences as sequences of real actions, we are getting to the heart of the belief system for which we have no texts. When, for example, a flower or plant with a symbolic value or ascribed meaning derived from its believed usefulness or efficacity is offered to a goddess it is because the goddess was believed – either specifically by the participant or generally within the culture – to influence or affect its usefulness. The Cretan plant dittany, for example, was considered helpful to childbirth and was offered to Eileithyia, and she in turn was believed to assist birth.

Who specifically, we may now ask, was or were the object of all these rituals? Since we have no Minoan religious texts, other than the untranslated, short, perhaps invocatory inscriptions on stone offering tables in shrines, this is a difficult question to answer. Surrounding peoples such as the Hittites, the Egyptians and, a little later, the Mycenaeans, all had polytheistic religions. Judaism was unusual in being monotheistic, but non-Hittite Anatolia (modern Turkey) had a great goddess, lion-guarded Cybele, perhaps extending back to the feline-guarded great goddess of Neolithic Çatal Hüyük. For Minoan Crete there are several classes of evidence, all problematical. The cult scenes on gold rings and their surviving clay impressions sometimes show a female seated and receiving offerings. She is to be understood as a goddess, portrayed in human form. A wall painting from Building Xeste 3 at Akrotiri on Thera shows a similar seated female, receiving crocus stamens. She is likewise a goddess, with attendant monkey and mythical griffin. Occasionally there is a standing female, supported by lions or other animals and in one case saluted by a worshipper as well. Again a goddess. But is she the same goddess as the seated figure? The Early Minoan statuette from Myrtos (see above) and others of the same Prepalatial period appear to represent one goddess with different aspects, or several goddesses. So far, then, a goddess or goddesses. A recently found impression of a ring from Khania shows a large-scale male figure standing on a town or religious building. He is probably a god who has arrived; one or two gold rings also show a male figure arriving or having arrived, and receiving worship. Needless to say, all these figures are nameless. Can we go further?

The Linear B tablets from the palace of Knossos list various divinities and are clear evidence from polytheism. But they belong to the period of Mycenaean Greek control around 1400 BC, and therefore need not, and almost certainly do not, describe pure Minoan religion. Later Greek writers are more helpful, but introduce the problem of the validity of back-reference to a period so far removed in time from their own. They refer to Rhea, mother of Zeus, who bore him in a cave in Crete; she is a great goddess of nature, later identified with Cybele. There were Greek temples dedicated to Rhea at Knossos, it may be noted, and elsewhere in Crete. We also learn of Europa-Hellotis, Diktynna, Britomartis, Eileithyia, Ariadne and Pasiphae – all divine names – and of a young male god, Cretan Zeus (not to be confused with Greek Olympian Zeus), and of Velkhanos and Zagreus, perhaps other names of Cretan Zeus. Some of the female names are of Greek derivation, some – Britomartis, Diktynna, perhaps Eileithyia – probably Minoan, and they may be thought to indicate a polytheistic religion. But the Swedish scholar A.W. Persson has argued that they are invocatory names – 'Very holy one', 'Visible to all' or 'All illuminating' – and as such are likely to have originally been epithets of one great goddess, rather than separate divinities with 'real' proper names, such as Athena later on. Furthermore, the contents of the Minoan religious sites and the iconography of the cult scenes on rings and gems give an impression of much unity and homogeneous identity of female divinity. And there is always Rhea. It is likely, therefore, that the Minoans worshipped one great goddess of nature (Minoan Rhea, as it were) under different aspects. They also had a male god, but his status in relation to the great goddess is uncertain. Later literature and comparable pairings in adjacent cultures suggest he was subordinate. But the cult scene on the clay impression from Khania and those on other rings where he appears give no indication of lower status.

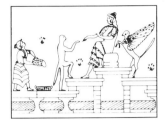

3.7 Drawing of wallpainting from Building Xeste 3 at Akrotiri, Thera. It shows a seated goddess, attended by a griffin and a monkey, receiving crocus stamens collected by richly dressed young women. 1500 BC

What, finally, was the meaning or purpose of the Minoan people's beliefs in their divinities? The immediate object was to translate their hopes and fears for their world into spiritual expression through ritual actions, and so to invoke the presence of the divinity and to gain communion with her in the sacred place. There the material world of cave, rock, soil, buildings and things was believed to house what was perceived or projected as beyond the human; it was a liminal zone, a point of interaction between two planes, human and divine. The divinity was believed to have control over all aspects of the natural and created worlds. To promote the fertility of these worlds and, conversely, to prevent damage or disaster to them was the general function of Minoan religion. Religious beliefs were thus an integral part of the whole living system. That system, the Minoan civilisation, was a success, not because of Crete's geographical position – important though that was, it was a necessary precondition rather than a primary cause of human success – nor even because the Minoan people understood the benefits of minimising or containing aggression (partly through ritualisation), again a precondition, but because, positively, they also understood and put into practice – and in this lay their brilliant achievement – the benefits of their system of social hierarchy without social divisiveness, a system permeated by their beliefs expressed in ritual. Their religion is a major explanatory mode for our understanding of their achievement: for religion and ritual were a major, positive force in creating and maintaining the civilisation.

CHAPTER FOUR

NEOLITHIC LAKE VILLAGES OF FRANCE

JOHN HOWELL

In the winter of 1921 the water-level of Lake Paladru, near Grenoble, fell to a record low. For Hippolytus Müller, a local archaeologist, this proved to be a fortuitous event: protruding through the mud of the fore-shore to above ankle height were the remains of the wooden posts of a prehistoric village, amongst which Müller could walk and collect artefacts which the mud and water had preserved. Müller had discovered the Neolithic site of Charavines, which we now know to have been inhabited around 2700 bc.

Müller's was not the first discovery of a lake village in the Alps. Early accounts of similar discoveries in Switzerland had been brought back to Britain in the 1800s by Sir John Lubbock (later Lord Avebury) and the distinguished scientist Sir Charles Lyell. Further discoveries also came from other Alpine lakes, from Austria to France and Italy to southern Germany. By the end of the nineteenth century, local archaeological societies had amassed large collections of artefacts from these sites and had undertaken some excavation work – industrial development along the edges of lakes and the damming of the Alpine rivers provided ample opportunity for the collection and study of the artefacts which were now revealed.

The main reason for this intense scientific activity was the unique level of preservation both of the artefacts and of the debris of everyday life. In contrast to sites on dry land, where in general the only artefacts found had been those made of robust materials such as flint, stone and pottery, the sterile conditions beneath the mud and water had perfectly preserved more fragile items, such as carved wooden spoons with all the elegance of Georgian silver ladles, fragments of cloth, the remains of baked bread, delicately carved and decorated wooden carding-combs, and apples, baked in prehistory, half-eaten and thrown away. Furthermore, instead of the slight remains of former post-holes recognised only by a faint discoloration in the soil, the posts themselves were still *in situ*, the debris of household activity scattered across the floor.

Such preservation and the immediate, visual impression provided by the sight of the wooden posts emerging from the mud led to romantic interpretations of the sites as 'Cities of the Lakes' (*cités lacustres*). Johann Hegi, the nineteenth-century Swiss painter, for example, depic-

4.1 A nineteenth-century view of life in a Neolithic lake village, by Johann Hegi

ted life in the villages with images reminiscent of the Vikings; tall, fair-haired, moustachioed heroes punting their way across the lakes to the distant smoke of the village chimneys. At the same time, however, a more serious debate was beginning as to how the villages should be interpreted. There were three possibilities: first the posts could have supported a platform on which the houses were built, the posts standing in the water like stilts. Second, the houses could have been built on the edge of the lake during a phase when the water level was lower. Third, wooden platforms could have been laid on marshy or peaty ground to act as a foundation for the construction of the houses on top.

Assistance in interpreting the sites came from two sources, one contemporary, one ancient: the increasing number of scientific voyages of discovery to the Far East and the Pacific brought back reports of contemporary lake villages built on stilts, notably in Papua, New Guinea; and the fifth-century Greek historian Herodotus had provided a detailed description of lake villages around Lake Prasias in Macedonia. Not all contemporary examples were, however, of villages on stilts. A diverse range of types of lake and lake-edge habitation was discovered. What all of these types of settlement shared, however, was a specialised adaptation to a particular environment which geographically was, and still is, rare. The reasons why people settled in these locations cannot be explained by one simple interpretation. In Benin, in West Africa, for example, lake-settlements on Lake Nokoué appear to have intensified among the indigenous population after the King of Abbomey's army, whose people observed a tabu against crossing water, invaded the area.

Quite commonly, then, the settlement of the lake-edges represented a forced move into areas which were not immediately favourable and may have required considerable technological, agricultural and social adaptation. This point is particularly relevant to the French Alpine lakes. For, when the first farmers settled there it was to all intents and purposes virgin territory. Their own agricultural way of life, however, was adaptable and, indeed, had already undergone some revolutionary changes since it had first been introduced into Europe.

A settled agricultural way of life (the Neolithic) was introduced into Europe from the Near East via the Balkans around 6000 bc. By 5000 bc, small villages practising a form of garden agriculture augmented principally by domesticated cattle, sheep, goats and pigs had spread along the valley bottoms of Europe as far as the Rhine and the Paris basin. These villages cluster in distinct settlement cells, located to take advantage of high ground-water and rich and fertile alluvium. These cells, in some cases, remained substantially unchanged for over a millennium. Although towards the end of this phase there is some expansion of settlement around the major Swiss lakes, such as Lake Zurich, the lakeside environments did not in general provide a congenial environment to this early agricultural way of life. The first substantial settlements around the lakes occur in the later fourth millennium bc and are part of a wider social and economic change.

The scale of this change is more pronounced in some areas of Europe than in others. In the Paris basin, for example, areas outside the valley bottoms, such as promontories and the plateau edge, were occupied for the first time and the settlements themselves became large, centralised sites often surrounded by a ditch and palisade, rather than open or lightly fenced villages. Pressure on resources seems to have produced a more warlike society, witnessed by the increase in weapons and by the concentration of wealth in a more mobile form – cattle.

These changes, although profound, were not, however, to revolutionise the agricultural way of life as much as those of a thousand years later, the middle of the third millennium. These changes were based on two principal technological developments: the plough and wheeled transport. With the aid of these two tools, settlement spread into a diverse range of environments and prehistoric man began to exploit a range of soils which had been previously inaccessible and too heavy to work. It is to the beginning of this phase that the site of Charavines belongs.

Two other major developments are linked with this expansion – the introduction of metal and the keeping of animals for their non-meat products, for example, sheep for their wool. These developments are not unassociated, for the wool produced was a ready cash crop to exchange for the new metal products which now appeared for the first time in the lake village sites.

It was in the context of this background that in the summer of 1983 I visited the lake sites in the foothills of the French Alps at Charavines, near Grenoble, and Clairvaux, further north towards Besançon in the Jura to record a programme for *Origins*. Charavines is a site now covered by the waters of Lake Paladru; excavation is conducted underwater by divers. By contrast, Clairvaux is covered by deposits of saturated peat and excavation resembles more that of a dry-land site. Nevertheless, both sites have provided exciting insights into the way of life of these communities.

CHARAVINES

The first village at Charavines appears to have been built around 2700 bc. This was not, however, the first appearance of farmers in the area. Beneath the first village, preserved in the mud layers, have been found the pollen of wheat and the weeds of cultivation which normally accompany agriculture. This suggests that intermittent farming was being practised in the area for about 600 to 700 years before the village was built. So far no traces of earlier settlements have been found, but the evidence points to isolated clearings hacked out of the forest, occupied only for short periods. In contrast, when the first village was built, the hard chalky fore-shore of the lake lay exposed, largely uncovered by vegetation and covered instead by fertile lake muds. It was an ideal site.

The extent of preservation of organic material on the site has provided an excellent opportunity for the application of a range of scientific techniques. One of the most important of these is the means of dating based on tree-rings, known as dendrochronology. Dendrochronology allows the identification of individual years within a relative time-scale based on a comparison of the width and colour of the annual growth rings seen in the cross-section of trees. The preservation at Charavines of large pieces of wood, and in particular the timbers of the houses themselves, has enabled a detailed chronology of the major events in the life of the village to be established. There were two phases of occupation of the village separated by a period of abandonment. In year one (the first year in which the village began), one house was built, approximately 5 metres wide and 12 metres long, very close to the water edge. In year two, three other houses were built around the first and the land side of the village was enclosed by a light fence. In year seven, rot appeared to have persuaded the owners of the first house to pull it down and rebuild it with new timbers. They also took this opportunity to enlarge the house. Major re-furbishment of the other houses appears to have taken place 16 years after that. Finally, after about 30 years, the two largest houses either caught fire or were burnt down and the first village was abandoned to be covered by the now rising level of the lake.

Variations in the lake levels were a common feature before the canali-

4.2 House plan and
reconstruction

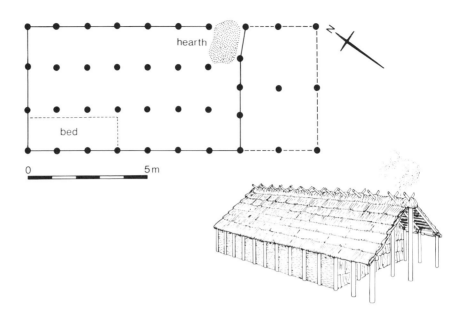

hearth

bed

0   5 m

sation and damming of the rivers which feed them took place in the nineteenth and early twentieth centuries. Indeed, it was one such temporary variation in 1921 which revealed the site of Charavines to Hippolytus Müller. The cause of these variations has been much debated and climatic factors, such as particularly dry spells and cold winters, have been the favourite explanation. Modern research, however, suggests that one of the most important factors was geomorphological changes in the lake itself and in the feed-rivers. Natural damming of the outflow of the lake, for example, by the deposit of debris washing out of the lake would have caused a rise in the lake level until the debris in turn was eroded away, and the level once more dropped.

After the rise in the lake level, the area of the first village remained deserted for about 30 to 40 years, the supports of the houses probably still visible above the water. Towards the end of this phase the lake level again dropped and new and larger houses were built above the remains of the first village. This village too lasted 20 to 30 years before the rising lake level once again covered the site and may have forced its abandonment, preserving it beneath the mud and water. This level of detail about the organisation and re-organisation of a Neolithic village is a rare insight into a prehistoric way of life.

The houses at Charavines were built on four rows of posts running along the length of the house. These seem to have supported a pitched roof covered with a thatching probably made from nearby reeds. At one end of the house the roof continued beyond the end wall to provide a covered open area. These areas would have been ideal for domestic chores such as pottery-making, flint-knapping and basket-weaving and indeed a large number of the artefacts found on the site do come from these areas. Inside the house a hard, baked clay area carried the open fire and cooking area. Along the walls were beds made out of a mattress of foliage covered by mats woven from reeds.

The rich variety of domestic activity can be seen from the artefacts found. Basket-weaving and plaiting, for example, have left examples both of pieces of the baskets themselves and rush mats. Rope made out of the twisted fibres of trees has also been recognised. In addition, cloth and the equipment on which it was made have been found. One method of producing cloth involved using the fingers to entwine the flax or wool around a spindle, weighted at one end, to produce a bobbin. Another involved weaving the fibres on a wooden frame and carding them with a wooden comb. The combs themselves are made from thin pieces of box-wood, the teeth sliced into shape with the aid of a flint blade. The handles of the combs are often carved with elegant curves and a central crescent-moon notch. Most of the cloth found was made from flax. No wool has been found at Charavines, although it has been found in small quantities on other sites. However, its rarity on these sites is probably due to the fact that it does not survive well, rather than to its lack of availability.

Amongst the wooden artefacts found on the site, special mention should be made of the wooden long bows and canoe paddles, as well as bowls and elegant serving spoons. In addition, axe handles carved from solid pieces of timber have been discovered. The working end was an intricate arrangement of an antler sleeve into which a stone blade was set. The whole sleeve was then inserted into a socket in the wooden haft and secured with glue. The blade itself could be detached when blunt and thrown away, something on the lines of a modern Stanley knife.

Of particular note were two exquisite daggers made from flint. The hafts on both of them were still bound with twining, and the end of one was surmounted by a small wooden pommel in the shape of a cardinal's hat. These beautiful and delicate daggers, however, are unlikely to have had any functional use. They, and the remains of a ceremonial axe-hammer, used perhaps as a sceptre – are rare glimpses in this village of ceremonial activity that was, possibly, associated with socially presti-gious objects. No funerary evidence can support this interpretation, however, since no burials at all have so far been found at Charavines.

Evidence of an agricultural way of life comes from three sources: the remains of pollen from edible plants or weeds from the plantain family, typically associated with agriculture; the remains of domesticated animal bones; and, in the case of the lake sites, the remains of the food itself. One example of the last source is the find at Charavines of a piece of bread, burnt in prehistory and preserved. The bread, resembling a modern pizza dough, was placed on a schist plaque and pushed into the flames to cook. With regard to domesticated animals, the animal bones

4.3 *Above:* A needle and thread recovered from the site at Charavines
Below: The handle of a flint dagger

found on the site suggest that sheep, goats and cattle were kept. The dominant animal, however, was the pig. This is not perhaps surprising. The pig is, after all, an excellent choice of domesticate in a forested environment. As well as keeping domesticated animals, the villagers hunted many wild animals, including a large number of wild pig. One of the most important hunted animals, however, was the deer, the antlers of which provided a diverse range of tools from needles to picks, the rest of the deer providing skins and, of course, meat. The lake also yielded a rich harvest of fish.

Where skeletal remains have been found on sites it is sometimes possible to identify family groups on the basis of hereditary traits in the bone structure. At Charavines this sort of analysis is impossible as no human remains have been found. The archaeological evidence does not provide sufficient detail to compensate for this. It is likely, however, that the village at Charavines would have accommodated about 30 people – all members of an extended family. Contact outside the village, particularly for reproductive purposes, would probably have been a necessity in view of the small number of people in the village.

The wider cultural affiliations of prehistoric groups are traditionally traced by archaeologists through the distribution of distinctive and recurring artefacts, usually the shape and decoration of pottery: sites with similar types of pottery or similar styles of decoration are classed as belonging to the same culture. Of course, these similarities may not always indicate a similar ethnic or tribal association. They do, however, usually indicate the area over which cultural and social contact was habitually maintained. At Charavines, a number of different pottery types have been recognised. One type consists of large, rough vessels about 30 centimetres high and with four small lugs near the rim. These pots – often bell-shaped – were probably used for storage, although traces of cooking have been found inside. By contrast, the smaller pots and saucers are usually finely made and seem to have been used for eating and drinking rather than cooking. A number of bottle-type pots have also been found. Only one pot had any decoration; all the others were plain. On the basis of the shape and style of these pots, the villagers of Charavines would seem to have been part of a cultural grouping that was restricted to the Saône-Rhône corridor and the Alpine foothills to the east. This group appears to have lasted for much of the later third millennium bc.

Charavines, therefore, was not self-sufficient and isolated from contact outside its immediate area. This can be demonstrated most clearly by the number of imported objects on the site. The import from the furthest distance is a small bead made of amber which came from the Baltic coast in southern Denmark. Other examples are the stone used for making the axe blades and hammers, from the Italian side of the Alps, and the rich, honey-coloured flint used for making long blades and daggers, from Grand-Pressigny in Touraine along the Loire. Finally, a bead and a small blade of copper which came from the Languedoc have also been found.

CLAIRVAUX

The site at Clairvaux can be contrasted with Charavines in many ways. To the modern visitor, the most obvious of these is the differences in the way the sites are being excavated. At Charavines excavation is carried on underwater at a depth of up to 2 metres by divers working in shifts up to four or five hours long. At Clairvaux, on the other hand, some of the sites are no longer covered by water but by layers of saturated peat. Excavation, therefore, although in a wetland environment, is not exclusively conducted underwater. More fundamental contrasts also exist between the two.

The area in which Clairvaux is located had a history of occupation stretching back to 3500 bc. In prehistoric terms it was an area of considerably greater population density than Charavines. A map of the surrounding area for about 20 kilometres shows a total of six to seven sites, some lake-edge, others inland. By contrast, the lake village at Charavines represents an isolated hamlet. Clairvaux, therefore, offers the opportunity of studying the site not only from the viewpoint of the internal organisation of the village, but also from that of the relationship of the village to the area of the population at large. As at Charavines, the sterile conditions provided by water and, in this case, peat have also provided an incredible level of preservation.

Although excavations at Clairvaux have now finished, the work on the artefacts, the general archaeological debris and the interpretation of the site is still progressing. As a result, a detailed sequence at the site, based on dendrochronology, has not yet been published. The overall sequence, however, would appear to be as follows.

Between 3100 and 2600 bc settlement around the lake at Clairvaux consisted of small settlements occupied for short periods; in other words, very similar to the later situation already seen at Charavines. Agriculture appears to have been based on small temporary clearings. As these became overgrown or less fertile they were abandoned and the village was frequently moved. Around 2600 bc, however, there is much evidence that the whole area became more densely populated: settlement occurs on the edge of promontories as well as around the lakes, and the lake sites became more stable – the true focus of a settled agricultural community. Around all the lakes, a variety of architecture would have been visible, with some houses built on dry land, others on marsh, and still others on posts over water. These villages, like the settlements on the edges of the plateaux, seem to have had a definite concern with defence:

4.4 Divers at work recovering objects from the lake

the plateau sites are often surrounded by ditches and wooden or stone palisades and the lake sites often barred the landward side of the village with a palisade.

The site at Clairvaux was occupied along a large expanse of the lake. However, this was not one vast township but a series of smaller hamlets of a few houses, each probably containing individual family groups. The position of these hamlets was subject to the regular fluctuations of the lake. This led to a continuously changing variety of site locations, from small islands, promontories and the lake edge itself. The organisation of the villages showed some individuality. In one case the houses were against the inside of the palisade. In another, they were organised in streets, rather like a modern terrace. This is of course a completely different picture to that at Charavines. Whereas Charavines was an isolated, temporary hamlet colonising a virgin landscape, Clairvaux was the focus of a dense occupation of an established and organised community whose sites included locations both around the lakes and elsewhere.

In addition to the habitation sites, a number of burials have also been found in the area around Clairvaux – the bodies were buried individually in simple shallow graves without grave goods. Some burials have also been found in caves or rock fissures. The absence of a complicated funerary ritual contrasts with other contemporary areas of Europe where burial is often made in a stone-built or megalithic tomb.

As at Charavines, the superb level of preservation has provided an opportunity to study aspects of the daily life of the village in a detail that is usually denied the archaeologist. Here, too, fragments of cloth have been found. Of particular significance amongst these is the presence of wool remains. Other interesting finds include a wooden whisk, weights for fishing nets (made by wrapping stones in tree bark), and a pottery colander. The latter, about 20 centimetres high, was riddled with small holes. It seems most likely that it was used as a strainer in the preparation of cheese.

The houses at Clairvaux were rectangular in shape and about six to eight metres long and three to four metres wide. A pitched roof was supported on three rows of posts made out of rot-resistant timbers such as oak – less-resistant timbers being used in other, drier parts of the construction. In other features, such as the internal clay hearths, there is a great deal of similarity with the houses at Charavines. Unlike Charavines, however, the architecture often shows considerable variation in the size and organisation of the houses within each village.

The cultural affiliations of the villagers at Clairvaux have, as at Charavines, been based largely on the shape and style of the pottery used. Many of the parallels for the later periods of Neolithic occupation at the site show that both Charavines and Clairvaux were, to different extents, part of the same Saône-Rhône cultural grouping. At Clairvaux and the neighbouring lake of Chalain, however, the pottery has a more individual and archaic character. This has prompted Pierre Pétrequin, the excavator at Clairvaux, to see the later occupation as the enforced settlement of more marginal environments by a local farming population forced out of its previous area either by new settlers or by other economic pressure. The earlier period, however, shows a mixture of influences that appear to suggest contacts both with the northwest and with the east, in Switzerland.

With such a wealth of material, fortuitously preserved, on these sites it is all too easy to look only at the objects themselves and not at what they tell us about the people who lived in the villages and their way of life. This is a particularly acute risk where, as in this case, the artefacts often show such aesthetic care in manufacture that their delicate lines and refinement cannot fail to impress. The ways in which these objects were made, the skills and thinking behind them are, of course, valid areas of pursuit. But there is something of still wider importance which the sites and the objects can reveal about the organisation of society and the quality of life in general.

The lake sites did not form a separate cultural phenomenon. Each site was part of a wider group or culture usually occupying a variety of landscapes, united in pottery styles, tool types, agriculture, and even style of

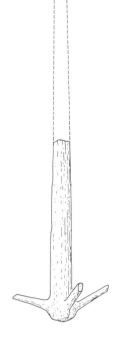

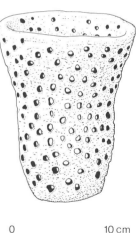

4.5 Wooden whisk and pottery vessel

dress. The closest the record comes to indicating a restricted lake-side culture is in the final phase at Clairvaux, where, as we have seen, there may be some evidence for the population being refugees, at least of an economic sort.

The changing settlement of the lake-edge – the rhythm of occupation – was not necessarily interrupted by the fluctuations of the lake level. The inhabitants of Clairvaux seem to have been remarkably adept at adapting their architecture to these fluctuations. The rhythm of occupation was, however, different from area to area. As we have seen, while at Charavines the settlement consisted of an isolated hamlet, the contemporary lake-edge at Clairvaux was a bustle of villages in stable occupation.

This wealth of detail, however, by no means provides a complete picture. The site remains a still photograph deprived of life and colour and, in parts, incomplete. Even the excellent conditions of preservation beneath the lake have been able to keep intact no more than a small fraction of the original objects which have been left behind. Some colour, however, can perhaps be added to the picture by drawing comparisons with those areas of the world where lake villages are still inhabited today. Recent studies of just this type of community in western Africa have provided a number of interesting glimpses into the possible way of life of the villages at Charavines and Clairvaux. Without the space here to go deeply into the details of these studies, it is interesting all the same to note the frequency with which the lakes were occupied as places of refuge and how, gradually, they developed a recognisable and special identity of their own. The exploitation of a lake-side environment has not, therefore, been confined simply to the Neolithic period.

A brief survey of some of the other historic and prehistoric types of lake-side occupation shows a vast diversity of settlement. In the Mesolithoc period, for example (about 5500 bc), the Wauwil marsh behind Lucerne had small hunter-gatherer encampments along the edge of the former lake shore. So far, about 30 sites have been found, although it is unlikely that all of these were occupied at the same time. These sites appear to have been specialist camps for the killing of deer which may have come to the lake as part of their annual migration. At one site alone, about 4800 animal bones were recovered. The culling was not, however, indiscriminate, since few of the animal bones related to young individuals. These sites, therefore, are unlikely to have been permanent settlements but occasional butchery camps.

Another example of settlement around a lake can be found nearer to home in Scotland and Ireland. From the later Bronze Age onwards (approximately 1000 bc), a number of artificial islands were created in the lakes by the dumping of earth and stone. Such islands are known as crannogs. Here the settlements seem to have consisted of circular wooden structures built on islands themselves measuring between 15 and 30 metres in diametre. Recent interpretations have suggested that in some areas the crannog represented a small fortified homestead of a particularly powerful Celtic warrior. Crannogs continued to be used throughout the Middle Ages.

A medieval example of lake settlement can be found, ironically, back at Lake Paladru on the edge of which was located the Neolithic site of Charavines. There is some argument as to whether the medieval sites, which can cover as much as 15,000 square metres, were built on the dry land of a promontory jutting out into the lake or whether they were built over shallow water. These sites appear to have had certain defensive characteristics which offer parallels to the motte castles of the same period. They also appear to have had a significant role simply as peasant villages.

Most of these sites also have a superb level of preservation which has added much to the study of the archaeology of their own periods. The Neolithic settlements, however, have a particularly important role to play in understanding the occupation of these areas since they represent the first settled agricultural habitation of the lakes. Within the Neolithic period, the sites also add a new dimension to our understanding of the organisation of society itself.

Clairvaux and Charavines themselves were both occupied during the late Neolithic period at various dates in the later third millennium bc. In much of western Europe, this period is characterised by an absence of settlement sites and a preponderance of funerary sites – either single, aristocratic inhumations or communal family vaults built of stone. This is, of course, partly an accident of preservation. The burial mounds which cover the inhumations and the stone tombs have survived much better than the flimsy settlements of which now only a scatter of surface flints remains. As a result of this, the ritual aspects of late Neolithic life, associated with burial, have been a magnetic focus of study.

The lake sites provide much evidence to balance this. Villages such as Clairvaux and Charavines are uniquely important, for they go some way at least in telling us less about the way of death and more about the way of life of the people who lived in them.

Note: The excavator of Charavines is Aimé Bocquet and of Clairvaux, Pierre Pétrequin. Both men have generously made available to me both published and unpublished information on their sites. I would like to take this opportunity of thanking them for their assistance in the writing of this chapter and the kindness they have shown in allowing me to extend the information about their sites to a wider audience both here and in the *Origins* series on Radio 4. I would also like to thank Mme. Françoise Vin, the assistant director of Charavines, for providing useful additional information.

CHAPTER FIVE

WARRIORS AND TRADERS: BRONZE AGE CHIEFDOMS IN CENTRAL EUROPE

ANDREW SHERRATT

WARRIOR SOCIETIES:
WEAPONS, CHARIOTS AND HILLFORTS

On 2 November 1907 György Czibere and three other labourers were digging a drainage ditch into a sandhill at Hajdúsámson, some 20 kilometres from Debrecen in northeast Hungary. About three-quarters of a metre down, they came upon a set of bronze weapons: a sword, and twelve battle-axes – several of them richly decorated with ornate, curvilinear designs. Keeping the best of the axes for himself, Czibere sold the rest to the museum in Debrecen for 110 crowns; and they may still be seen there today.

The hoard had not been left haphazardly, abandoned in time of danger. It had been carefully arranged, with the sword aligned north–south (its tip pointing north) and the axe-heads laid across it, their blades to the west. It was a deliberate offering, a ceremonial dedication, and it represented the disposal of a considerable concentration of wealth and craftsmanship. The weapons were not mass-produced types of the kind which any warrior might have possessed. The sword, 0.53 metres long, was especially fine. Its leaf-shaped blade with a prominent midrib was ornamented by elegant lines of opposed C-scrolls on either side. The solid bronze hilt was cast on and secured by five rivets, the grip ornamented by arcading and terminating in a fine, lozenge-shaped pommel. The technological expertise in casting the hilt was as remarkable as the wealth of decoration lavished upon it. So too with the axes, surely weapons rather than working tools, with a striking elegance of line; three of them bore decoration in the same style as the sword. The two most impressive had a disc-shaped terminal which offered a circular field in which to develop a fourfold motif of linked C-scrolls, and its sense of rhythm and movement compares with the achievements of later, Celtic bronzesmiths.

Although spectacular, this hoard was not to remain a unique discovery: in 1939, just across the border at Apa in Romania, two suc swords and three finely decorated battle-axes, along with a spiral arm-guard, came to light in digging defence works at the outbreak of the last war. Other finds of decorated axes had been known since the nineteenth

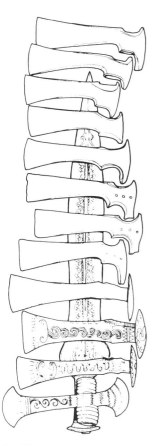

5.1 The hoard of bronze weapons from Hajdúsámson, as found (reconstruction)

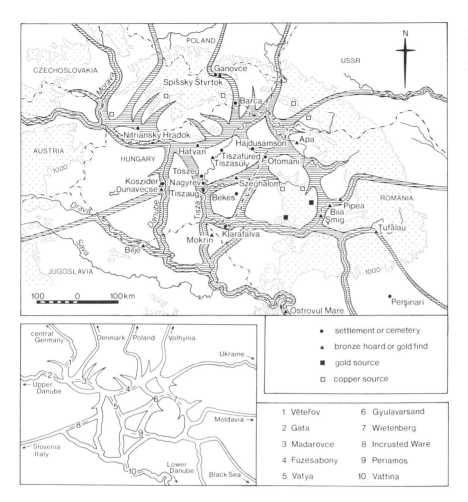

5.2 The Carpathian Basin showing principal sites and trade routes, with names of local groups (inset)

century – usually single finds or pairs, sometimes associated with other weapons such as spearheads made by the advanced technique of casting a hollow socket – and they were eagerly sought by collectors. Examples were purchased by English archaeologists such as Sir John Evans or General Pitt Rivers, and are now in archaeological collections.

Although each one of these weapons is different in detail, and each was an individual creation rather than a standardised product, they all nevertheless fall into well-defined types, with a clear pattern of distribution, concentrated in the area where Hungary, Romania and Czechoslovakia meet, around the headwaters of the River Tisza and its tributaries. That they were local products is demonstrated by fragments of the clay moulds used in casting them, which have been found on settlement sites in this region; and examples of the axes themselves have also been found as grave-goods in the richly endowed cemeteries of the north Tisza region, at Megyaszó and, more recently, at Tiszafüred. The group to which the makers of these weapons belonged has been named by archaeologists the Otomani culture, after a fortified settlement

5.3 Gold arm-ring from Bilje, northern Yugoslavia. It is 5cm across, and carries incised curvilinear ornament

5.4 Clay model wheels from early Bronze Age sites in Skovakia belonging to the Madarovce and Větěrov cultures. The four-spoke wheel in the middle is clearly that of a light chariot

site of this period in northwest Romania.[1]

The wealth of this area was not confined to bronze, however. Goldwork, too, has been found, ornamented with the same curvilinear style of decoration – notably the elegant arm-rings (of which the most splendid is undoubtedly the example from Bilje near Osijek in northern Yugoslavia, just outside the main concentration of the other finds but clearly an export from that area) and, even more importantly, a gold cup from the former County Bihar,[2] the heartland of this style of metalworking. Since the manufacture of sheet-metal vessels demands sophisticated workshop techniques, this cup and other gold vessels testify to a particularly high level of skill.

Even more surprising, perhaps, is the find of an iron knife-handle with bronze rivets, which came from a well at Gánovce in Slovakia. This object, securely dated by its association with other material in a sealed context, was not an import but reflects the experience of Carpathian bronzesmiths at smelting copper sulphide ores in which iron was a major impurity to be removed by slagging. (As an occasional novelty, this by-product was apparently made up into small objects – an interesting early use of a technology whose time was yet to come.)

The elegance in design which typifies the metalwork is similarly manifested in the whole range of products found associated with these metal types: the pottery forms, although hand-built rather than thrown on the wheel, are some of the most striking three-dimensional plastic shapes encountered in prehistoric Europe, and include bowls, jars and cups with conical bosses joined by swinging spirals. Another medium for this kind of ornament was antler- or bone-work, extensively used for small items of horse-gear such as the cheek-pieces of bridle-bits. On these items it is clear that this curvilinear ornament was constructed by using a small compass to lay out regularly disposed circles. It is possible that this technique lay behind the development of this whole system of curvilinear ornament, which may be why it seems to foreshadow some of the elements of the Celtic style which was to appear over a millennium later. Interestingly, objects decorated in this compass-work style were found in the Shaft Graves at Mycenae, dated to *c.* 1600 BC.

The occurrence of decorated items of bone and antler horse-gear (cheek-pieces, strap-junctions, possible whip caps) indicates the importance of horses in a region singularly well fitted for breeding them because of its extensive open plains and eastward links to the steppe homeland of the domesticated horse. Moreover, the occurrence of clay models of spoked wheels (and, somewhat later, a complete representation of a two-wheeled vehicle, on a pot), shows that the people of this area were some of the first in Europe – and perhaps in the world – to make use of the light, spoke-wheeled chariot: the first use ever of the harnessed horse. These vehicles, probably of a simple, bentwood construction, where the first means of rapid transport in combat and demanded expertise not only in building them but in breeding and training their draught-horses.

How did these people live, and what was the basis for their remarkable burst of artistic activity? What kind of sites did they inhabit? Over much of Bronze Age Europe, settlement sites and traces of architecture are notoriously rare – the result of relatively impermanent forms of construction, along with the destructive effects of 3000 years of subsequent agriculture. But here in the Carpathian Basin – a convenient geographical term used to encompass Hungary, parts of Romania, and Slovakia – the evidence is more abundant, and we have a good picture of the way of life of Bronze Age populations.

What is notable on sites of all sizes is the need for defence. The population was concentrated in small, fortified villages, usually round or oval in shape, and surrounded by one or two ditches and banks. In low-lying country, as along the rivers, these take the form of low mounds consisting of the remains of closely packed timber and mud houses sheltering behind their earthworks. Successive generations of village-dwellers rebuilt their homes within this confined space, so that later occupants looked out from the top of a low, artificial hillock – useful as a defence against floods as well as against human invaders. But even in hill-country, on the terraces and foothills around the plain, fortification was still necessary: isolated elevations and promontories were selected, and defended by ditches and walls of stone where this was available. A good example of the former, lowland type is the famous tell of Tószeg, now cut by the River Tisza itself: a striking, naturally defended site is the hill of Békés Várdomb, with its well-preserved log cabins.

Beyond the plain, in the valleys reaching up into the Carpathians and leading to important passes northwards through the mountains, lines of fortified sites are particularly evident. On the River Nitra, in western Slovakia, sites like Nitriansky Hrádock, with its 4.5-metre deep ditch and timber-laced earthen rampart, contained notable concentrations of decorated bonework and also a bronze hoard consisting of five axes and a spearhead. In an analogous position in the valley of the Hornad in eastern Slovakia, the fortified site at Barca near Košice was occupied for a considerable period and several levels of occupation have been distinguished in an occupation deposit 2.5 metres deep. In Level 2, a regular pattern of close-packed rectangular houses, in rows of different sizes, has been recovered. Twenty-three houses survived, out of an original total of perhaps 30 or 40, laid out in a grid within a circular bank and ditch. A later phase of occupation had been destroyed by fire, and was remarkable for the richness of finds, presumably from within houses: a finely decorated bronze dagger, several caches of bronze ornaments, a heavy amber necklace, 3 necklaces of gold beads, 20 sheet-gold hair-rings. These finds give some impression of the wealth of such settlements, on an occasion when personal possessions could not be

5.5 Antler cheek-piece of a bridle bit, 9cm long, with incised compass work, from Százhalombatta, Hungary. This kind of ornament seems particularly associated with horse gear

salvaged from destruction and have survived to give a rare snapshot of their quality and variety.

It is noteworthy, however, that none of these sites has yielded any trace of a 'palace', or even a substantial 'chief's hut', standing out from the rest. Some evidence of cult places survives, like the structure at Sălacea in Romania, but there is no obvious distinction among the secular buildings. This may suggest that these societies were organised not so much under the rule of single powerful chiefs as under some form of oligarchy of wealthy families, perhaps within a framework where religious sanctions played an important part. This might explain why the remarkable concentrations of warrior wealth at Hajdúsámson and Apa took the form of ritual deposits rather than accompanying the burials of particular prominent individuals. (It is characteristic of this area throughout the Bronze Age that ritual deposits – 'hoards' – were more spectacular than burials.) It is important not to project backwards to this time any stereotype of social organisation derived from the historical period: we simply do not know how these societies operated, and they may well have been fundamentally different from later 'barbarian' groups.[3]

What is clear is the extent to which the inhabitants of the Carpathian Basin stood out from their contemporaries, not just by their wealth and skills but more particularly by the emphasis on defended settlements – a pattern which only became common elsewhere in temperate Europe during the Urnfield period of the Late Bronze Age (1400–700 BC). This is most spectacularly evident from a group of sites above 600 metres in the Spiš, a fertile valley high up in the Carpathians whose northern end overlooks the steep descent towards the upper Vistula and the North European Plain beyond. One of these sites, Gánovce, has been largely destroyed by travertine quarrying but is noteworthy for waterlogged finds from a well, dug down to a thermal spring, which demonstrate otherwise missing organic components such as bark containers as well as bronze and gold objects apparently deposited for ritual purposes. Ten kilometres away from Gánovce is the defended settlement of Spišský Štvrtok, which seems to have been a 'fortress', attached to a larger agrarian settlement, dominating the major trade route northwards through the mountains. It was protected by a massive, stone-built wall which in places acted as a revetment to a rampart 7 metres thick. The construction of fortifications around an area of 6000 square metres argues for a considerable concentration of labour, and indicates the crucial nature of the Carpathian passes in connection with trade.

The routes leading northwards from the Carpathian Basin are marked by stray finds of the distinctive axes and other weapons, and by their local limitations further north. The East Slovakian route led to the Vistula and the eastern Baltic; the West Slovakian route passed up the

Elbe or along the Oder to Scandinavia. Southward connections, too, are evident (at a slightly later phase than the northward one); they are marked, for instance, by finds of daggers decorated in a curvilinear style that go through Slovenia (e.g. sites in the Ljubljana Marsh) down to northern Italy. This route, important throughout later prehistoric times and becoming a major artery of the Roman Empire, is also reflected in the distribution of decorated antler horse-gear and the curious but highly distinctive stamped clay tablets, which may be counters or tallies of some kind, and are known to archaeologists as *Brotlaibidolen*. Were these connected with a trade in horses, for which this route was famous in later times?

These warrior societies in the Carpathian Basin, with their fortifications, their chariots, their metal wealth and their range of long-distance contacts, stand out clearly on the map of Bronze Age Europe. Their influence was felt throughout the continent, and provided the basis of later development in many adjacent areas. But what was their date? What was their relationship with the Bronze Age civilisations of the Aegean? Who were these people, and what was their name?

The last question is the most difficult to answer, and this difficulty is, in some part, responsible for their lack of recognition in popular accounts. Later peoples, such as the Celts or the Scythians, or contemporaries such as the Mycenaean Greeks, have an image and a personality which is known from written texts. At the very least they have a name. For Bronze Age Europe outside the Aegean, we have no such labels. We can try to project backwards the main linguistic groups known to have existed in the first millennium BC, and to which Bronze Age groups were clearly ancestral. Thus, Bronze Age Scandinavians were broadly Germanic, or at least 'proto-Germanic'; the Bronze Age inhabitants of southern Germany, known from their tumulus burials, were perhaps partly 'proto-Celtic'. Following the same reasoning, our East Carpathian Bronze Age societies were perhaps northern members of a 'proto Thracian' group — ancestors of the peoples known to Herodotus as the Agathyrsae and the Getae, and to the Romans as the Dacians. But this does not tell us much about them, and still less explains their prominence in the ethnography of Bronze Age Europe. One factor was clearly their mineral wealth — the massive copper sources of Transylvania and Slovakia, the gold of Transylvania — and perhaps also the suitability of the adjacent plains of livestock-rearing. Yet such wealth was not necessarily exploited – Bronze Age Ireland, for instance, had the same set of resources, yet only achieved a comparable degree of sophistication in the late Iron Age, and then only under the influence of southern neighbours. Was it the Mycenaeans who were responsible for the Carpathian Basin's rise to prominence?

Traditional accounts of the period used to provide a simple answer. Mycenaean prospectors, searching for metal supplies, discovered the rich ore-bodies of Transylvania and the tin deposits of Bohemia. They opened up these sources, on which a flourishing local industry developed, and at the same time introduced elements of Mediterranean sophistication, reflected in the curvilinear ornament style, weaponry and the fortifications and elements of town planning. It was their impetus which began the local florescence of Carpathian culture. Extending further, their demand for exotic materials opened up the amber route, carrying this precious substance from Jutland and the Baltic coastlands southward to Greece.

A new generation of archaeologists, mostly British, has challenged this interpretation. Many of the supposed 'Mycenaean' features in the temperate European Bronze Age – such as the rich graves of Wessex and central Germany – can be dated by the tree-ring calibration of radiocarbon to a time *before* the Mycenaean period. Furthermore, critical scrutiny has revealed very few indisputable traces of direct Mycenaean influence on Europe outside the Mediterranean. Such archaeologists would see no evidence for contacts, trade or the transmission of new features between the Aegean and central Europe.

Continental archaeologists however, have by and large resisted this challenge to older views. They emphasise the uncertainties associated with the radiocarbon timescale for the Bronze Age, and point to resemblances between compass-decorated items in the Mycenae shaft graves and those in central Europe as demonstrating a connection, and hence giving a more reliable date for the Carpathian material than the earlier dates indicated by radiocarbon. They thus uphold the view that the Mycenaean intervention, some time around 1600 BC, was critical.

Can these views be reconciled? I think that both have some measure of truth, and that a fully satisfactory interpretation must account for all aspects of the evidence. The following picture is a personal view of what happened in central Europe, and how it affects our understanding of Bronze Age development as a whole. It does involve Mycenae, but in a very different way from that which either side has suggested so far.

TRADE AND CONTACT IN BRONZE AGE EUROPE

The Carpathian Basin had long been one of the most technologically advanced areas of prehistoric Europe. Already by the fourth millennium BC[4] it was the scene of a flourishing copper industry, making massive shafthole tools whose forms owed nothing to contemporary Near Eastern industries. With large herds of cattle on their open plains, and a desirable metal for export to less advanced regions, these Copper Age communities had intermittent long-distance links with areas as far away as Denmark and the Ukraine, where objects of Carpathian copper have been found. From surrounding territories the inhabitants of the

Carpathian Basin acquired small amounts of good-quality flint for long dagger-blades, and also a few of the horses then being domesticated by neighbouring steppe tribes to the east. Greece at this time was far less advanced, with only small amounts of copper made into relatively primitive tools.

In the later fourth millennium, however, this picture began to change. The growth of trade links from the expanding, newly urbanised societies of the Near East (with their need for precious metals like silver) had opened up the routes into what is now Turkey, and on the periphery of this sophisticated new world were flourishing trading centres like Troy, well placed to command the passage to the Aegean and the Black Sea. Many novelties spread along these routes, including innovations in farming and transport technology, as well as more sophisticated craft skills such as alloying, complex casting and the manufacture of fine gold jewellery. Luxury items, like wine made from grapes and metal vessels for drinking it, also came into use. Some of these elements spread further west, to Troy's European neighbours. Greece was drawn into this commercial network and developed its own small fortified craft centres, perhaps gaining their wealth by supplying silver to Troy; but in the northern Balkans and central Europe only the most basic features were acquired, such as wheeled vehicles and that other useful application of draught oxen, the plough. The pottery, however, shows clearly the impact of southern sophistication, in shapes that are direct imitations of metal vessels – probably used for drinking some local alcoholic drink such as mead or honey-beer.

Links with the steppe people – who themselves had acquired certain aspects of Near Eastern technology via the Caucasus – also became more important. Stock-rearing tribes with horses and ox-carts (perhaps bringing the first wool-bearing breeds of sheep) seemed to have moved west to settle in areas of Romania and eastern Hungary, bringing their own metallurgical techniques and the practice of burial in large, circular mounds that still dot these steppe landscapes. They may have been among the first speakers of Indo European languages.

Impulses from these two areas were absorbed by local populations, and caused fundamental changes in society. Old areas of settlement were abandoned, and new sites appeared on the sandy ridges of the plains and in the mountain fringe. Metals were more intensively worked, and made into new types of weapons, made possible by more advanced manufacturing techniques: battle-axes, long daggers, and spears. Bridle equipment and clay models of spoked wheels testify to the first use of the chariot: and everywhere, communities sheltered behind newly thrown-up fortifications. Radiocarbon dates demonstrate that this pattern was well underway by the early centuries of the second millennium BC – before the emergence of major centres of power on the Greek mainland like Pylos and Mycenae.

5.6 Routes of trade and contact in Bronze Age Europe (2000-1500 BC). Indirect overland contacts in central Europe (traceable by the distribution of distinctive types of bronze weapons) were mainly focused on the Carpathian Basin, although there was another network centred in the Upper Danube. Not all routes were active at the same time. Seaborne trade in the Mediterranean (traceable by exported Mycenaean and Cretan pottery) was more organised, and channelled through major centres. The two systems were potentially in contact in Italy, and on the Black Sea coast

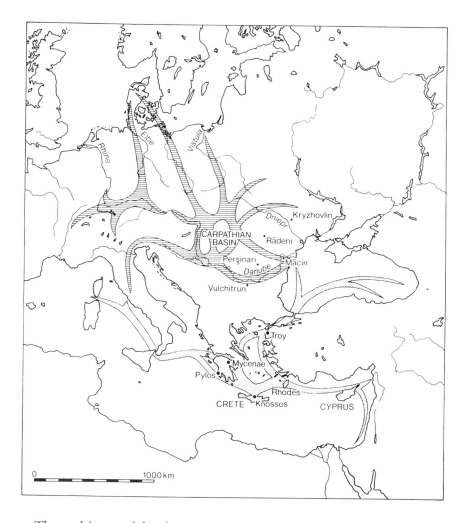

5.7 Impression of a stone seal, c. 1cm across, from Crete (LM III period) showing a masted ship. The introduction of the sail from the east Mediterranean around 2000 BC made possible the kind of seaborne trade which supported the Bronze Age palaces of Crete

The real focus of development in the Aegean by this time had shifted to Crete, where a truly urban lifestyle gained its first foothold in Europe. Palaces like Knossos, Phaistos and Mallia, surrounded by small towns inhabited by craftsmen working under the direction of the palace elite, were centres at which the products of the countryside and surrounding islands were made into objects which were in demand by the sophisticated consumers of the East Mediterranean. It was Syria, now more directly accessible by means of the sailing ships which had replaced earlier log canoes, that provided Bronze Age Cretans in the early years of the second millennium with an outlet for their products and a source of novel ideas, as well as rare but basic commodities like tin. This trade grew, and after 1750 BC began to include processed agricultural products such as scented oil, wine, (and perhaps fine cloth) which were produced on Cretan country estates. The inscribed clay tablets of this period, written in a script called Minoan Linear A, cannot yet be read; but the later distribution of special containers for liquids (the so-called stirrup jars) is mute testimony to this growth of trade.

So far, these two areas of Bronze Age development – the 'barbarian' societies of the Carpathian Basin and the palace-centred societies of Crete – have each been described without reference to one another. Although their backgrounds had common elements, they were essentially independent and very different in character. It was only in the later part of the second millennium, especially after 1600 BC with the emergence of power centres in mainland Greece, that a new pattern is evident in which their spheres of influence had become to some extent interlinked. The mainland centres formed a bridge between the central European chiefdoms, in touch with a north and east European hinterland, and the South Aegean societies with their Near Eastern connections.

Let us return to the Carpathian Basin and the communities which produced the Hajdúsámson hoard, with which we began. These were some of the most advanced groups on the European mainland at that time, which we have dated to the earlier second millennium. The northward connection to Scandinavia, first evident as far back as the Copper Age, was by now especially strong. The developing Scandinavian bronze industry took many of its models – and probably much of its raw material, since it had no natural copper and tin sources – from the Carpathian Basin. Swords and spearheads, and their local version of curvilinear and geometric element, can be related directly to types represented at Hajdúsámson and Apa. The fortresses on the Carpathian passes controlled a massive transfer of material and expertise across the mountains and on to the growing population of Scandinavia, probably in exchange for items like furs and amber. Commodities moving northwards included metalwork and probably also horses and perhaps woolly sheep and their products. While Mycenae was still a relatively unimportant regional centre on the edge of the Aegean trade routes, the communities of the Carpathian Basin had already established their industrial and military base and set up long distance trade links with their northern neighbours.

There was then a major re-alignment of trade routes in central Europe. The northern fortresses went out of use, trade with Scandinavia slackened, and instead the southern routes came into prominence. The metal supplies of Transylvania were no longer exported northwards, yet local prosperity continued, as shown by bronze hoards like the group from Koszider on the middle Danube. North Italy shows an influx of Carpathian bronze types, and also horse-gear. Had trade now switched southwards, to the Mediterranean?[5]

In the Aegean at this time there are signs of the growing importance of the southern Greek mainland. Two areas became especially prosperous: Messinia, centred on Pylos and well placed for trade with Italy; and the Argos plain, centred on Mycenae with its northward routes to

5.8 Trade routes bringing European commodities to Crete and the Aegean passed through peninsular Greece, where they were funnelled along an important artery from Corinth to the Gulf of Argos. This map is based on the distribution of major Mycenaean sites and sections of Bronze Age roads. Mycenae rose to prominence because of its position dominating both this route and the fertile Plain of Argos. (Note that the coastline has since shifted because of silting, leaving the site of the Mycenaean port of Tiryns land-locked)

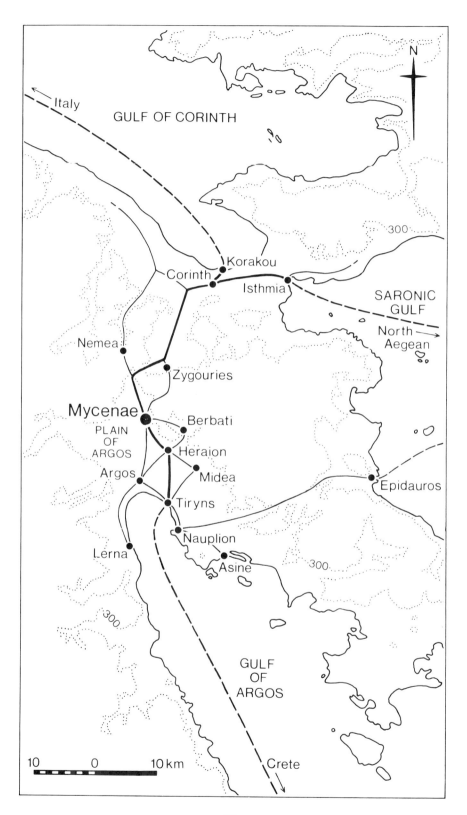

Corinth and access to routes both west to Italy and northeast across the Aegean to the Black Sea. Both areas show new, ostentatious forms of burial – the first stone-built beehive (*tholos*) tombs near Pylos, and the famous circles of shaft graves at Mycenae. At both there are traces – alongside the massive evidence of Cretan craft goods – of northward contacts with central Europe: amber beads and objects in the enigmatic, compass-decorated style which we have seen were especially associated with horse-rearing groups in the Carpathian Basin. Were central European metals reaching the Aegean network, then being shipped via southern Greece to Crete? Were Pylos and Mycenae getting rich on the proceeds? Did Greeks also acquire – however indirectly – elements of horse-gear (and perhaps breeding stock) from expert chariot-using groups on the sandy plains of Hungary?

5.9 Mycenaean two-handed gold cup from Romania, probably of the Shaft Grave period (16th century BC): its regular profile shows that it has been finished on the lathe

There is some further evidence that this may have been so. Early Mycenaean pottery turns up both in southern Italy and at Troy. From the lower Danube is a series of items of goldwork, like the Perşinari dagger, the Măcin halberds, and the early gold vessels from Vulchitrun, Rădeni and Kryzhovlin (the first accurately centred, lathe-smoothed gold vessels from temperate Europe) which have no background in that area but would fit easily in the treasures of the Shaft Graves. A two-way traffic, with basic commodities going south and a few sophisticated items going north, may be envisaged. After all, if Hungarian copper and Bohemian tin could reach Denmark, then why not Greece – the same distance in the opposite direction?[6]

This reconstruction (in which Mycenaean Greece first rose to prominence as an intermediary between two very different types of trading systems – the Aegean palace-centered maritime trade and the simpler overland transfer of goods in central Europe) solves a number of problems. On a technical level, it removes the puzzle of the date of the compass-decorated horse-gear and that of the Hajdúsámson hoard. If it was not a Mycenaean feature going northwards but a Carpathian feature coming south, then its early radiocarbon dating in the north and its relatively later appearance at Mycenae would make sense. At the level of economic history, it explains why southern Greece rose to prominence within the Aegean world, and neatly pinpoints the two main centres of growth on the principal trade routes. And it reconciles the otherwise conflicting convictions of different scholars, some of whom assert the independence of European development and others who point to the evidence for some kind of links. In a way, both are right.

In subsequent centuries, it was the mainlanders who were to wrest control of Aegean trading networks from the Cretans, to the extent even of invading Crete and implanting the Greek language, awkwardly written in an adaptation of the old script called Linear B. They then adopted for themselves some of the techniques of Cretan palace accountancy and introduced them into their mainland capitals. They expanded the eastwards trade, selling their own wares and gaining access to other supplies of copper. Their northern links dwindled, and their former Carpathian suppliers experienced recession and relative isolation, as well as competition within Europe from their western neighbours in southern Germany. An episode in the economic history of central Europe had come to an end.

The effects of this episode on the prehistory of Europe, however, were long-lasting. Many of the elements of later developments had been assembled. Central Europe had gained its first experience of the effects of Near Eastern civilisation on its southern neighbours, and had used its position as the crossroads between other cultures – on the steppes, in northern Europe, and in the Aegean – to take advantage of its local resources and participate in a wider world.[7]

1   Formerly in Hungary, when it was spelt Ottomány. Hungarian archaeologists distinguish other groups of this culture, again named after fortified villages of the period, such as Füzesabony and Gyulavarsánd.

2   This find, made before the break-up of the Austro-Hungarian Empire, is only recorded under the name of the country where it was found. County Bihar is now split between Hungary and Romania.

3   The term 'chiefdom' used in the title of the chapter implies that these societies included elite groups capable of mobilising wealth and organising trade, but that they did not have the coherence and continuity characteristic of early states. In reality, however, the definition covers a wide variety of types of society, and the significance of 'chiefdoms' has been much debated by archaeologists.

4   All radiocarbon dates and date-ranges quoted in this article are based on the tree-ring correction to ensure consistency with historical dates (e.g. for the Aegean region) which are based ultimately on Egyptian written sources.

5   A rather similar phenomenon occurred during the first millennium BC, by which time Carpathian copper was again supplying Scandinavia. The diversion of metal flows southwards between the seventh and fifth centuries BC in response to the growing demand of the resurgent Greek city-states, had the effect of cutting off the north from its bronze supplies and so precipitating the shift to iron.

6   As fig. 5.7 shows, the two routes in question were the east Alpine route and the Black Sea route: the Adriatic was little used as a transport artery at this period. Links within Italy show that northern Italy was connected overland with the west coast, where a concentration of Mycenaean finds suggest that commodities were there transferred to Mycenaean vessels. The Black Sea route is less documented, and was perhaps used only intermittently by the kind of entrepreneurs later depicted in the legend of Jason and the Golden Fleece.

7   This account is based on a number of papers, unpublished or in press, two of which have been written in collaboration with Sue Sherratt and Tim Taylor. I am grateful to them for their comments on what is written above.

CHAPTER SIX
LEFKANDI AND THE GREEK DARK AGE

MERVYN POPHAM

The early history of Greece, which culminated, after many centuries, in the civilisation of Classical Greece, is obscure. The later Greeks themselves had little recollection of it. Epic poetry and myths had handed down stories of a glorious past, such as the siege and capture of Troy, when kings lived in glorious palaces and warriors fought in chariots with weapons of bronze. There were vague memories, after this, of confused conditions, when races moved location and people migrated overseas; these may have been preserved in folk memories and family pedigrees. But there was clearly a lack of any real knowledge of events until the establishment of the earliest Greek settlements in Italy and Sicily in the years between 750 and 700 BC, a gap of nearly 500 years after the traditional date of the Trojan War.

This gap has become known as the Dark Age, not only because of Greek ignorance about it but equally because what was known of it archaeologically indicated an age of depopulation, poverty and isolation – depressed conditions from which the communities of Greece only slowly emerged.

In this emergence, we can now see from recent excavations that an important part – perhaps a leading role – was played by Euboea, the large island which lies along the north coast of Attica and Boeotia.

6.1 Cup with semi-circle decoration

67

6.2 Principal sites on the island of Euboea and the Greek mainland

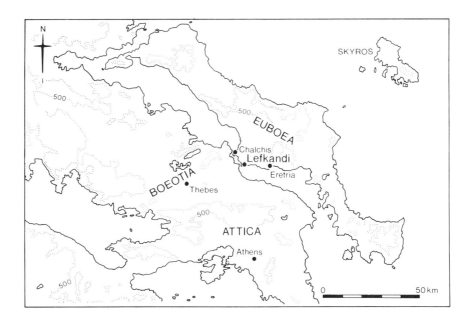

Euboea's early importance was hinted at by the literary records which show that it sent out the first colonies to Italy and Sicily. It was also known to have settled the region of northern Greece still called Chalcidice after the name of one of Euboea's main cities, Chalcis. There are also references to a war of more than local impact between Chalcis and Eretria, the other major city of the island – a conflict which probably exhausted both sides and led to the eclipse of Euboea's early pre-eminence, shortly before 700 BC.

Archaeology has been able to fill out these meagre literary references. Excavations at Ischia in Italy have uncovered part of the earliest Euboean settlement in that region, founded around 750 BC. At Eretria, Swiss and Greek archaeologists have revealed part of the large contemporary settlement there. Other finds have been made at Chalcis; and Chalcidice, too, is in the course of investigation. But the impetus which started this interest in Euboea came from an earlier excavation, that of Sir Leonard Woolley at Al Mina in northern Syria, where he discovered the earliest Greek trading post overseas – established jointly, it seems, with Cypriots soon after 800 BC. The identity of these venturous Greek traders was uncertain until John Boardman, now Professor of Classical Archaeology at Oxford, recognised the earlier pottery at the site to be Euboean. Evidence from that island itself was slight, but this has now been made good, and of those vases exported to Al Mina we can point to one type in particular as being a hallmark of Euboean trade – a two-handled cup with concentric semicircles painted below the rim.

This knowledge is but one of the results of the excavations at Lefkandi, a site on the south coast of Euboea, roughly halfway between Chalcis and Eretria. More importantly, they have shown that the people of Euboea were actively trading with the Near East still earlier, at a time when Greece was thought to be stagnating in isolation from the outside world. These trading ventures brought their leaders wealth unknown at this time in the rest of Greece, as their tombs testify, while their prosperity, and perhaps experience abroad, provided them with the resources and stimulus to build the first monumental building we know of in Greece.

Lefkandi, where these discoveries have been made, was a small fishing village and a centre of brick-making when we first went there in 1954 to begin three seasons of excavation carried out by the British School of Archaeology at Athens in the large ancient settlement which is now known as Xeropolis ('the deserted town'). Since then Lefkandi has become a popular seaside resort, with restaurants, blocks of flats and hotels strung out along its beaches. Every year more summer bungalows spring up on the slopes of the hill above the harbour, in the cemetery area of the ancient town. Damage to the antiquities is inevitable, despite careful supervision, but all this activity also brings to light new discoveries, as we shall see later.

We do not know the ancient name of the settlement, which is strange since its unusually large size shows it to have been a town of considerable importance throughout its long history. It occupies the whole of a long, rather narrow plateau with abrupt cliffs some 17 metres high facing the sea and having a somewhat gentler incline on the landward side. On its two other sides are small bays; that to the west being deeper and larger, and used until recently as a harbourage for visiting caiques which loaded bricks from the nearby factories, and transported them mainly to the Cycladic islands.

Not only was the site well-chosen for its ready access to the sea but it had very considerable agricultural advantages too, being situated not far from the mouth of the River Lelas, either side of which a fertile alluvial plain stretches for several kilometres inland. Now divided up into vineyards and orchards of cherry and fig trees, the plain is also a rich source of fine clay used for making bricks and pottery. Known in antiquity as the Lelantine Plain, it was said to have been one of the points of conflict between Chalcis and Eretria which led to their war. (Later it was coveted by the Athenians, who, in the sixth century, after defeating the Chalcidians, took over the plain and planted settlers there. Two millennia later the Venetians made it part of their maritime empire and thought it sufficiently valuable to protect with three watchtowers and an impressive castle built on a steep hill which dominates the region.) At the time of the war between Chalcis and Eretria, it may have been partly left as expensive pasturage for the horses of the aristocrats of Chalcis who, we are told, were called the Horse-rearers, a title which they may have earned even as early as the Dark Age, to judge from two horse burials at Lefkandi.

The tombs in the cemetery area, some 600 metres away from Xeropolis, have been more informative about this stage than the settlement itself, where subsequent rebuilding may have removed much of the evidence. A dump there of clay moulds, however, discarded after use in a bronze-foundry, told us that the inhabitants were already capable of sophisticated metalworking as early as 900 BC. We learnt, too, that the site had been finally destroyed and abandoned shortly before 700 BC, presumably in the course of the war between its neighbouring cities; and this, if so, gives us a more exact date for that important event.

But it is on the earlier history of the region that our quite limited excavations on Xeropolis have shed most light, revealing that it was occupied almost continuously for over 1300 years from its settlement in about 2000 BC, in the later stages of the Early Bronze Age, throughout the Middle and Late Bronze Ages up to its destruction and abandonment. In this we were fortunate; for we found that in the area we had chosen for our main investigation the remains of the successive settlements had accumulated one above another for a depth of 8.5 metres – typical of a Near Eastern tell site, but most unusual in Greece.

The pottery of the earliest settlers indicated that they were immigrants from northeastern Asia Minor who slowly assimilated with the local population in the neighbourhood. Thereafter we could trace five successive stages of the Middle Bronze Age up to the introduction of Mycenaean pottery. Perhaps the greatest contribution to our knowledge, however, came from the deep accumulation of levels belonging to the years between about 1200 and 1100 BC, that stage of the Mycenaean Age following the destruction of its palaces and many of its towns and continuing up to the point when Mycenaen civilisation, finally exhausted, fades away almost entirely in Greece and we enter the Iron Age and a new beginning. That intriguing final stage was little known archaeologically and could be regarded almost as part of the Dark Age, or, at least, as the immediate prelude to it.

Around 1200 BC, Xeropolis was rebuilt after receiving a large increase in its population, probably refugees from the troubles and dangers on the mainland. This settlement was burnt down, and the pots and many of the inflammable contents of the houses were found intact as they had been at the time of the destruction: in this, too, we were fortunate. There were corn, olives and figs in their storage bins, a bath, a range of storage jars and kitchen pots, together with the finer vases in use for the table. We were most excited, however, by the discovery of a small quantity of hand-made pottery alien to Greece and which resembled vases at home in southern Italy. Could it be that the refugees on Xeropolis included aliens from that region? And if so what were they doing in Greece? Similar evidence has since been found on other sites and the answers to our questions are still being debated.

6.3 Excavation of the settlement mound on Xeropolis

After its burning the town was entirely rebuilt on a different plan, almost grid-like in the regularity of its houses and rooms. Then it, too, suffered some disruption, the danger of which perhaps led its inhabitants to bury their dead inside the houses close to the walls of the rooms, a practice virtually unknown in Greece. Yet they were not foreigners, to judge from the vases they used, which continued in the old Mycenaean tradition, but with one interesting innovation in particular: they delighted in decorating special vases with natural and mythical animals, birds and warriors. Only one such vase survived intact, an alabastron depicting two griffins feeding their young in a nest and accompanied by a sphinx and a stag. Other fragments showed the range of their interests, including a kilted warrior armed with his sword. This settlement, too, did not last for long and was, in turn, partly built over by other houses in which there were signs of a severe run-down in standards. And then, it seems that the settlement was temporarily deserted, just when the real Dark Age begins.

We pick up the story again, not long afterwards – say some 50 years later, soon after 1100 BC – in the cemetery area which was first used at this stage. At least six burial plots have so far been located just above the village of Lefkandi, on the slopes of a hill overlooking the sea. Probably the whole of this area was used as a cemetery by the inhabitants who either cremated their dead on funeral pyres or buried them in cist tombs constructed of large stone slabs, sometimes even combining both practices by placing a token number of cremated bones in a cist tomb together with the offerings. Later they gave up the laborious practice of building their tombs and were content with digging a simple shaft into the rock over which they placed a cover of stone slabs. The burials, of which some 177 tombs and 91 pyres have been investigated, are often packed so closely together that one tomb has been cut into another. The earliest belong to the so-called Sub-Mycenaean stage, soon after 1100 BC, when our evidence fails on the settlement. And this raises

6.4 Vase depicting two griffins feeding their young, accompanied by a sphinx and a stag

6.5 Lefkandi and its environs

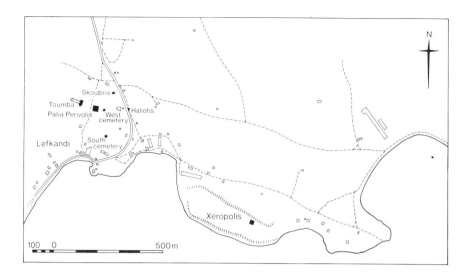

some problems. Were the people living on Xeropolis at this time, and if not, where else, since we have found no trace of another settlement? And were they descendants of the last Bronze Age inhabitants or newcomers, since their pottery, though in the same Mycenaean tradition, has marked differences?

The burials enable us to trace developments in the evolution of the inhabitants over 250 years. Initially the offerings in the tombs, though fairly lavish in pottery, contain little in the way of luxury items: some finger rings – occasionally of gold wire but more often bands of bronze – dress pins of iron and fasteners for their clothes, called fibulas (a kind of large safety pin), made either of bronze or iron.

The situation so far seemed to fit the picture we had been led to expect, of depressed conditions and isolation. But a surprise came in a tomb dating around 1000 BC, the burial of a warrior which contained his short iron sword and, in addition, a plain undistinguished-looking vase but whose shape and fabric made it certain that it had come from Syria or Palestine. Then, a somewhat later, and otherwise ordinary, burial contained a necklace composed of beads of glass paste and one of cornelian, again an exotic object brought from the same region of the Near East. Unexpected as this evidence was for contact of some kind with distant overseas countries, there were still no signs of any wealth or very unusual progress until another discovery shattered all our preconceptions.

In the cemetery area is a small but prominent hillock, appropriately called by the inhabitants Toumba ('the mound'). It looked a possible site for a small settlement, which surface sherds seemed to support. However, a test on one of its slopes uncovered another cemetery, though one which was markedly richer than the others. It was not until 1980 that the true nature of Toumba was revealed, when the owner of its summit applied for permission to build there. This required the District Office of the Greek Archaeological Service to make preliminary test trenches, and these brought to light part of a building, apparently Protogeometric in date, a period (1050–900 BC) of which architecturally little was known and certainly nothing with such substantial walls. A combined Greek and British full-scale excavation was planned, but,

6.6 Plan and reconstruction of the Heroon

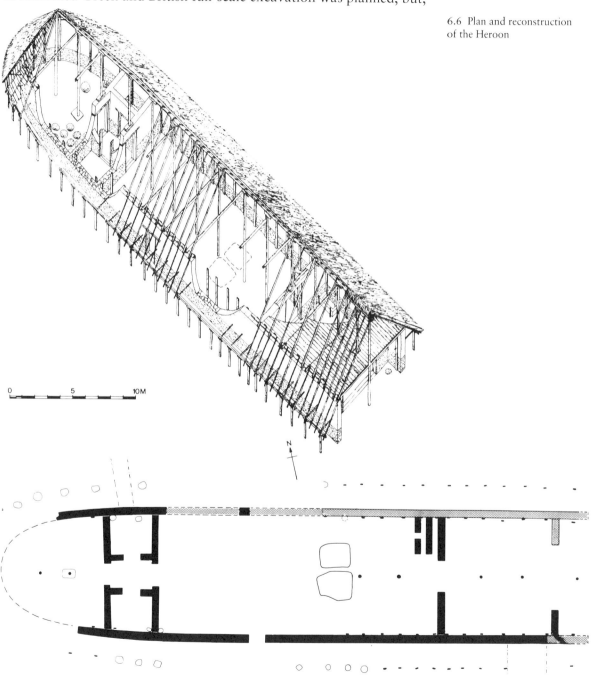

0   5   10M

before that could take place, the owner brought in a bulldozer on a feast day when the authorities were on holiday and he cleared nearly the whole of his plot, digging in places well below rock surface. In some hours a third of the building was destroyed. Fortunately, however, most of the walls had previously been planned and the surviving part of the building has recently been uncovered in three seasons of excavation.

These have revealed a monumental building, 10 metres wide and at least 47 metres long, of a size and quality far beyond what the Greeks of that time were believed to be capable of constructing. It had been erected on a large artificial platform of levelled rock and given well-built walls with a high stone base on which was set the mudbrick superstructure, and their inner faces were finished with plaster. Unfortunately, both ends of the building and sections of its walls had been badly damaged by recent stone-robbing and road-making, but its original plan is reasonably certain. It had a shallow porch at the east end, mainly destroyed, with a wide entrance leading into a nearly square 'anteroom' through which was approached the long, rectangular 'hall' beyond. From this, a corridor led, between two small flanking chambers, into the apsidal western end, also badly destroyed, but with its series of pits, presumably to hold storage jars, still preserved. A series of 11 substantial circular posts of wood ran down its centre, about the size of telegraph posts, and these had supported a thatched roof. Wooden supporting posts, rectangular in shape, were set at closer intervals along the inner face of the walls, while around the outside of the structure ran a further row of similar posts, clearly to support a veranda. The shape and size of these posts are often visible in the refill of the pits into which they were set, and even remains of the wood is sometimes preserved in the form of silvery dust. Enough details, indeed, survived to enable a reasonably accurate reconstruction of it to be made in drawing.

At first we thought that such an imposing building might have been a temple but a further discovery discounted this idea. Two adjacent deep shafts had been dug into the rock, roughly in the centre of the building. One contained the skeletons of four horses, two with simple iron bits still preserved in their mouths. The other had been carefully finished with a lining of mudbricks and clay plaster and held the body of a woman, laid out along one wall, and a decorated bronze amphora which was found to contain cremated bones, cloth bands and a rolled-up garment – clearly the burial of a warrior since his iron sword and spearhead, together with a whetstone, had been placed alongside the urn. The bronze vessel had collapsed under the pressure of the earth above it but its stout rim and handles were sufficiently well preserved, despite corrosion, to make out most of their decoration – a series of bulls, lions and other animals with hunters aiming their bows interspersed among them, on the rim.

The woman's skeleton was lavishly provided with jewellery: two gilt

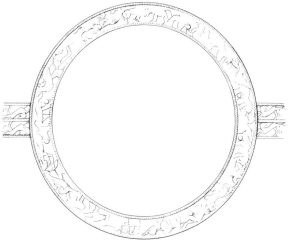

hair coils, a gold necklace, bronze and gilt iron pins, and two embossed gold discs, one over each breast with a lunate-shaped sheet of decorated gold, perhaps for the collar. Two rings of gold and of silver were on her fingers while by her head had been placed an iron knife with an ivory handle.

6.7 *Left:* Rim and crushed body of the bronze vessel in situ
Right: Reconstructed drawing of decoration on rim

The goldwork was quite unexpected for that period, but still more so were two of the offerings, both with a foreign origin. For the bronze amphora is likely to be of Cypriot manufacture and somewhat of an heirloom, but not such an antique as the gold necklace with its pendant finely decorated with granulation, which is exactly matched by ones from Babylonia belonging to around 2000 BC.

If these burials exclude the possibility that the building was a temple, what was its purpose? Under the clay floor near the burial shafts was a scorched area of rock covered with ash, which looked like the site of a funeral pyre, while in the nearby corner of the room a clay box had been constructed, which was found to contain wood ash and small fragments of cremated bone, suggesting they were sweepings-up of the pyre, carefully preserved. But had the building already existed, any pyre in this location would have set fire to the wall timbers and the roof, and this had not happened. So, if this was the site on which the warrior was cremated, the building must have been constructed after the funeral. It seems, then, that the building was intended as a monumental house for the persons buried in it – a Heroon, at least in the sense that it honoured a warrior who had been given a burial of a kind remarkably similar to that provided for the heroes in the poems of Homer.

There is no evidence for cult worship; indeed, the structure was found almost empty with nothing to indicate its use. But its extraordinarily early date can be determined from the pottery it contained. For, very soon after its construction, perhaps following some structural damage,

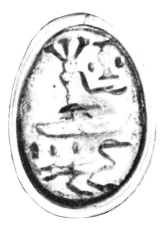

6.8 Gold mounted scarab

a decision was taken to partly dismantle its walls, fill it in and cover its remains with a mound of earth. To facilitate this great undertaking the porch was closed with a rough blocking wall, a ramp was heaped up against the outer walls, composed largely of mudbricks and earth, and then a fill of stones, pebbles and earth was tipped into the interior of the building from above. This process was clear from the section across the central room cut by the bulldozer; the medley of differently coloured mudbricks used in constructing the ramp against the south wall was especially conspicuous. Part of the earth fill must have been brought from the communal rubbish dump since it contained a mass of broken pottery. It is this household pottery, together with the few vases of identical character left on the floor of the building, which date its abandonment to around 950 BC or somewhat earlier. In also helps date a monumental clay krater which had been set up beside the burial shafts which otherwise would have been difficult to place chronologically because of its unique size and decoration.

The name of the warrior honoured in this extraordinary way is unknown. His memory may be hidden somewhere in later Greek myth but, if so, there is no obvious candidate. We are told, however, that even 200 years later there was still a king at Chalcis, so it is not too fanciful to call this extraordinary burial a royal one, perhaps even that of the founder of a particular royal dynasty. This would certainly help to explain the special character of the burial ground in front of the building which began to be used soon after the Heroon was covered over. The tombs there are far richer in gold objects and contain an unusual number of fine vases from the nearby region of Attica with which its dead must have had close relations; they may even have intermarried, to judge from four of the burials: three of these were of warriors who were given tombs of an Attic type, with their cremated bones placed in an amphora which was set in a hole dug into the bottom of the rock-cut shaft.

But their external contacts reached much further afield than this, as can be seen from the large number of luxury objects from the Near East. Far from living in isolation, the inhabitants were actively trading with Syria, Palestine and Cyprus at least by 900 BC, and profiting considerably from their transactions. A bichrome flask in one of the other burial grounds is an undoubted import from Cyprus, and it was not the only one since the local potters imitated other Cypriot types. From that same island came a gold fibula and at least the idea for the design of a pair of earrings with gold granulation, which closely correspond to the description by Homer of those worn by Hera with their three mulberry-like clusters. Cyprus, too, may have been the source of an enigmatic pair of large bronze wheels, while Near Eastern models, if not actual manufacture, are indicated in the case of two crescent-shaped pendants of gold, decorated with minute cones of granulation. A gold necklace, too, is strung with spiral beads of a type which has a long history in that area of the eastern Mediterranean, which may also be responsible for a related pair of spiral earrings. The uncertainty in ascribing a definite source for some of this goldwork is due to the surprising fact that there must have been a jeweller already working at Lefkandi since he produced a series of objects known only on Euboea and the nearby island of Skyros, objects we call vaguely 'attachments' since their exact function is uncertain.

Another group of objects resemble Egyptian work but are usually regarded as Phoenician imitations; these include a gold-mounted scarab, an inscribed cuboid seal, two other seals in the shape of a lion with hieroglyphs incised on the base, and a necklace with over 50 faience pendants of seated figures, one depicting the goddess Isis, the others a lion-headed god.

The contents of one tomb in particular widened the possible scope of overseas contacts still further, to Egypt itself. This burial, of around 900 BC, was supplied with many vases, including six from nearby Attica, one from northern Greece and a unique pot with a handle in the form of a human leg – of additional interest in that it tells us the type of footwear being worn at the time. Apart from the curious pair of bronze wheels, mentioned earlier, the tomb also contained an iron sword, adze, and two bronze fibulas as well as several necklaces, gold bands and four of those puzzling gold 'attachments'. Its large cover slabs had impeded all but a little earth and water from seeping through to the burial, which was fortunate since this had protected its surprising group of faience objects, comprising five vessels, a plaque and a ring. While necklaces of imported faience and glass beads are a common feature of the Toumba burials – there are over 20,000 disc beads, for instance – a collection of objects of this kind would be extraordinary even at a much later date in Greece. The colouring of two vases, in the shape of a bunch of grapes, the small jar and the ring vase are particularly well preserved, as too are the amiable features of a recumbent lion or cat on the plaque. Suspicions of a possible Egyptian origin, however, arose more directly from the faience ring with its bezel moulded in the form of a ram-headed god of that country, wearing an elaborate pectoral and crowned with a solar disc.

A similar ring was found in last year's excavations and if these are of Egyptian manufacture, they may not be alone, because the same origin has been suggested for several of the bronze vases in the tombs, two jugs with lotus-bud handles (one from the tomb with the faience vases), a *situla* (bucket) engraved with an Egyptian offering scene and a spouted jug with a similar rounded base.

A different source, probably northern Syria, has been suggested as the home of another particularly fine bronze vase, unfortunately somewhat crushed and corroded, but still retaining its finely incised and embossed decoration of winged sphinxes and elaborate trees. This bowl was found with one of our finest Attic vases, which helps date the burial to shortly after 900 BC.

The presence of these exotic imports at Lefkandi does not, of course, in itself prove that they are the result of Euboean seafaring. Indeed, some scholars have preferred to regard them as evidence for early trading by Phoenician merchants in Greek waters and cite Homer in their support – essentially one passage in the *Odyssey* of dubious location and date. In any case, this alternative view must be weighed against the known outcome of this activity, the establishment by Euboeans of the trading post at Al Mina in Syria, and the widespread distribution of the island's pottery in other areas of the Aegean and the eastern Mediterranean. This, in turn, can be regarded as the prelude to the still longer voyages by Euboeans to the West in the next century.

Moreover, as the burials show, the island's interests extended to other areas as well, particularly to northern Greece. Actual imports from Thessaly and Macedonia were placed in the tombs and the potters of Lefkandi imitated vases which they had seen from those regions. Interest in this area may have spurred one potter to fashion the figurine of a centaur – one of the mythical creatures, half-man, half-horse, whose traditional home was on Mount Pelion in Thessaly. It has been called one of the great artistic achievements of the Dark Age and was certainly prized in its day; for, after being broken, its head was placed in one tomb and its body in another. To facilitate trade in this direction, the Euboeans may even have established a settlement on the small island of Skyros, off its north coast. Here the burials from at least 900 BC onwards are remarkably similar to those at Lefkandi: the same sort of pottery, dress ornaments, jewellery and, even, the surprisingly early occasional Near Eastern import. The island lies well positioned for trade in the shipping lanes of the North Aegean, and Euboean interest in this region may, again, be the prelude to its later colonisation of Chalcidice.

No further burials were made in the Toumba cemetery or in any of the other excavated burial grounds after 825 BC. Part of the settlement may have been destroyed about the same time and it seems thereafter to have dwindled in size and importance. The neighbouring cities of Chalcis and Eretria now develop and take over the leading roles in Euboean history. Why this should be, we do not know. But it was a fitting conclusion to our final season of excavation in the Toumba cemetery last year that we found one of the latest vases deposited in that burial ground which admirably illustrates the maritime interests and enterprise shown by the people of Lefkandi in its heyday. It is a *pyxis* (pottery vessel), sadly incomplete, painted with one of the earliest pictorial representations on pottery known in Greece: its artists chose to depict a ship.

6.9 Figurine of a centaur

The excavations at Lefkandi have thrown much light on many stages of the history of Euboea, on the Early Bronze Age and the foreigners who came then to settle, on the people who took refuge on the island in the closing stages of the Mycenaean Age, and on the date of the much later major conflict between Chalcis and Eretria in which the settlement is likely to have been destroyed and then abandoned around 700 BC.

The greatest contribution, however, has been to dispel some of the gloom which surrounds the Dark Age. We can now trace, in outline at least, the evolution of a particular community which for over a century must have been one of the most adventurous and progressive centres in Greece. Its sailors made occasional contact early on with distant overseas territories which they eventually intensified into regular trading ventures, bringing to the community, or at least to its rulers, a prosperity unknown in the rest of Greece. By the time Lefkandi lost its pre-eminence, the experience, skill and venturesome spirit had already been acquired which were to enable its successors, Chalcis and Eretria, to go on and exploit yet further trade with the Near East and to be the first to send settlers to the West, the highspot of Euboean enterprise. The island's fortunes were, however, shortly to be eclipsed in rivalry and war, leaving only a dim recollection of its great achievements. This marked, too, the destruction and abandonment of our site which has added so much to our knowledge of the early history of Greece.

Note: The excavations of the settlement were carried out, and financed by the British School of Archaeology at Athens and were under the direction of the author and Mr L.H. Sackett. The excavation of the cemetery area was a joint undertaking by the Greek Archaeological Service and the British School, the Greek director in recent years being Mrs E. Touloupa and later Mr P. Kalligas, both of whom I warmly thank for generously allowing me to mention and illustrate material not yet fully published.

CHAPTER SEVEN

CITIES, STATES AND THE TRANSFORMATION OF EUROPE
BARRY CUNLIFFE

The collapse of the Minoan-Mycenaean cultural systems in the decades following 1200 BC heralds the beginning of the Greek Dark Age, a period about which, until comparatively recently, very little was known. On the Greek mainland, the Aegean islands and the west coast of Anatolia (Turkey) it was a time of folk movement and of consolidation. Indigenous communities, the successors of the Mycenaean Greeks, were probably augmented by other Greek-speaking peoples known to us through vague mythology as Aeolians, Ionians and Dorians.

In the ripples of folk movement which followed the great collapse of the thirteenth century, communities of these peoples spread eastwards from Greece to establish new settlements on the Aegean islands and the adjacent coasts of Asia Minor. The Aeolians moved to the Troad, the Ionians to central western Asia Minor and the Dorians to the islands of Kos, Rhodes and the southwest corner of the Asian mainland. Some of the settlements, like that at Old Smyrna, near Izmir, were established on virgin sites, while others, like Miletus, chose locations already well used by traders in Mycenaean and Minoan times. By about 900 BC these folk ripples had subsided and the scene was set for the emergence of the second great European civilisation – the Graeco-Roman – which was to grow and flourish in the next 1500 years.

The study of the formative period, c. 1100–700 BC, is very much in its infancy but great strides forward have been made by archaeologists in recent years. One of the most important of these is the excavation at Lefkandi on the island of Euboea, just off the coast of Attica, which Mervyn Popham describes in the previous chapter. What we glimpse here is a native community emerging from the ruins of the Mycenaean world and gradually re-establishing an extraordinarily widespread network of trading contacts, not only with other parts of Greece but also with Egypt and the Near East.

By the end of the eighth century BC, Lefkandi was in decline, but by then its Euboean neighbours – the cities of Chalcis and Eretria – were emerging as powerful entrepreneurs. Soon after 800 BC a trading post was established on the North Syrian coast at Al Mina and from the pottery found in its earliest levels it is clear that the principal overseas

7.1 East Mediterranean: major trading sites of the 8th century BC

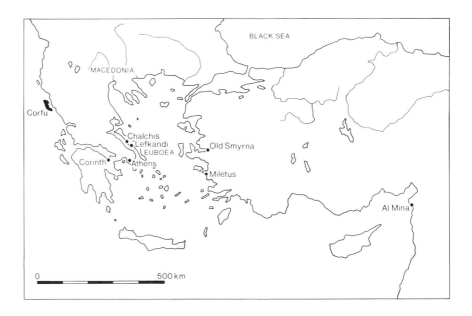

visitors were Cypriots, which is hardly surprising considering the proximity of the island, and Euboeans prepared to brave a sea journey of about 1200 kilometres. Nor was this all: in the west, colonists from Chalcis and Eretria were spearheading the opening up of the western Mediterranean, establishing trading settlements at Corcyra on Corfu; at Naxos, Leontini and Catane on Sicily; and Pithekoussai and Cumae in central Italy, all around the middle of the eighth century BC. It looked very much as though the cities of Euboea were poised to lead the emergence of Greek civilisation, but local jealousies led to a period of conflict between the two cities and by 700 BC their energies were exhausted.

By then, however, other Greek cities were emerging as leaders in a variety of fields. Throughout the seventh and sixth centuries the enthusiasm for colonisation abounded. While Ionian cities like Miletus were busy spreading their colonies around the shores of the Black Sea, others were concentrating on the sea routes to the west by consolidating their hold on the vital Straits of Messina between Sicily and Italy. Southern Italy and Sicily came so much under Greek influence that the region became known as Magna Graecia – Greater Greece. Colonies spread up the west coast of Italy to the Bay of Naples. One of the earliest, at Pithekoussai on the island of Ischia, was soon balanced by Cumae, established on the nearby Italian mainland. Together they lay on the interface between Magna Graecia and the barbarian north, whence came a variety of desirable commodities like tin and copper from Etruria and iron from the island of Elba. By 600 BC Phocaean colonists from the Anatolian coast had become so confident of their knowledge of the western Mediterranean that they established a permanent colony at Massilia (Marseilles), from where, a few decades later, a daughter colony was sent out to found another trading post, Emporion (Ampurias), in Catalonia on the Spanish coast. These western adventures had a considerable effect on the barbarians of central and western Europe, as we shall see later.

The colonial enterprise sprang from a variety of causes. One was undoubtedly the rapid growth in population which took place in the Greek homeland in the period 1000–700 BC. A few cities like Athens and Corinth, set in comparatively fertile hinterlands, could accommodate the growth and so took little part in sending out colonies. Others, in less hospitable lands, such as the occupants of the volcanic island of Thera (Santorini), following a series of poor harvests, had no option but to draw lots and force a tithe of their reluctant populations to sail off in search of new lands on the North African coast.

But while population pressure, and the social unrest which it generated, was certainly a significant cause of migration there were others of equal importance, not least the desire to establish control over the supply of raw materials coming from the barbarian periphery. The Black Sea colonies, for example, were vital in supplying corn to the Greek cities as well as luxury goods like furs, and, as we have seen, it was through the cities of Magna Graecia that metal supplies from the West, including Iberia and even Britain, were drawn. The barbarian communities also provided ready markets for consumer goods produced by the artisans and craftsmen of the colonies. In other words, the colonial settlements played a vital role in maintaining the socio-economic equilibrium of the emerging Greek world.

While colonisation was at its height a number of far-reaching developments were underway in the Greek core. One of the most significant was the creation of an alphabet. Here the Greeks showed their particular skills as innovators. There was no attempt to go back to the awkward and limiting syllabic script of Mycenaean times. Instead, the Phoenician alphabet was taken over and modified to suit the subtleties of the Greek language. By the mid-eighth century BC the transformation was complete. The Greek alphabet was widely adopted and underwent a variety of local modifications until, in the fourth century, the Athenian version became the norm.

Another advance of long-term importance was the development of regular coinage in the seventh and sixth centuries, an innovation probably copied from the idea developed in Lydia, Asia Minor, in the eighth century. Coinage of widely accepted value offered a considerable advantage in facilitating the increasingly complex commercial transactions and paying the bands of mercenaries now being employed on some scale.

Alongside these 'enabling' innovations there was a tremendous upsurge in the development of the arts, particularly among the cities of coastal Asia Minor. In the eighth century the Homeric epics were composed in one of the coastal Ionian cities, possibly Old Smyrna, providing the Greeks with a flamboyant ethnic identity. Later, in Miletus in the sixth century, a brilliant school of philosophers emerged – men like Thales and Anaximander, who began to develop hypotheses to explain the natural world, consciously breaking away from the mythological explanations of the past. All branches of science flourished in this small corner of the Aegean: Hecataeus the geographer came from Miletus, as did the great town planner Hippodamus, medicine was systematised by Hippocrates on the island of Kos, and Europe's first historian, Herodotus, came from the city of Halicarnassus. It was a remarkable flowering of talent, a product of the varied gene-pool created by the migrations, stimulated by the constant movement of travellers and traders through the port cities, spilling information for the hungry minds of the resident scholars to feed upon. It was in these cities of the Asia Minor coast that the Greek genius came into being.

On mainland Greece developments of a different kind were underway. The two great commercial cities of Corinth and Athens were fast evolving craft skills – particularly in the mass production of fine pottery – that put them in the forefront of exporting cities. Their products flooded the Mediterranean and penetrated deep into barbarian Europe. In Athens, too, new democratic forms of government evolved and internal stability was further underpinned by the copious supplies of silver to be found virtually on her doorstep (the exploitation of which John Ellis-Jones discusses in the next chapter). Thus, when the crisis came at the end of the sixth century, Athens was ready to take the lead.

The crisis in question was the increasing threat of the Persian advance through Asia Minor and into mainland Europe. In 546 BC the Persian armies destroyed the kingdom of Lydia and in doing so gained control over the Greek communities of the Asian coast. Some, like the Phocaeans, abandoned their cities and fled overseas, but most stayed, reluctantly, under Persian overlordship. Meanwhile, the Persian armies had crossed into Europe and by the end of the campaigning season of 512 BC had gained control over much of Thrace. The presence of the Grand Army posed a considerable threat to Greece, not only of military intervention but also of commercial strangulation through the disruptive effect it had on Greek trade with the Black Sea coastal cities through which much of the Athenian corn supply was acquired.

The opportunity to act came in 499, when the cities of Ionia rebelled against their Persian overlords, supported, and probably encouraged, by Athens and Eretria. The rebellion failed and was finally put down in 494 when the Miletians, leaders of the revolt, watched helplessly as the Ionian fleet was destroyed at the Battle of Lade, an island in full view of the city.

Right: Aerial view of the palace of Knossos in Crete. Neolithic occupation debris upon which the palace was built has been excavated below the Central and West Courts, visible in the centre and at the right of the picture (chapter 2)

Right: A faience statuette of a
goddess with cat and snakes
or a priestess in the role of a
goddess, from Knossos
(chapter 3)

Far right: A rhyton, or
pouring vessel, in the form of
a bull's head carved from
serpentine, from the Little
Palace of Knossos (chapter 3)

Far left: A fragment of basket, from the underwater excavation of a Neolithic lakeside village at Charavines, near Grenoble (chapter 4)

Above: The citadel of Mycenae seen from the air, looking south. The walls were extended in the 13th century BC to include the earlier ring of 16th-century royal tombs, the Shaft-Graves of Grave Circle A, which can be seen to the south of the main entrance, the Lion Gate, on the far right of the picture (chapter 5)

Left: Circular gold mount ornament, found by Heinrich Schliemann in Shaft Grave III at Mycenae. It is 6 cm across, and may have been part of a piece of horse gear (chapter 5)

89

Above: A gold necklace strung with spiral beads from Lefkandi (chapter 6)

Right: Xeropolis, on the south coast of Euboea, from the west (chapter 6)

Far right: The burial of a woman from the 'Heroon' at Lefkandi. She was lavishly provided with jewellery, including gilt hair coils, a gold necklace, bronze and gilt iron pins, and an embossed gold disc over each breast with a lunate of decorated gold, perhaps for the collar (chapter 6)

90

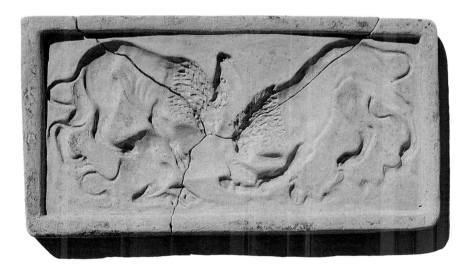

Above: A cistern near an ore-washery at Soureza, in the Laurion hills, where silver was mined for the Athenian coinage. Its diameter and depth can be judged from the height of a man standing at the foot of the far wall (chapter 8)

Right: A terracotta relief mould of two male lions mauling an ox. It was found complete, though in three fragments, at the bottom of the draw shaft of a cistern at Agrileza (chapter 8)

Far right: The temple of Poseidon on the summit of Cape Sounion, a prominent landmark for sailors (chapter 8)

Right: Vergina, where the Macedonian royal tomb was discovered, showing the village, mound and Haliacmon Valley from the site of the palace (chapter 9)

Below: The body armour of Philip of Macedon from the tomb at Vergina, now in the Archaeological Museum at Salonika (chapter 9)

Far right above: A gold head of a gorgon, from Vergina (chapter 9)

Far right below: The gold casket, with the Macedonian star symbol on its lid that showed it contained a royal burial. Analysis of the charred bones inside provided overwhelming evidence that these were the remains of Philip of Macedon (chapter 9)

Above: A reconstructed view of the Punic harbour at Carthage, *c.* 150 BC (after Peter Connolly) (chapter 10)

Right: The Punic harbours today, taken from the air (chapter 10)

Above: A detail, showing Alexander the Great in battle, from the Alexander Mosaic at Pompeii (chapter 11)

Left: Two pendant heads of polychrome glass, found at Carthage and perhaps manufactured there. 4th century BC (chapter 10)

97

Right: A wall painting from the House of the Vettii, Pompeii (chapter 11)

Far right: The head of a boy, a detail from a wall painting in the Villa of Mysteries, Pompeii (chapter 11)

Above: Silver cups from an Iron Age chieftain's burial at Welwyn. They were made in Italy during the reign of Augustus and imported as part of a set of wine-drinking equipment (chapter 12)

Right: Hengistbury Head, in the Solent, the site of a major Iron Age port, was a dominant landmark easily seen by approaching ships (chapter 12)

In 490 the Persian army led by Darius the Great set sail for Greece to take its revenge, landing first on Euboea where it destroyed Eretria and then on the mainland, on the Plain of Marathon, to confront the Athenians. Athens's famous victory was indeed great and brought her well-deserved renown. Ten years later, however, the Persians were back in force, led this time by Xerxes. Athens was sacked, but in the remarkable sea battle of Salamis, not far from the city, Xerxes looked on as his fleet was torn to pieces by the Athenian navy. The land battle that followed at Plataea drove the Persians from Europe for good.

Athens's leadership in the period of crisis and her subsequent victories brought her a brief moment of triumph. In art and literature as well as military prowess, she led the civilised world. It was a brilliant period of achievement but one in which Athens showed her inability to rise above the politics of the city-state. In striving for power and empire she rode roughshod over her allies: funds collected for the pursuit of the war against the Persians were commandeered and spent instead on the rebuilding of the city, including the temples of the Acropolis. Further political ineptitude led to the débâcle of the Athenian expedition against Syracuse and eventually Greek energy was dissipated in the petty squabbles of the long-drawn-out Peloponnesian War.

While Athens was enjoying her brief moment of triumph in the fifth century BC, a new power-base was growing to the north in the barbarian fringe of Macedonia. By the middle of the fourth century this kingdom was significant enough to be used as a pawn in the power struggle between Athens and one of her rivals, Thebes, and it was from the Thebans that King Philip of Macedon was to learn the military skills that allowed him to build Macedon into one of the great powers of the ancient world. That story, in the light of recent archaeological revelations, will be told by Richard Tomlinson in his chapter on 'King Philip of Macedon'.

In 336 BC Philip was assassinated and his son Alexander became king. Alexander's achievements in the brief 14 years of his reign are truly astonishing. In that time he not only drove the Persian army from Asia Minor but took control of Syria and Egypt and campaigned far into the East to the fringes of India. The vast empire he created at such speed was doomed to failure, however, and on his death it rapidly fragmented into rival states whose constant squabbles kept the whole of the eastern Mediterranean racked by internal conflict. In the West, however, new power blocks were emerging and it is to the western Mediterranean, seven centuries before Alexander's death, that we must now turn.

The Iberian peninsula was a vital source of metals in the ancient world. Copper, silver and some gold were to be had in quantity in the southwest in the mountains around the lower reaches of the Guadalquivir River, while in Galicia in the northwest lay one of Europe's most abundant sources of tin – a comparatively rare metal and an essential component of bronze. It was in southern Spain that one of Europe's earliest copper industries developed independently and by *c.* 1000 BC the kingdom of Tartessos (probably the Tarshish of the Bible) was renowned throughout the ancient world as a source of metals. Tartessos probably lay in the region we now know as Andalusia in the lower Guadalquivir valley, perhaps somewhere close to Seville, and it was to this kingdom that traders came from the eastern Mediterranean.

The Greek Phocaeans are known to have maintained friendly contact, and, indeed, the trading bases they established at Massilia in *c.* 600 BC and later at Emporion lay on the route they would have taken. The other entrepreneurs interested in Iberian resources were the Phoenicians, a Semitic people from Tyre and Sidon (now in Lebanon). While the Greek sailors were passing westwards using the route between Sicily and Italy, and coast-hopping along the northern shores of the western Mediterranean, the Phoenician merchants were using the southerly route along the North African coast. Along this route they established a number of ports. Traditionally the earliest were Utica in Tunisia and Gades (modern Cadiz) in Spain, close to the mouth of the Guadalquivir; both were said to have been founded before 1000 BC.

Gradually, the Phoenicians developed their routes and ports, spreading to western Sicily, where a base was founded at Motya, and to Sardinia, where the archaeological evidence from Nora suggests a presence as early as the ninth century BC. Towards the end of the century, traditionally in 814, the Phoenicians established a port at Carthage (now in the northern suburbs of modern Tunis). Carthage was to grow rapidly in importance and in about 650 BC, as the home cities in the Lebanon collapsed, it became the centre of Phoenician power in the Mediterranean.

The Phoenicians, or Carthaginians as we can now call them, have had a bad press – partly because their implacable foes, the Romans, did their best to wipe out their memory, and partly because, since they produced little art of significance, archaeologists brought up in the classical tradition have tended to overlook them. Moreover, virtually nothing of their once-extensive literature survives. Now, however, the mood is changing and in Tunisia, in particular, much new work is in progress. One of the most interesting of these projects is the international campaign at Carthage itself, sponsored by UNESCO, and in a later chapter Henry Hurst, director of the British excavations at Carthage, presents a new view of the Carthaginian achievement.

In the early part of the first millennium the western Mediterranean was large enough to accommodate the trading activities of Carthaginians, Greeks and cities of Etruria, but by the beginning of the sixth century tensions began to emerge between the Greeks on one side and the Carthaginians and Etruscans, sometimes working in collaboration, on the other. Matters came to a head when the inhabitants of the town of Phocaea on the coast of Asia Minor fled the Persian advance and made for their colony at Alalia on Corsica, greatly swelling its numbers. This was seen as a threat to Etruscan interests and, after a sea battle fought in *c.* 535, the Greeks gave up their interests on Sardinia and Corsica while still maintaining their old colonial settlements along the French and Spanish coasts from the Maritime Alps to the River Ebro.

Meanwhile, the Carthaginian hold on the Straits of Gibraltar was strengthening to such an extent that, after the Battle of Alalia, Greek shipping was excluded from these waters. The result was that the metal wealth of Tartessos was now entirely in the hands of the Carthaginians and the Greeks had to look elsewhere for their metals. It is in this context that the Greek cities of southern Gaul began to take on a new significance as trade with the barbarians of central Europe intensified. The impact of these developments on the barbarians is a theme to which we shall return.

Our attention now passes, however, to a new focus of innovation – the Italian mainland. As the Greek colonists were establishing themselves at the southern end of the peninsula, the inhabitants of Tuscania, to the north of the Tiber, were developing an urban-based civilisation of their own. These Etruscans clearly benefited from their mineral resources and their geographical position – beyond the fringe of Magna Graecia and commanding both the coastal route north and the trans-Apennine route to the Po valley and barbarian Europe beyond. The remarkable growth of the Etruscan civilisation from the eighth century until the fifth was based largely upon the intensification of Mediterranean trade in this period. The Etruscans benefited from the presence of the Greek colonists but were in constant conflict with them and, as we learn from the gold tablets found at Pyrgi, the port of the Etruscan town of Cerveteri, they allied themselves with the Phoenicians against the Greeks.

But by the end of the sixth century the power of Magna Graecia was in the ascendancy and in two sea battles the Etruscans were beaten. Soon after this we find them changing the direction of their trading activities – the old cities of the coast begin to decline while those inland, controlling the routes through the Apennines, increase in prosperity. The Etruscans were now extending their influence to encompass the Po valley and in doing so were to take command of the trading routes leading northwards from the ports of Spina and Adria at the head of the Adriatic (near Venice) to the Alpine passes. It was a short-lived enterprise that was shattered by the migrations of the warlike barbarian Celts who poured out of western Europe in the latter part of the fifth century, settling first in the Po valley and, by the end of the century, moving south through Etruria.

7.2 West Mediterranean: some major trading sites of the 8th–5th centuries BC

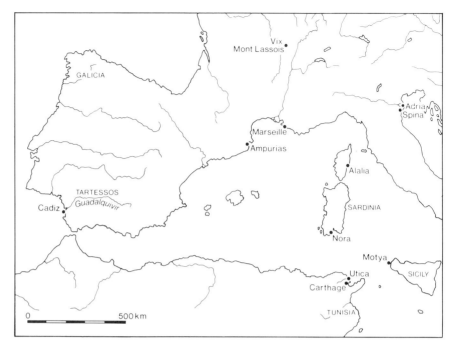

Before continuing the story of Italy's rise to supremacy some mention must be made of what was going on in barbarian Europe at this stage. The breakdown of the Minoan-Mycenaean world in the thirteenth century dislocated the long-established trade networks which had hitherto held the disparate communities together in some kind of equilibrium. The details of what happened we shall never know, but the overall impression, gleaned from the archaeological evidence, is of a much greater cultural unity developing in central Europe, covering a vast tract of territory from Hungary to France and from Poland to Italy. In archaeological terms this cultural continuum is referred to as the Urnfield Culture, based on the fact that the near-universal burial mode consisted of cremations placed in urns and arranged in large cemeteries. The tradition originated in Hungary in the thirteenth century BC and spread to the West to the region between the Elbe and Vistula, to the Alps and southern Germany and to the Po valley and much of Italy. By the tenth century much of this vast region, though composed of hundreds of different ethnic groups, was showing a broadly similar culture and was bound together in a complex of trading networks. Elements of this Urnfield Culture spread further west, to France and the Low Countries, to southern Britain and into Spain. Old views, that this was brought about by the westward migration of 'Urnfielders' are no longer generally accepted, most archaeologists now believing that cultural transmission was by means of reciprocity and exchange.

Judging by the array of metalwork surviving from this period, Urnfield society was warlike and aristocratic. By the seventh century BC these trends had become even more apparent. In the heart of Europe, from Czechoslovakia to eastern France, it is possible to recognise a series of elite burials: the paramount aristocrats were buried with their wagons, horse-gear and a range of personal equipment, often beneath large barrows. Lesser nobles and warriors, accompanied by weapon sets and sometimes horse trappings, were interred in greater numbers in less ostentatious graves. By this stage iron was coming into general use. We can now legitimately refer to these people as Celts, the ethnic name by which the later Greek historians knew them.

The foundation of Massilia, close to the mouth of the Rhône, in *c.* 600 BC was a turning point in the history of the Celts since it brought them, for the first time, into close proximity with the classical world. By means of the River Rhône, the Saône and the other river systems of western central Europe, commodities could be trans-shipped with ease between the Mediterranean and barbarian communities. Raw materials and slaves could be brought out while luxury goods such as wine and all the metal and pottery vessels needed in the wine-drinking ritual, made in Greek workshops throughout the Mediterranean, could be sent in to adorn the courts (and the burials) of the Celtic nobility.

After the Battle of Alalia in *c.* 535 BC Greek commercial enterprise in the Mediterranean was seriously circumscribed and, as we have seen, the Greek traders were forced to rely far more heavily on the barbarian markets of the north. Trade along the Rhône routes intensified and from about 530 BC onwards we find an impressive range and quantity of Greek imports in the hillforts and burials of the paramount chieftains occupying a compact territory stretching from eastern France to southern Germany. Near the French village of Vix, in the valley of the upper Seine, a remarkable group of sites of this period has been found. On the hilltop of Mont Lassois lay the fortified residence of the nobility, its rubbish deposits producing quantities of fine black-figured vessels made near Athens, together with amphorae from Massilia in which the wine was imported.

Nearby, in the valley below, the tomb of one of the 'royal' family, possibly a female, has been excavated. In addition to the cart and personal ornaments, including a massive gold diadem, the grave was furnished with a complete set of wine-drinking gear, ranging from small Attic cups to a huge bronze krater – probably made in one of the cities of Magna Graecia and transported in sections by sea and river to be reassembled in the barbarian court at Mont Lassois. The Mont Lassois complex is only one of a dozen or so similar residences which flourished in the decade around 500 BC. They owed their magnificence entirely to their ability to control the barbarian end of the trade route to the Mediterranean.

By the beginning of the fifth century, the Etruscans, as we have seen, squeezed out of the western Mediterranean, were extending their sphere of influence into the Po valley and beginning to develop their own network of contacts, through the Alpine passes, to the barbarian courts of Germany. By *c.* 480 flagons made in Etruscan towns like Vulci were being traded northwards in some quantity. It is quite possible that this Etruscan enterprise was tapping off some of the supply of raw materials which previously had passed further westwards down the Rhône to Massilia. If so the commercial conflicts of the Mediterranean were now being fought out at one remove among the Celts.

It was at this stage that a highly volatile situation began to develop in the northern periphery of the western central European zone of the Celtic aristocracy. A more warlike society began to evolve and there is some evidence to suggest that the population had grown considerably. To what extent these changes were the result of stress caused by the trading patterns with the Mediterranean, established by their southern neighbours, is a matter of lively debate, but the effects are not in dispute.

In the middle of the fifth century considerable segments of this warrior Celtic population moved off in a mass migration. Many of the old chieftains' residences were destroyed, presumably as the hordes passed through the once-rich zone. One branch moved south, perhaps along the Rhône and through the Alpine passes, to carve out new lands for themselves in the fertile Po valley. More and more arrived, leapfrogging over newly settled Celtic communities and thrusting deep into Italy. Another branch forced its way eastwards along the Danube and into the Balkans, a tip of it reaching the Greek shrine of Delphi in 279 BC before being deflected into Asia Minor. For about 200 years from *c.* 400 to *c.* 200, Celtic marauders were a force to be reckoned with on the borders of the classical world.

It was these people, in the full flood of their barbarian energy, who swept down on the Etruscan cities in the early years of the fourth century at the very moment when the Etruscans were being attacked from the south by their neighbour, Rome.

Rome was a native town that had by this time begun to increase its power and influence in the region, gaining much from the nodal position it occupied, commanding the crossing of the Tiber. Although Rome suffered in the Celtic migrations, she was a youthful energetic state that soon bounced back, unlike the Etruscans, who now fell under Roman domination. The north secured, Rome turned her interests east and south, overcoming Samnites and Latini and eventually gaining control of the cities of Magna Graecia on the Italian mainland and in Sicily. In doing so, however, she had now brought herself into direct confrontation with the two great Mediterranean powers, Carthage and Greece.

Rome's struggle against Carthage was a long-drawn-out affair spread over three periods of outright warfare, known as the Punic Wars. The First Punic War, from 264 to 241 BC, was fought out for the control of Sicily. The victory was hard-won but as a result Carthage agreed to prevent her ships from entering Roman waters, not to attack Roman allies, to give up any claim to the island of Sicily, and to pay a high indemnity. The Second Punic War began in 218 BC with a confrontation between Roman and Carthaginian interests in Iberia, but Hannibal's famous march brought the Carthaginian army to Italy itself and only with great difficulty did the strength of Roman arms prevail. But by 204 the situation was sufficiently restored for the Roman general Scipio to land in North Africa and, two years later, to rout the Carthaginians at Zama in the Tunisian hills. Half a century later, in 149 BC, the Romans landed again in North Africa, this time intent on wiping out Carthage altogether. It took three years to reduce the already weakened state and in 146 the city of Carthage itself was taken and totally destroyed.

The year 146 BC was a turning point for Rome, for not only was her only western competitor, Carthage, brought to heel but in the east the campaigns in Greece and Macedonia culminated with the destruction of the other great maritime city – Corinth. At both ends of the Mediterranean Rome was now firmly in control. But for the final act she had to wait another 13 years, until 133. It was then that a difficult and extended campaign in Iberia culminated with the capitulation of the besieged Iberian stronghold of Numantia, while at the other end of the Mediterranean the kingdom of Pergamum, one of the most powerful of the successor states of Alexander's empire, was bequeathed to Rome in the will of its last king, Attalus III. Thus, by the end of the second century BC, Rome had become virtually master of the Mediterranean.

But already, in civil strife and widespread unrest, the political, economic and social systems of the nascent empire showed themselves to be incapable of supporting the edifice. The revolution which brought Augustus to the throne in 27 BC did much to correct the socio-political imbalances but the vast megastate of the Roman Empire had to be constantly fuelled from without with raw materials and manpower, drawn in from the barbarian periphery, if the system was to be kept in operation. Roman entrepreneurs were quick to make the most of the commercial opportunities which this provided, and in a later chapter I shall examine one small part of this system – the wine trade – at work.

Inevitably, the productive peripheral zones were soon absorbed, one after the other, to become provinces of the empire until Rome had reached the edge of the exploitable world. To the south and east lay desert, to the west the ocean, and to the north were vast tracts of Europe – much of it forested, and so different in its social and economic systems that Rome, try as she might, could not bring its people to heel. Reluctantly, the empire settled back behind a densely garrisoned frontier to observe its own decay.

CHAPTER EIGHT

THE SILVER MINES OF ATHENS
JOHN ELLIS JONES

Of all the city-states of ancient Greece, Athens must be the best known. Apart from now being the capital of modern Greece, Athens possesses those instantly recognisable symbols of the classical age: the Parthenon and the Acropolis. (Several other settlements had an acropolis or citadel, but spelt thus with a capital A, the term seems in the popular mind to belong by right to Athens.) Again many, perhaps, indeed, most of the remembered great and good of Greece were Athenians or had some close personal connection with Athens: the lawgivers Draco and Solon; the statesmen Themistocles, Aristides the Just, and Pericles; the philosophers Socrates and Plato; and among the historians, if not Herodotus, 'Father of History', a visitor and admirer rather than a native, then certainly Thucydides and Xenophon. As for Greek drama, Athens holds all the extant aces: the tragedians Aeschylus, Sophocles, and Euripides, the old joker Aristophanes and the new comedian Menander.

It is no wonder that more books have been devoted to the history and antiquities of Athens than to those of any other Greek city, nor that J.C. Stobart gave so much weight to Athens in his justly popular survey *The Glory that was Greece*. It was, he declares, 'a liberal education even to walk in the streets of that wonderful city, to worship in her splendid shrines, to sail the Mediterranean in her fleets'. Indeed, elsewhere he reminds us 'that we are apt to forget that Athens was not Greece'. Here, in this chapter, you are invited to turn away from the familiar and glorious aspects of ancient Athens, to penetrate to the remoter ends of Attica, to delve among the silver mines of the Laurion district, and contemplate the grime and grit upon which that glory was founded.

When we consider the history of Greece as it is known to us in the classical age (here understood to mean not the whole of Graeco-Roman antiquity, but its narrower connotation of the fifth and fourth centuries BC), we realise that we have an Athens-centred view of events. In the preceding Archaic period – the eighth to sixth centuries BC – when the world of the Greek *polis*, or city-state, was developing, other cities seemed more prominent than Athens. Other cities had been more active in that process of colonisation which resulted in the establishment of Greek cities along the coasts of much of the central and eastern

Mediterranean and the Black Sea. Other cities – particularly those involved in the expansion of maritime commerce in the Archaic period – had seen the early emergence of tyrants; those thrustful leaders, dynasts of one or two generations, upset established aristocracies in many city-states and their own fall brought a variety of oligarchic and democratic governments into being. Athens too in the sixth century BC was to have her own dynasty of tyrants, that of Pisistratus (560–527 BC) and his two sons Hippias (527–510 BC) and Hipparchus (527–514 BC). The expulsion of Hippias led, after factional strife, to the establishment of a democratic constitution by Cleisthenes. That constitution, modified by other statesmen and adapted to varying circumstances, allowed Athens to develop into a full democracy. Then a great many citizens took part in public affairs at local and central level, in popular assemblies and large jury-courts, and as magistrates and members of councils elected on merit or selected by lot. The Acropolis, the lofty citadel where once kings of Athens had their palaces and seats of power, gradually became a preserve of the religious and ceremonial activities of the city, while political and commercial life centred on the *agora*, an open area fringed with sacred and public buildings in the lower part of the city. The same system of government extended over all Attica; all its free citizens were regarded as Athenians, since those early days when Athens had unified the whole peninsula.

It was a democratic Athens, then, which faced the threat of conquest and domination by the forces of the King of Persia in the fifth century BC. One ship-borne invasion of Attica in 490 BC was defeated by the Athenian citizen army at the Battle of Marathon – the lighter-armed Persian horde gave way before the armoured and disciplined Athenian hoplites and was drive back to the shore and its ships. A second land-and-sea invasion was aimed through northern Greece in 480 BC, and was resisted by an alliance of some of the Greek city-states under the formal leadership of Sparta. The Persian forces were held at bay for three days, on land at the coastal pass of Thermopylae and at sea off Cape Artemisium, but then, overwhelming the rearguard, they overran Boeotia and later captured and sacked Athens, destroying public and private buildings in the city and the temples on the Acropolis.

That was not, however, the end of free Athens. Most of the population of the city and threatened districts had been evacuated to the islands of Salamis and Aegina and to Troezen on the Peloponnesian mainland, while the men of military age manned the 200 ships of the new enlarged Athenian navy. In the autumn of 480 BC they and their Greek allies won a great naval victory in the confined waters of the Bay of Salamis. This was one of the crucial battles of that century, a turning point in the history of Athens and of Greece. It led to the retreat of the King of Persia and a great part of his army, and to further Persian defeats in 479 BC, on land at Plataea on the northern borders of Attica,

8.1 A map of Greece showing cities and battlesites of the Persian wars (490–479 BC)

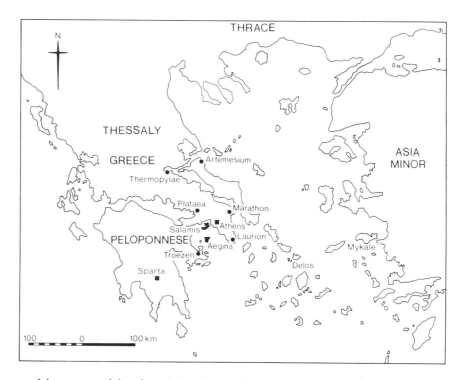

and by sea and land at Mycale on the western coast of Asia. Sparta withdrew from supreme command of the Greek alliance, and other Greeks looked to Athens for leadership in a continued war to effect the liberation of the Greek cities of the islands and coasts of the Aegean. Thus was created the Confederacy of Delos, which was to develop into an Athenian maritime empire that was dominant but not unchallenged in Greek affairs for 50 years after the victory of Salamis.

All this was made possible by the natural resources of Attica and the resourcefulness of the Athenians, particularly of their wartime leader Themistocles.

Herodotus, in his *Histories* (Book VII, chapter 144), writing a generation after the event, describes how it was Themistocles who persuaded the Athenians not to share out between all the citizens the great wealth derived from the mines of Laurion, but to devote it to the building of a fleet of 200 ships, intended at first for a war against the island Aegina which occupied Athens between the two Persian invasions. Other ancient accounts differ as to the number of ships but agree both as to Themistocles' part and as to the resources involved. The biographer Plutarch in his *Life of Themistocles* (chapter 4) makes a specific reference to the silver mines of Laurion, while Aristotle's *Athenian Constitution* (chapter 22, 7) adds further details, suggesting a date for the event (483 BC) and linking it to the opening-up of mines at Maroneia (a district in the Laurion area) which produced a profit of 100 talents. But by far the earliest reference to this connection between the glorious victory of Salamis and the silver mines of Laurion is found in the play which the poet Aeschylus wrote some eight years after the battle. In his *Persians*, he depicts Atossa, mother of the Persian king, receiving from the Chorus the news of her son's defeat:

8.2 An 'owl of laurion': the silver coin of Athens

QUEEN: But first, my friends I wish to hear where in the world do men say that Athens lies.

CHORUS: Far to the west where sets the light of our god the Sun.

QUEEN: Was it this city that my son desired to sack?

CHORUS: Aye, for so would all Greece then be subject to our king.

QUEEN: So, has its army such a multitude of men?

CHORUS: An army of a sort that brought great harm upon the Medes.

QUEEN: And what else have they? Great wealth at home?

CHORUS: They have a fount of silver, the treasure of their soil.

QUEEN: And is it the bow-bending arrow that fits their hands?

CHORUS: Not so! They stand with spears in close array and shield on arm.

QUEEN: Who is their shepherd? Who is master of their host?

CHORUS: No mortal man may call them his slaves or vassals.

Thereafter the control that Athens exercised over her allies depended on the strength of her fleet and the ample supply of her silver coinage, and that hegemony brought yet more wealth in the form of tribute and service. Her silver coins became current through much of the eastern Mediterranean, recognisable to all from their device – the helmeted head of the goddess Athena on one face and her symbol the owl on the other. From the late sixth century BC until Roman times all issues are modifications of this familiar design. 'Owls of Laurion' was how Aristophanes referred to these coins in his comedy *The Birds* when enumerating the rich blessings that would accrue to the judges if his comedy won the prize:

> First, what every juror sets his heart on,
> Little Lauriotic owls will never leave you.

The Laurion area is a region of hills and narrow coastal strips rendered remote from Athens by distance and, even more, by difficulties of communication. The traveller coming by the main, easterly, route from the Mesogaia, the 'midlands' as the central plain of Attica is now called, has to negotiate a pass – the Plaka Pass – in order to reach the plain and bay of Thorikos and the modern town of Laurion on the southeast coast. (The revival of the mining industry in the last century brought a road and the first Greek railway to make this route an easier one.) On the western side of the peninsula hills rise steeply from the sea, and up to 50 years ago there were only unpaved tracks along parts of this coast. Not until the 1950s was a brand-new motor road made, terraced and tunnelled through the cliffs, and today tourists can admire

8.3 The mining area of south-eastern Attica, showing sites mentioned in the text

the sunsets from the Temple of Poseidon on Cape Sounion, and sup in Athens. In antiquity, the trip from Sounion to Athens was easier by sea. Yet within the district itself there are many traces of ancient roads. Some are indeed impressive, such as the terraced way which is to be seen in the Agrileza valley – doubtless built to transport to the coast the produce of the mines and marble blocks from the local quarries, which provided some of the material for the temples at Sounion.

Mining in the area was confined to the central hills and eastern coast from north of Cape Sounion to the level of the Plaka Pass. The geology of the area has been much studied, and can be described here as a succession of alternate layers of whitish limestone and marbles, and of micaschists, grey-green in colour and with a micaceous glint. The minerals were generally found at the contact level between the different rock strata. As the schists were less porous than the limestones, mineral-rich fluids forced upwards during geological changes had left richer deposits where impervious schists overlay limestone. The significant contacts are, therefore, numbered downwards: the first, where an upper schist layer caps a main upper limestone layer, and the even richer third contact between the lower schist and the lower marbles below. The intermediate second contact between the upper limestones and the lower schists is poor in mineral content.

The silver ores of the Laurion are normally found in association with much greater quantities of various lead ores. The term nonetheless applied by the ancient Greeks to the mined ore was *argyritis* (silver ore), for it was the precious metal which was the object of their search rather than the lead (some use was certainly also made of lead for building and domestic purposes, although it was not till Roman times that it was required in large quantities). The main argentiferous lead ores were oxidised and carbonated ores, such as the tawny-coloured cerusite (Pb CO_3), found in some quantity in the first contact, and lead sulphide, or galena, a glistening grey-black mineral, most often found in the third contact. The chief silver ores were silver chloride (cerargyrite, Ag Cl) which occurred mainly with cerusite, and silver sulphide (argentite, Ag_2S) mixed in with the galena. It has been argued that the opening-up of mines in Maroneia shortly before the second Persian invasion represented a large new exploitation of the ores of the third contact.

Other profitable minerals in the Laurion area, such as copper and iron, and zinc, arsenic and manganese, exist in lesser quantity. The Greeks certainly exploited both the copper and the iron, but zinc was not used for commercial purposes until the Roman period, when brass, alloyed from copper and zinc, began to be manufactured. Even trace elements of iron and manganese proved of indirect use to the ancient prospectors, for iron stained the rock to an ochre or rust colour and manganese to black, and such discolorations showed where the contact layers emerged on or close to the surface.

Mining in antiquity started with open-cast extraction of ores where they were traced on the surface. Then tunnelling would follow, and galleries were driven deeper into the hillsides to follow the level or inclined planes of the contact, and these would open out into larger chambers if ore-rich rock existed in quantity. Long galleries would require the sinking of air-shafts, and, finally, exploratory pits were sunk, from which galleries were driven out below ground when the contact level was reached.

Of the techniques used in mining, smelting and metallurgy in the Laurion area during classical times, the literature of the period tells us little. There are a few descriptions of mining as conducted elsewhere – in Egypt and Spain – and these are useful for comparison. Such references as do exist to the Laurion mines tell us more about their social and economic importance. They show that the mines were state-owned, but concessions were leased to individual entrepreneurs who would work specified mines for set periods with free and slave labour. Some men had large mining interests, others kept huge gangs of slaves for hire as miners, others still built and leased surface installations for the washing and treatment of ores. There are references also to property disputes involving mines and workshops.

Archaeology has added a great deal more to this fragmentary picture. To begin with, there was much exploration of the Laurion area, of its surface remains and underground workings, in the nineteenth century. A revival of interest in the exploitation of the minerals led to prospecting, the reprocessing of ancient dumps of spoil and slag, and the re-opening of the mines from 1865 onwards. Much more recently – indeed, in the last 20 years or so – there has been much excavation in the area, undertaken by Greek and foreign archaeologists, and some of the results are described here.

As a visitor to the Laurion area crosses from the Mesogaia and descends the Plaka Pass, he sees ahead of him two centres of the mining industry, one modern, one ancient. Further off are the buildings of the modern town of Laurion, a creation of the nineteenth century, originally called simply Ergastiria ('works') but then renamed in classicising style after an ancient place-name of the district. Osbert Lancaster, in his *Classical Landscape with Figures*, remarked that Laurion had a peculiar ugliness all of its own, and the visitor can soon identify the evidence of its recent industrial past – great black slagheaps, a flue snaking uphill to a high chimney smoking against the sky, and the stark grey pile of a smeltery, the very model of a dark satanic mill.

Nearer at hand and on the very shore is a high twin-coned hill, bleak and bare, known to the locals as Velatouri ('Watch Tower'). That was the site of ancient Thorikos, one of the chief townships of southern Attica and a main centre of mining in classical times. Earlier it had been perhaps the seat of an independent prince, and legend knew it as the home of the great hunter king Cephalus and his queen Procris, and as the place where the goddess Demeter had first set foot on Attic soil after sailing from Crete to establish her mystic cult at Eleusis, its new home a few kilometres beyond Athens. By the first century AD the prosperity of Thorikos had ended. It had become a ghost town, and the Roman geographer Pomponius Mela dismissed it as a place 'formerly a town, now no more than a name'. The efforts of Greek, American, and Belgian archaeologists over the last hundred years have revealed impressive remains of several periods, implying occupation for well over a thousand years. On the col between the two peaks of Velatouri are princely tombs of oval plan, and on a shoulder below was a round Mycenaean 'beehive-domed' tomb. Also on the upper slopes are Bronze Age houses and, lower down on the west, a cemetery of the Geometric period; in both areas evidence was found for pre-classical metallurgy in contexts of about 1500 BC and 900 BC – namely fragments of litharge, a lead oxide by-product of the process of separating silver from lead. On the lower slopes in 1885 a theatre had been uncovered; not one of the semi-circular or horseshoe-shaped plan assumed to be the classical norm, but one with an auditorium quite straight in the middle and irregularly curved in at the ends. Since 1963 the Belgians, led by Professor Hermann Mussche and Dr Paule Spitaels, have reinvestigated this theatre, showing it to have been built early in the fifth century BC

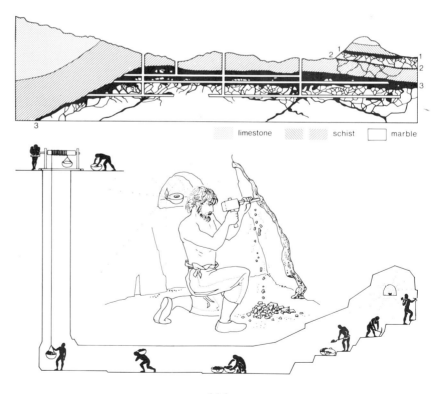

8.4 The geology of the Laurion area: a simplified diagram showing the alternation of schist and limestone layers and the contact levels between them. Lower diagram shows the manner of working in one of the mines

limestone   schist   marble

8.5 In the 'Industrial Quarter' of Thorikos: washery no. 1, as restored, seen from the north (1977) with a view across the Thorikos plain to the Laurion hills

and extended in the fourth, and have uncovered a considerable part of the classical township also, finding much evidence for the mining activities of the populace.

A visitor to Thorikos may gain an insight into ancient mining techniques by entering a derelict modern quarry just south of the theatre. In the vertical face he will see, as in a giant archaeological section, a row of black holes, all set on the line of a horizontal fissure, a contact level between two layers of rock. These holes were galleries, driven inwards from the surface of the hill and much later transected by the modern quarry. They are low and narrow, in places cut as neat rectangular or trapezoidal tunnels just large enough for one man to crouch in, but elsewhere linking up with each other and enlarged into rough chambers where much ore was extracted. Further exploration of these galleries reveals tool marks on the walls and roofs, seeming as fresh today as when they were scored by the chisels and hammers of the slaves of ancient times. They are now visible in the light of powerful electric torches and can be recorded in flash-lit photographs. In antiquity the slave worked here by the light of a wick-flame burning on the spout of small clay oil-lamps, no larger than would fit into a man's palm. Some lamps resemble old-fashioned ink-wells; they are a type characteristic of this region, and perhaps were intended to hold enough oil to last a workshift. To squat far underground in such a gallery brings home to one the grit and endurance that was needed to work long hours there – to chip and hammer at the rock face in the shadowy light, to pick over the rubble and select the lumps of ore, to collect it into leather bags or rush baskets and drag these in the semi-dark back out to the light.

Not far off, just north of the theatre, the Belgians have cleared part of

115

another mine-gallery, one of larger cross-section. Pottery sherds recovered from the rubble inside range in date from the Early Bronze Age, in the third millenium BC, right down to late Roman times, represented by lamps of the fifth and sixth centuries AD. But there are significant gaps, suggesting long periods of inactivity. The gallery was certainly in use in the classical period. On the hillside outside the mine entrance were structures of industrial use, including two ore-washeries, cemented floors with tanks and channels, of a type common in the Laurion district. One badly eroded example (no. 4, according to the Belgians' identification list) has been restored in great part and now gives a fine impression of what an ancient washery looked like. The other (no. 11) is of less regular plan, though the basic concept is the same. Yet another washing-table (no. 1) has been cleared and partly restored in that large area of streets and houses located further north, called from the presence of such installations the Industrial Quarter. This washery is built up on a terrace within a roughly triangular compound sited between converging streets, and has at a lower level various adjoining rooms, some perhaps used as living-quarters for the workmen. One room seems to have been the grindery where crude ore was brought to be pounded and then milled to a fine sandy consistency. It contains two large limestone boulders, worn smooth and hollow on top from the constant hammering of lumps of ore into small chips, and resembling in their degree of wear well-used butchers' blocks of the old-fashioned sort. Such 'chopping-blocks' or 'anvil-stones' may be seen abandoned in many parts of the Laurion district, most being made of white limestone but not a few of the even harder iron-impregnated brownish limestone known locally as *sideropetra*. The room also contains an upright cone-shaped stone, made of a very hard porous dark-grey rock, probably trachyte; it is the vertical axle or 'spindle' of a rotary quern. Fitting over it there would have been a high cylindrical stone of hourglass shape with an open funnel top to hold the material for grinding. It is of a type known to have been used elsewhere (such as at Pompeii in

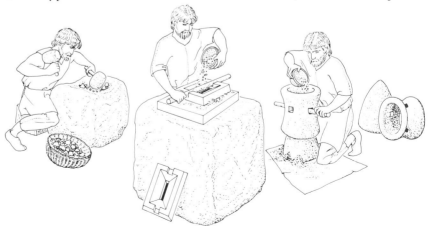

8.6 An anvil block, a rotary mill, and hopper querns being used to grind ore

Italy) for grinding corn, but was used here to grind the ore chips into a fine gravel. More commonly found in the district are fragments of a different sort of handmill, the so-called 'hopper-quern'. This had two rectangular trachyte blocks set flat, one on the other, the upper hollowed on top to form a tapering container with a slit at the bottom; through that the ore would drop as the hopper-stone was moved to and fro by a lever arm, and it would be ground small between the striated surfaces of the two millstones. And all this was done by hand! The hollows of the boulders and the polish on the tough quern fragments represent days and months of hard labour, whole lifespans spent in unremitting toil.

The ore so arduously milled would then be ready to be washed in a flow of water, so that the heavier grains of argentiferous lead ore would settle and the lighter particles of useless stone and earth flow away in the current. This function was carried out on washing-tables such as the three examples noted above on the lower slopes of Velatouri. Other washeries have been excavated or part-cleared on the fringes of the Thorikos plain by officers of the Greek Archaeological Service. These washeries are all much of the same type, though displaying differences in their state of preservation, their overall size, and the form and location of their various tanks and channels. What is lacking in these as in the three on Velatouri, however, is clear structural evidence for the provision of the large reserves of water required for the washing process. As a result it has been suggested by some that sea-water was brought up from the shore in containers – which would have meant yet more back-breaking work for men and mules!

For such evidence we must visit the hills above Laurion, where the builders of ancient washeries had to make elaborate provision for water-storage, for this whole area has very little average rainfall, no permanent watercourses, and topsoil that is thin and unretentive. Let us leave the coast just north of Laurion and follow the branch road which ascends westwards up-valley towards Kamariza, and at the edge of that village turn sharp south at a white marble shrine and follow a new road towards the church of Hagia Triada (Holy Trinity). South-west of the church and set at the upper end of a deep valley may be seen a whole series of surface works, represented by piles of rubble, cemented walls and hollows, almost as raw and stark as if they were the relics of modern rather than classical industrial archaeology. Several installations have been cleared in 1985–6 by Dr Evangelis Kakavoyiannis, Curator of Antiquities for the Laurion area, and include ore-washeries and deep water-cisterns, rock-cut, stone-built and cement-lined so as to store the winter's rainstorm water for use throughout the dry months. An unexcavated cistern not far off preserves the high remains of a central column intended to support a roof so that the water will not turn green and slimy (as open stagnant water does), nor evaporate too rapidly.

Further down-valley, and approachable by a dirt road leading directly south from the church, there is another area of excavated remains, cleared in 1976–8 under the general direction of Dr C.-E. Conophagos, then Professor of Physical Metallurgy and sometime Rector of the National Technical University of Athens. Here, at the site called Soureza (named after a nearby mining hamlet abandoned 40 years ago), three ore-washeries have been cleared, all three served by their own cisterns. Two of them form part of two distinct compounds, each with its own yard and surrounding rooms, some obviously workshops, others serving the domestic needs of staff and workmen. One compound had a small bathroom with two embedded terracotta hip-baths, and the other a small plaster-lined room recognisable as a dining-room, having a low dais around its walls to accommodate couches for diners to recline on in the Greek style; both were doubtless amenities reserved for the managerial staff. The cisterns are notable for their depth and good preservation, and were set in interlinked pairs – a smaller, shallower basin serving as a clarification tank, and a deeper reservoir.

Following the same trackway further south, we reach another group of remains, a stone tower and three compounds, set high on the slopes of Mount Michaeli. Here, at the site called Agrileza from the valley which it overlooks, I directed excavations between 1977 and 1983 under the aegis of the British School at Athens. The first two compounds (distinguished as A and B) appear to have been basically rectangular in plan, but for the most part only the visible surface-remains – the rubble foundations of the mud-brick walls – were noted. The washery of compound A was cleared and proved to be (at 6 by 12 metres overall) very similar in size and form to washeries at Thorikos and Soureza; its waterproof cement floors had been badly damaged but several features were preserved in detail.

Such washeries had certain features in common. At one end was a long stand-tank (a) which held the water in actual use, and had a row of funnel-shaped holes half-way up its front face for the emission of jets, pressured by the short head of water. The front wall of this tank, formed of two long limestone slabs set on edge, was complete but for its cement facing, and had three jet-holes. At the foot of the tank was a slightly inclined floor, the 'washing floor' (b), projecting about two metres forward. Beyond that was a larger flat area, the 'drying floor' (c), surrounded on all four sides by a system of water-channels (d), and with deeper sedimentation basins (e) at the outer corners. The last channel ended in another deep basin, the rebaling tank (f), set in front and below a solid platform with an inclined 'draining-board' (g) top at this end of the stand-tank. This elaborate form was developed not only to wash the ore and concentrate it by separating the profitable material from the sterile grit and silt, but also to reclarify the water and recycle it for further use.

The method of use was as follows. Milled ore was placed below the jets, not directly onto the 'washing-floor', but into inclined wooden troughs which had a series of riffles and hollows to catch the heaviest granules of best ore. The rest flowed on with the muddied water into the nearest channel. Held back in the channels by end-stops so that there was time for sedimentation, the water circulated in an anti-clockwise direction, depositing ore, gravel, grit and silt in the various channels and basins, until it reached the rebaling tank in clearer condition. From there it was lifted in buckets and poured onto the draining board so as to return into the stand-tank gently, without turbulence.

The third compound was revealed only in the course of excavation, for beforehand no more than a part of the washery was open to view, below a cover of loose rubble and scrub. Even so, this washery was so large (14 metres square) that it almost demanded investigation. This also proved to have the various elements described above, but mostly on a larger scale: the stand-tank, although not extending right across the washery, had as many as seven jet-holes. The sedimentation basins were round, the rebaling-tank rectangular, and there was space for an open-fronted room at the northeast corner of the washery, possibly to hold tools in use. Beyond that was a side-room, opening off the washery through a narrower doorway, but cement-lined throughout, just like the washery itself, and so perhaps a temporary store for the concen-trated ore. Three column-bases embedded in the washery floor, and finds of tile fragments, suggested that a shed roof had extended across the north-end of the washery to provide shade and shelter for the area of greatest activity. To one side of the washery was discovered a level court with rooms along its north and east sides, some judged to be workshops from the traces of burning and crusted deposits on their earth floors, others with cement floors and a small stand-tank thought to be used for washing and bathing (fragments of displaced terracotta baths were found).

As more was uncovered, it became clear that this third compound had been extremely large, a rectangular area 45 by 50 metres overall, carefully planned and built in terraces on a sloping site with walls retaining the level floors of yards and rooms. There was only one entrance, a narrow corridor-entry on the east side of the south court, and from there a sloping ramp passed through a range of rooms into a higher north court behind. This was totally enclosed, by a great round reservoir behind the washery, and by further sets of rooms. One room was clearly a workshop with two pairs of limestone slabs forming supports for some kind of working surface; around them was a 'carpet' of dense cement, edged with a shallow runnel leading down to an oval basin at one corner. Other rooms were perhaps for domestic use. In the northwestern corner room was a second round cistern, used not to clarify water for the reservoir but to hold a domestic water supply. An underground tunnel (8 metres long) led to the bottom of a draw-shaft

8.7 A general view of Compound C in its setting, looking downhill over it and southwards across the Agrileza Valley

(6 metres deep). At the bottom of this shaft there came to light a remarkable find – a complete terracotta relief mould depicting two lions attacking an ox. The type can be paralleled by numerous small fragments of such moulds recovered from the excavations in the ancient Agora of Athens, but by no other perfect example.

The pottery fragments found in the Agrileza excavations show that these great installations were built and used in the later fourth century BC, and represent efforts to expand the exploitation of the Laurion mineral sources at a time when Athens was making an economic and political recovery.

Finally, a passing glance may be cast at one of the three sites where remains of ore-smelteries have been located and explored. All three exhibit a similar lay-out, having a row of fairly small furnace-rooms, built against a long terrace or loading-platform. At Puntazeza Bay, between Laurion and Sounion, several furnaces were exposed, set into the rear wall of rooms terraced on a hillside. The high chute-like back of the furnaces preserve the fused and crusted clay lining, multicoloured from the great heat which the stokers produced from packing the ovens with ore briquettes and wood for fuel. At such smelteries a mixture of lead and silver was produced, and it remained to reheat this 'work-lead' under a blast of air, and to oxidise the lead content, bit by bit, and separate it as litharge (PbO_2) from the metallic silver.

That silver, transported to the mint at Athens, would produce those magnificent coins of remarkable purity which filled the purses of generations of free citizens and the coffers of the state, and maintained the glory of Athens in peace and war. To the slaves of the mines was left a wasteland of dross and slag, of dust and grime.

CHAPTER NINE

KING PHILIP OF MACEDON

RICHARD TOMLINSON

The kingdom of Macedon formed the northern frontier of classical Greece. Compared with the Greek cities (and by the sophisticated and civilised inhabitants of those cities) it was a backward region. Its political system, dominated by an old-fashioned monarchy, was primitive. Its economic system flourished only when it controlled the gold and silver mines of the region, and the trade in the timber which grew on its mountain slopes. But this seemed only to arouse the interest of the other Greek states and Macedonian exploitation of these resources was fitful and precarious. The more progressive of the Macedonian kings had sought to integrate their kingdom into the civilised Greek world of the city-states. At the beginning of the fifth century BC, Alexander I, his kingdom briefly incorporated into the Persian Empire, had sought the friendship of the Greek cities. He had demonstrated to them his Greek pedigree, claiming descent from the former kings of Argos, though he had based this on a genealogy which was almost certainly fictitious, and which depended on nothing more than the apparent similarity between the name of his family, the Argeadai, and that of the city he adopted as their place of origin.[1] On the strength of this he had been admitted as a participant to the Olympic Games, which were normally reserved strictly for Greeks, and his dubious interventions as go-between (wholly in the Persian interest) of the Persian King Xerxes and the Greek cities, particularly Athens, earned him the unwarranted title of the Philhellene.[2]

At the end of the fifth century, after a long period when Macedon was dominated by the Athenians, King Archelaus undertook the modernisation of his kingdom. He probably introduced military reforms, inspired by the Greek use of the heavily armoured infantryman, the hoplite – acknowledged by friends and potential foes alike as the most effective soldier of the time. He also attracted Greek artists to his court: his palace at the city of Pella (which he developed as his capital in place of the traditional centre at Aegeae) was decorated by the famous painter Zeuxis, and the Athenian tragic poet Euripides, fleeing from a city which had become uncongenial to him wrote his final plays at Archelaus' court – one, now lost, called *Archelaus*, and presumably in some way celebrating the king's own ancestry; another, *The Bacchae*, which survives, reflecting the untamed world into which its author had come.

Archelaus was assassinated in 399 BC, and thereafter Macedon relapsed into relative insignificance and, at times, disaster. A series of weak kings, disputed succession, assassinations and coups d'état left the kingdom vulnerable to its neighbours, at a time when the Illyrian tribes, inhabiting the area northwest of Macedon, were united under a formidable leader, Bardylis. Macedon thus became a pawn in the rivalries of the Greek cities to the south: Athens (hoping to re-establish her old domination of the North Aegean), and Thebes (the rising power among the Greek cities, anxious to prevent Athenian resurgence). A Theban army invaded Macedon in 368 BC, to arbitrate between the legitimate king, Alexander, and a rival claimant to the throne, Ptolemy. Alexander was confirmed as king (with the result that Ptolemy sought the help of Athens), though as a pledge for his continued goodwill, the Thebans insisted on being given hostages: 30 sons of leading Macedonians, and the king's youngest brother, Philip, who was then about thirteen or fourteen years of age. At Thebes Philip was placed in the care of a prominent politician, Pammenes: he remained in Pammenes' household for three years.

Alexander's reign was among the shortest – he was assassinated at a religious festival within months of the Theban intervention and another brother, Perdiccas, who was older than Philip, succeeded. Perdiccas continued to cooperate with Thebes (and so secured the eventual release of Philip), in all probability supplying the Thebans with the ship timber for the fleet they built in 363 BC to rival that of Athens. In the process, however, he also incurred the anger of the Athenians, who promptly invaded and forced him to accept their conditions of peace. The weakness of Macedon is apparent; and no more so than in the activities of an Athenian exile, Callistratus, employed by Perdiccas, who succeeded in doubling the revenue of the kingdom from harbour dues. But even so, these were paltry compared with the wealth of the Greek cities to the south, and the Macedonian state remained, in general, impoverished.

Early in 359 BC, complete catastrophe fell upon the Macedonians. Bardylis of Illyria attacked, and in a pitched battle Perdiccas was killed, together with more than 4000 Macedonian soldiers. Macedon was completely exposed to Illyrian invasion. Although Bardylis came in search of plunder rather than for permanent conquest, this, combined with economic weakness and the incessant intervention of the Greek cities, brought the kingdom to its weakest point, and the prospect of immediate disintegration.

It was Philip who saved the kingdom; and, in any assessment of him, the measure of his greatness must be the point from which he started – as leader of a state shattered by internal dispute, trampled on and manipulated by rival Greek cities in their own interest, and now utterly defeated with many of its soldiers killed in a major battle inflicted by a powerful neighbour. No king can have come to the throne in more disastrous circumstances.

His first need was to rebuild the Macedonian army. During his time as a hostage at Thebes Philip had been in close contact with the men who had perfected the Theban army, introducing new tactics with hoplites massed in depth who crashed, like human tanks, through the thinner ranks deployed in the more traditional armies such as those of Sparta and Athens. Philip learned the military lessons well, but developed and improved them for his Macedonians, equipping his infantry, with their larger Macedonian lance, the sarissa, as a massed force on the Theban model, but combining them with the cavalry, which he possessed in greater numbers and, in all certainty, better quality than the Greek cities of the south.

The first battle fought by the reformed Macedonian army was not against the Illyrians, but a lesser enemy, Philip's own half-brother Argaios, who, supported by an army of 3000 Greek mercenaries and an Athenian admiral, put in an inevitable bid for the kingdom, thus continuing the debilitating civil strife which had so weakened Macedon. Philip won an easy victory, chasing Argaios away from the old capital, Aegeae. In the following year there was more serious work, a pitched battle against Bardylis, whom Philip sought out to attack. After a hard battle the gap needed for the Macedonian cavalry to deliver the decisive blow was opened up in Bardylis' infantry, and Philip was left the victor, with perhaps 7000 of the Illyrian army — three-quarters of its total — dead on the field.

Philip had given the Macedonian state the breathing space it needed. His own contribution to the success of his Macedonian soldiers was immense, for it consisted not only of the expertise which had enabled him to reform and retrain the shattered army, but in addition the character and power of leadership which turned it into an effective fighting force. From this time there can be no doubt that the majority of the Macedonian people were wholeheartedly behind him, and though the kingship was from time to time disputed (two other half-brothers, kept by Athens as potential claimants to the throne, lived in the nearby Greek town of Olynthus, and were one of the reasons why Philip attacked and destroyed it in 348 BC), the previous weakness which disputes for the throne had caused no longer detracted from the development of the Macedonian state.

Philip's progress was steady, though not without interruptions, for he had the good sense to know when he might achieve more by restraint and quiescence before returning to an invigorated attack. His immediate aim was to enlarge the Macedonian state by incorporating the various adjoining regions, each in effect a petty kingdom in its own right, into his own domains. To the north and west this was hardly a concern to the Greeks, but he also had Greek neighbours, Greek cities on the Macedonian coast and the whole district of Thessaly. These he attacked one by one, leading his armies in person. It was at the siege of the Greek city Methone, on the coast of Macedon below the slopes of Mount Olympus, that Philip was hit in the face by an arrow as he stood prominent amongst his troops under the walls, suffering a disfiguring wound and losing the sight of his right eye.

Philip's incorporation of Thessaly increased the size of his army – the Thessalian cavalry was as good as the Macedonian – while the conquest of the Greek cities worried Athens, who had previously controlled many of them. The Athenians, on the whole, underrated Philip. They had always (and hitherto with much justification) regarded the Macedonians as uncivilised and unsophisticated by their standards and assumed that Philip was just another Macedonian – Philip the Barbarian – whom they could easily hoodwink and dominate. Intellectually, however, Philip was more than a match for any Athenian: at Thebes he would have attended the philosophical circles with which the Theban leadership was associated, and he himself chose Aristotle as the most suitable person to be tutor to his son, Alexander. Philip was never a mere soldier, dedicated to fighting (as perhaps, despite his upbringing, Alexander should be regarded) and his skills in diplomacy and wiles in deception enabled him to consolidate and extend his military gains. He quietened the suspicions of the Athenians by offering to recapture for them their former colony Amphipolis in Thrace, at the mouth of the River Strymon and controlling access to the rich hinterland with its gold and silver mines. He did indeed take Amphipolis – but kept it for himself.

Philip's final, and greatest, battle was fought in 338 BC, at Chaeronea in Boeotia, against a combined army from Thebes and Athens led by the man who had become the focus of opposition to him in Greece, the orator Demosthenes. It was a hard battle, particularly against those Theban soldiers who were the successors of the army from which Philip had learned so much himself, but the expert discipline and training of the Macedonian infantry opened up a gap between Thebans and Athenians; and into that gap rode Philip's son, Alexander, at eighteen years of age commanding the Macedonian cavalry.

Philip's victory was followed, immediately, by a less than edifying drunken rampage, but, more importantly, by skilled diplomatic negotiations with the representatives of most of the Greek cities, which resulted in the acceptance of a treaty alliance giving Philip effective control over the whole of Greece (except Sparta, which refused to sign and was simply ignored) while, at the same time, allowing the Greeks a reasonable pretence that their freedom was in fact guaranteed. Philip was appointed as the leader – *hegemon* – of a joint Macedonian–Greek military expedition, directed against the Persian Empire in revenge for

Xerxes' invasion, a crusade which Greek propagandists such as Iso-crates had earlier promoted as a means of bringing unity of purpose to a divided Greek world. Preparation for the invasion was put in hand.

Philip's lifestyle was hardly a peaceful one: despite the veneer of Greek civilisation which Macedon had acquired, at least among the royal family, the hard drinking and personal violence was never far away. In a difficult country, ruthlessness was needed if a king were to survive, let alone be successful. This turbulence can be seen in his family life. The murder or execution of half-brothers who were rival claimants to the throne was inevitable, and presumably extended to Macedonian nobles who were their supporters. Monogamy was never a Greek virtue, particularly in the aristocratic families, but Philip took poly-gamy to extremes. He married at least seven times, several of the marriages apparently being concurrent. Some were clearly for political purposes, however – marriages to the daughters of rulers whose terri-tory was being incorporated, by conquest, into the Macedonian state – and Philip's 'official' wife seems to have been Olympias of Epirus, in northwestern Greece. She stayed with Philip the longest; other wives were 'introduced' to her, apparently in recognition of her superior status, and she was the mother of Alexander who was clearly marked out as Philip's heir. She was herself a woman of violent and stormy temper, and was eventually banished from the court, along with Alexander. This occurred when Philip married for the final time. His last bride was a young Macedonian noblewoman, Cleopatra. Certain circles in Macedon obviously preferred such a marriage to that with the Epirote Princess Olympias, and at one drinking party Cleopatra's uncle expressed the hope, in Alexander's presence, that this marriage would produce a legitimate heir to the throne. There was a quarrel in which the drunken Philip disgraced himself; but it was enough to drive Alexander and Olympias away. Perhaps as part of a reconciliation, Philip arranged a marriage between his own daughter by Olympias (Alexander's full sister, another Cleopatra), and her uncle the King of Epirus. A splendid ceremony took place in the theatre at the old capital, Aegeae. Images of the 12 Olympian gods were brought in, and then a thirteenth image, that of Philip himself, enthroned as though he were himself the equal of the gods. But the gods were immortal. As Philip himself entered the theatre he was struck down by an assassin. Why he was murdered is not clear: whether it was through a personal, private quarrel, or organised by (or, at least, on behalf of) Olympias.

It is one of the most dramatic events of which we have a record in classical history. Alexander overcame the intrigue of rival claimants to succeed to the kingdom, and gave his father an appropriate burial – concealing any rifts that may have existed between them – among the tombs of the Macedonian kings at Aegeae. These graves were later plun-dered by Gallic mercenary soldiers employed by a later king of Epirus,

9.1 Map of Macedonia and surrounding area

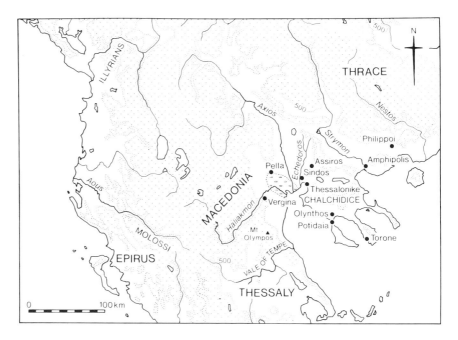

Pyrrhus, and it was usually assumed that Philip's own grave was amongst those desecrated in this way, the goods buried with him long scattered and vanished.

Despite the importance to Greek history of Philip of Macedon and his son, Alexander the Great, until recently Macedonia has not been a region where major archaeological discoveries have been made. There was nothing comparable with the great classical sites of Delos, Delphi and Olympia, for example, where large-scale excavations were started in the nineteenth century; or Knossos, where, at the beginning of the twentieth century, Arthur Evans discovered a wholly new prehistoric civilisation. Until 1912 Macedonia was part of the Ottoman Empire, and as a result finds from excavations carried out before that date, such as the splendid marble doors from the vaulted Macedonian tomb at the Langadas Pass north of Salonika, are now on display in the Istanbul Museum. The chief reason for the lack of archaeological discoveries, however, was that there were no places of obvious archaeological importance: Pausanias' guide book to the cities and sanctuaries of classical Greece, written in the second century AD, did not extend to Macedonia. No ancient buildings – with the exception of the late Roman and Byzantine buildings in Salonika – were visible as ruins. This was the result, it is now clear, of very thorough destruction of the Macedonian cities by the Romans in the second century BC, the use of generally inferior building material (especially, on a large scale, unbaked mudbrick), and the relatively high rainfall of Macedonia, which has washed down deep layers of deposit over the ruined remains: at Dion, for example, the principal religious sanctuary situated at the eastern foot of Mount Olympus, a river has changed its course and buried under several feet of mud the remains even of the Roman period.

However, in recent years, large-scale excavations have been conducted, by the Greek Archaeological Service and the archaeologists of the University of Salonika in particular, which are totally changing our knowledge of ancient Macedon, its cities and its inhabitants – including Philip, its greatest king. At Edessa, where a small town including several medieval buildings is perched on a hilltop by the side of the most spectacular waterfall in Greece, traces of extensive city walls, surrounding a considerable area on the south side below the modern town, were uncovered in the 1960s. This site was believed to be the ancient Aegeae, the original capital of the Macedonian kings and the place of their burial. Edessa, it was argued, was its late antique name: the fact that there was no sign of the tombs of the Macedonian kings was the result of the pillage by the Gallic mercenaries of Pyrrhus.

The 1960s also saw the beginning of large-scale excavation at Pella, the subsequent capital. When I made a preliminary visit to the site of Pella in 1955 with Photios Petsas, then an assistant in the Greek Archaeological Service in Salonika, no buildings were visible, but we were shown three statues – one a fine, realistically carved hound, which had been found in the area of the ancient cemeteries. It was clear that the ancient city covered an enormous area (in its day Pella was one of the largest Greek cities), and subsequently several extremely grand and spacious courtyard houses, with their columns and splendid mosaic floors, were excavated. These houses date to the late fourth century BC, to the days of Macedonian prosperity which resulted from Philip's military and diplomatic successes, as well as from the subsequent conquests of Alexander. They are far more substantial than the houses of any other Greek city: larger and more splendidly built than the houses of Athens, and certainly on a more magnificent scale than those of Olynthus, the Greek city of Chalcidice destroyed by Philip in 348 BC and excavated by D.M. Robinson in the 1930s.

The work at Pella continues: close to these houses, the area of the *agora*, the civic centre of ancient Pella, is being excavated, though all this bears traces of the thorough destruction inflicted on the city at the end of Macedonian independence. Some distance away from them, but still well within the city limits, excavations have revealed the royal palace where Philip lived and Alexander was born: here the destruction has been particularly thorough. The building consists of two large courtyard structures, with a single monumental entrance. Whether this was the site of the palace built by Archelaus when he made Pella his capital is not yet known; the excavated building is that of Philip, though extensive work was carried out by his late third-century successor Philip V. It must still have been the palace of the Macedonian kings when they embarked on their series of disastrous wars against the rising power of

9.2 Dog from grave at Pella (now in Museum)

127

9.3 Tomb excavated by Professor Rhomaios at Vergina, with Ionic facade based on the Philippeion at Olympia

Rome, and this would explain the particularly thorough destruction of it after the final war.

The most important and spectacular finds, however, have been at the village of Vergina, on the northern slopes of Mount Olympus, by the River Haliacmon. The first archaeological discoveries here were made by Leon Heuzey and Henri Daumet, in the 1870s: they carried out excavations at a courtyard building identified as a palace, and which would appear to have given its name to another neighbouring village, Palatitsia, where there was also a small vaulted tomb of a distinctively Macedonian type (the tomb excavated at the Langadas Pass was a much larger example of a similar tomb). The palace site was reinvestigated in the 1930s by K.A. Rhomaios: one of his young assistants was Manolis Andronikos, then a student at the University of Salonika. Rhomaios also excavated a new Macedonian tomb, a rather splendid example, decorated on its buried exterior with an Ionic façade, with painted embellishment whose colours were still fresh and clear when it was first uncovered.[3] Inside the tomb (which had been robbed) was a large throne, carved from solid stone. Clearly this was the tomb of a prominent person, and the details of the façade, particularly the distinctive form of the Ionic columns and the entablature they support, recalled those of the monument to Philip – the Philippeion – that Alexander had erected at Olympia in honour of his father. This tomb, though, and the adjacent palace, were both judged to belong to the Hellenistic period that followed Alexander's death in 323 BC. The palace was thought to have been built by Antigonus Gonatas, who ruled Macedon in the first half of the third century at the time of Pyrrhus' invasion, and the tomb was possibly his as well, though there was no proof of this.

Manolis Andronikos returned to Vergina in 1952. Since then he has completed the excavation of the palace, which is now dated to the late fourth century BC: it is a large formal building, with a central entrance, probably echoing that at the palace of Pella. The rooms round the court, with its peristyle of 16 Doric columns on each side, seem dedicated to feasting – the formal, drunken banquets which were such a feature of Macedonian royal life. Some rooms, decorated with splendid mosaic floors, may be identified as those used by distinguished feasters, presumably the king himself and his closest associates: other rooms, substantially larger (their roofs have the largest unsupported spans known in Greek architecture), but with floors made of marble chips rather than mosaics, were probably used by lesser members of the royal court.

Below the palace, on the flatter ground towards the Haliacmon River, is a substantial area of low tumuli extending over a square kilometre. Many of these have been excavated by Professor Andronikos (others, by Professor Petsas) and proved to belong to an extensive cemetery of the early Iron Age, from 1000 BC, down to the Early Hellenistic period at the end of the fourth century. They demonstrate the arrival at Vergina, at the turn of the second and first millennia BC, of new settlers, perhaps from the the northwest, who were already familiar with the use of iron. Though the contents of the graves indicate fluctuations in the fortunes of the community whose dead were buried there, this must have been an important place. Its identity, however, was quite uncertain. Rhomaios suggested it was the town called Balla, but this was little more than a name mentioned in the ancient sources whose precise location was uncertain: its possible identification with Vergina told us nothing more about the site.

At the first International Symposium of Macedonian Studies, in 1968, Professor N.G.L. Hammond, of Bristol University, read a paper arguing that this ancient site at Vergina, rather than Edessa, should be identified with the ancient capital of Macedonia, Aegeae.[4] The evidence for Edessa was in fact slight in the extreme, and Vergina fitted much better. Gradually the identification came to be accepted; and it was of paramount importance in the future development of Professor Andronikos's work. Below the palace, and west of the main cemetery area, was an exceptionally large tumulus, 110 metres in diameter and over 12 metres in height. Chance excavations (military, rather than archaeological) had already brought to light fragments of grave stones from it, and Professor Andronikos had dug his own trenches in it in the 1960s, finding more pieces of broken tomb stone, but not much else; otherwise the mound seemed to be made of sterile debris. But its outstanding size, and the fact that if Vergina was Aegeae the royal tombs were almost certainly a part of the ancient cemetery, suggested that an important grave, at least, was buried under the mound which, in all probability had been thrown up over the graves at a later date than the original burial, perhaps by Antigonus Gonatas, as a consequence of the threat of plundering by Pyrrhus' Gauls: this would explain the broken pieces of gravestones found in it.

Thus encouraged, in 1977 Professor Andronikos set about the complete excavation of the mound. Vast quantities of spoil had to be taken away, by lorry-load rather than wheelbarrow, for the only way to discover the burials, which might be anywhere within its perimeter, was to remove the whole of the mound. It was an expensive and at first (as Antigonus must have planned) unrewarding task, but at last, when the vital financial support was about to run out, remains of ancient walls began to appear. Walls, rather than tombs. Then came indications of sacrifices made for the dead, and, eventually, the vaulted tombs themselves.

The first tomb entered was a small one, with a chamber about 3.50 by 2.09 metres. It had been completely robbed, but its former quality and importance were amply demonstrated by the superb paintings on its northern wall, depicting the rape of Persephone. Nothing quite of this quality had ever been found in the other Macedonian tombs.

Close to this tomb another began to emerge: much larger, and with a façade decorated in the Doric order, half-columns supporting an entablature and an upper attic section, with a painted frieze. This façade was carefully cleared, revealing the rough stone blocks which are normally used as a final protection to the doorway opening. These did not reach the full height of the doorway and behind them could be seen, not the usual unblocked spaces through which tomb robbers would have entered the tomb, but the closed marble door, made of two marble slabs, like those from the Langadas tomb. Thus the possibility arose that the tomb was unrobbed, and Professor Andronikos rightly hurried on with his work so that he could enter the tomb before the end of his digging season. He entered it, not through the door, since this would have caused much damage, but by removing one of the blocks from the vault over the main chamber, peering in through the resulting gap – as he later recalled – like a tomb robber himself.

What he saw was incredible. The tomb was indeed unrobbed, and filled with the richest imaginable collection of grave goods – metal vessels in silver and bronze, a helmet and other pieces of armour, including what appeared to be a large round bronze shield, an iron cuirass, eaten by rust but still recognisable and decorated with gold ornament. All over the floor were the decayed remains of more perishable offerings. Amongst all these was the sarcophagus – a small plain marble box with a lid, obviously to hold a cremation burial. Compared with the elaborate and decorative sarcophagi of Hellenistic and Roman times this was not particularly exciting, but when the lid was raised it revealed the casket in which the ashes had been placed, a chest of gold with the Macedonian star symbol on its lid. Inside it, not only the expected charred bones, but a purple cloth wrapping, and a gold wreath. For safety's sake the casket was immediately lifted from the sarcophagus and the tomb, and taken to the Salonika Museum.

Such a tomb had never been found in Greece and the discovery was reported, first in the local Macedonian papers, then in the Athens press, amid great excitement. The BBC broadcasted an interview with Professor Andronikos, and in 1978 the excavations were the subject of an *Origins* programme. Since then much discussion in scholarly circles has been directed to the question of the identity of the occupant of the tomb. Some of this speculation was undoubtedly premature, and judgements were passed before the full significance of the material in the tombs was appreciated.

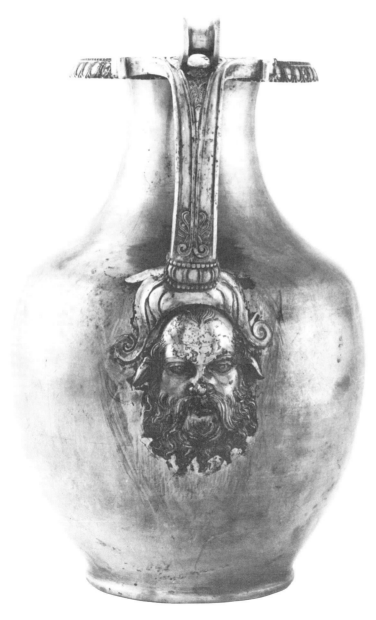

9.4 Silver wine jug from Vergina, 325 BC

9.5 Silver *gorytus* (bow and arrow case) from Vergina (detail)

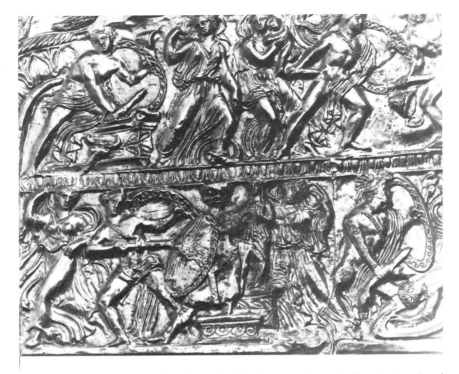

Much still remains to be done. A whole team of specialists is involved in piecing together the remains, in conserving the material (much of which is incredibly fragile), and in cleaning the more substantial of the grave goods. What has been found is still in the process of study: with so rich a find so much work remains that the final account of the tomb is still years away.

Even so, much more is now known than at the time of the *Origins* broadcast; and much more is certain. That the occupant of the tomb was royal has never been seriously in doubt. The vaulted type of tomb, with a funerary chamber and antechamber decorated in the forms of Greek architecture, is quite frequently found in the area of the Macedonian kingdom – well over 50 of them are known, and more have been discovered at Vergina itself. Not all are as splendid as this tomb, but others are larger and equally, or more, elaborate in their decoration. Clearly not all are the tombs of kings, but it is not the form of the tomb which betokens the royal character of its occupant. It is the contents.

Admittedly, most other tombs of this type have been thoroughly robbed in antiquity, and so, as far as we know, may have contained offerings of equal quality (though this cannot be true of the smaller, less elaborate tombs). But now that the offerings from the Vergina tomb have been cleaned and reassembled and put on view in the large room devoted to them in the Salonika Museum, we can see their true significance. The silver gilt diadem, embossed with a knot of hair, is similar to diadems depicted in portraits of the Hellenistic kings, as well as contemporary portraits of Philip. The iron cuirass, decorated with bands of gold and lion's head buttons, is identical in appearance to that worn by Alexander the Great in the mosaic that shows him at the Battle of Issus known to us from a copy made at Pompeii of an original fourth-century painting which must have been similar in style to the painting over the façade of the tomb. Finally there was the large bronze circle, believed at first to be a shield, which proved to be only a cover – within was revealed the most spectacular shield to survive from ancient Greece, elaborately decorated with fittings, patterns and figures in relief in gold and ivory, a parade piece which marked out its bearer as a man of outstanding importance. In Macedon this could only be a king.

9.6 Small ivory head of Philip II of Macedon from Vergina, 4th century BC

More hotly disputed was the identity of this king. Many of the objects in the tomb can be given an approximate date for manufacture – but they could already have been heirlooms when they were deposited in the tomb (one, a bronze tripod with an inscription on the rim proclaiming that it was a prize from the games of Argive Hera, and dated to 430–420 BC, most clearly was an heirloom and provides an interesting link between that city and the Macedon royal family). The more homely objects – fragments of pottery that may have been left in the tomb by accident rather than placed there as offerings – must be closer to the date of burial; this all points to the third quarter of the fourth century BC. Thus the obvious candidate was Philip: and the discovery of a pair of greaves in the antechamber, one larger than the other, was held to confirm this, since Philip was known to have been lame.

Nevertheless, there was no absolute proof; and the possibility that the tomb was too late to be Philip's was argued by some scholars. In particular, there was the form of construction – a built chamber and antechamber of equal width, each roofed with its own barrel vault. Such vaults play no part in classical Greek architecture, and it was argued that they could only have been introduced from the Near East; that is, they must have belonged to a time after Alexander the Great's conquest of the Persian Empire, to the Hellenistic Age that followed Alexander's death in 323 BC, and that they could not have been used on a building in which Philip's remains were buried, in 336 BC.

This is not, in fact, a sound argument. One of the other graves in the Vergina mound – also unrobbed – contained objects which seemed to be even earlier in date. There is a vaulted passageway at the stadium of Nemea which belongs to a time around 325 BC. In fact, the vault seems to be not a borrowing from Near Eastern architecture (where its employment is not common and its method of construction not the same as in these tombs) but a Macedonian invention: it is, of course, a method of roofing ideally suited to underground chamber tombs.

The decisive argument comes from a study of the remains in the gold casket. Though cremated, the bones were not consumed and although slightly distorted, the pieces could be reassembled. Enough survived of the skull to enable R.A. Neave of Manchester University, an expert in the forensic reconstruction of the actual appearance of individuals from skeletal remains, to rebuild the face of its owner. The discovery that the dead person, a mature male aged 40 to 50, had been seriously wounded, almost certainly blinded, by an arrow which had grazed the skull bone before penetrating the right eye was overwhelming evidence for it was just such a wound that Philip had received through his recklessness at the siege of Methone.

There is now no doubt that this is the tomb of Philip, buried with his armour, with a feasting couch once decorated with ivory figures, depicting himself and members of his family. In the antechamber, in a smaller gold casket, but wrapped in an elaborately embroidered cloth, were the ashes of a young (20- to 30-year-old) female – probably the last of his wives, the true-born Macedonian Cleopatra, who may, unwittingly, have been the cause of his death. The tomb was built by Alexander; close by are the remains of the place where he cremated his father. Perhaps he commissioned what was then a new form of tomb, newly designed with a roof intended to be more durable than that of earlier graves: certainly, he deposited in it offerings worthy of his father.

Philip himself now lies, on view to all, in a showcase in the room of the Salonika Museum in which the splendid objects consigned to his tomb still accompany him. It is, in a way, a sad conclusion for one of the greatest of the Greeks, and certainly the most important of the ancient Greeks whose mortal remains have survived to the present day. Should archaeologists consider the feelings of the individuals whose resting places provide us with so much information about the past? Perhaps Philip would be more pleased that the discovery of his tomb has stimulated interest in Macedon and its remains. Aegeae is now one of the major archaeological sites of Greece. More – much more – remains to be excavated, but since the discovery of Philip's tomb, Manolis Andronikos has excavated a shrine of the goddess Eukleia, dedicated by Sirra, wife of Amyntas III and mother of Philip, as well as the theatre nearby, where Philip himself made his last living appearance, after the procession of 12 gods, only to be struck down by the blow which consigned him to his tomb.

1   The account of the origin of the Macedonian kings is given by Herodotus (Book 8, 137) and contains much which is obviously fairy story. N.G.L. Hammond accepts the descent from the kings of Argos as factual. (*History of Macedon* II, pp. 3 ff).

2   Alexander's doings are described by Herodotus. His qualifications for the Olympic Games are discussed in Book 5, chapter 22.

3   K.A. Rhomaios, *The Macedonian Tomb of Vergina* (Athens, 1951) (in Greek).

4   N.G.L. Hammond, *Ancient Macedonia I* (Society for Balkan Studies, Thessaloniki).

CHAPTER TEN

CARTHAGE: THE PUNIC CITY
HENRY HURST

If someone was to go to Carthage every day of his life and occupy himself only with looking at it, each day he would find a new marvel that he had not seen before

(EL BEKRI, 11TH CENTURY AD)

Our first thought of Carthage is as the great power which Rome fought in three bitter wars and eventually defeated and destroyed in 146 BC. We see it secondly, perhaps, as the home of the Christian bishop St Augustine, in the first decades of the fifth century AD. These two instances, separated by more than five centuries, span little more than a third of Carthage's life. Traditionally the foundation date is placed at 814 BC, though the earliest archaeology dates from about a century after that. The demise of Carthage as a great city (the site was probably never totally unpopulated) came in the decades surrounding the Arab takeover of AD 698. A history, then, of one and a half millennia, stretching from the foundation of Rome until the last gasp of classical civilisation in the central Mediterranean.

For nearly 15 years now, the site of the ancient city has been an international laboratory of archaeology. The background is a familiar one: the threat of modern building development. Ancient Carthage occupies a coastal location just 12 kilometres from the modern capital, Tunis. It is the ideal place to have a pleasant villa for those who work in Tunis, and it is here that the President of Tunisia has his official residence. Carthage is therefore a prestigious address and the pace of building has accelerated with each decade of this century, starting from a near virgin site around 1900. This intensifying development was highlighted in a study of the general urban development of Tunis and its vicinity carried out by UNESCO and first published in 1972 (Projet Tunis–Carthage). This study stressed the threat that was being posed to the archaeological heritage of Carthage, and as a result the Tunisian government and UNESCO jointly launched the 'Save Carthage' project. Member states of UNESCO were invited to send teams of archaeologists, first to work at Carthage – generally by doing excavations in specific locations, though there have also been wider environmental studies – and, after the scientific work, to assist in the presentation and

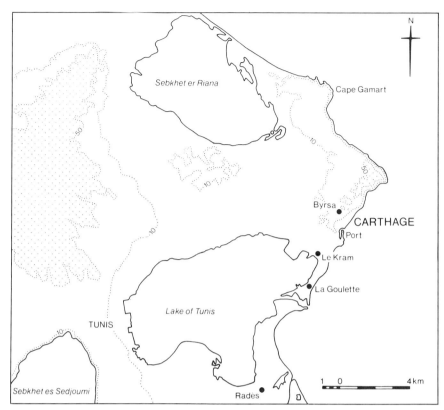

10.1a Location plan of Carthage

10.1b Carthage, showing the Lake of Tunis and La Goulette

display of the excavated sites. The intention was that the displayed remains would at once enhance the interest of Carthage to visitors and serve as a protection against further development.

Foreign archaeologists started work in 1973 – a Polish team which carried out geophysical surveys and limited excavation was the first. Between then and 1986 teams from a dozen different countries have been at work. A British team excavated on two sites in the harbour area and on a third inland, close to the late Roman city wall; another small British group carried out underwater survey work and more recently a third British group has done valuable 'salvage recording' on the archaeological remains exposed by the sewerage system being inserted throughout Carthage.

The results of all this work, which still continues, have revolutionised our knowledge of Carthage. Over 200 articles and books have been published in different countries since the project began and the flow has far from dried up. In this chapter, given the limitations imposed by lack of space, we shall focus on the city before its destruction by the Romans, since in many ways this was the greatest 'unknown' before the present work began. But in making this selection it must be emphasised that one could write equally about the Roman city or about Late Antique Carthage. A positive characteristic of the present state of knowledge is that it reflects the richness and complexity of the city's archaeology in all periods in a way which is unusual for many of the great urban centres of the Mediterranean. This is a reflection of the newness of the study, by contrast with the tendency of earlier times to hack straight through the unimpressive remains of later centuries to earlier Roman or, in many cases, pre-Roman times.

Carthage's origin as a Phoenician colony (the Phoenician name Kart Hadasht means 'new city', in this case founded from Tyre in the Lebanon) is expressed in its setting. The city is located at the seaward end of a peninsula, as if to stress that from the outset its business was with the sea. This type of setting, at the end of a peninsula, or on an offshore island, is typical of the most famous Phoenician cities, from Tyre and Sidon in the East Mediterranean to Tharros in Sardinia, Motya in Sicily, or Cadiz on the Atlantic coast of Spain. There is at once a contrast with Athens and Rome and many other inland cities of the classical world, which were established as the centres of rural territories. For Carthage, a landholding was a secondary consideration to its founders, though later on the city's relationship with the rich rural hinterland of northern Tunisia was to be one of the bases of its wealth.

The peninsula which Carthage occupies is itself a recent formation. The city lies at the southeastern tip of what was initially an offshore island joined to the mainland by sandbars on three sides. From descriptions in the ancient authors we know that two of the sandbars – the main one on the west and that which defines the present Lake of Tunis on the south – existed in classical antiquity (though both were smaller than now); the third, on the north, did not exist in the second century BC and the salt-lake of Ariana which it defines was an open bay of the sea. When were the earlier two sandbars formed? The hypothesis which has traditionally been advanced is that they were an indirect consequence of the introduction of agriculture into the area c. 5000 BC. The natural vegetation was destroyed in the river valleys, especially that of the largest river, the Medjerda, which flows into the sea c. 30 kilometres northwest of Carthage. Soil erosion resulted from this and silts and mud were discharged into the sea by the Medjerda at an estimated rate of 16 million tonnes annually until recent conservation measures were carried out. Long-shore currents then created the coastal formation around Carthage and indeed the process is still at work. At the present time the history and mechanics of this formation process are being looked at in a geoarchaeological study, combining archaeology and geology.

Until the 1980s one of the most obvious gaps in our knowledge of Carthage was the precise location of the original city. Since the discovery of the sacrificial site, known as the Tophet or Sanctuary of Tanit (Tanit was the Phoenician goddess Astarte, the consort of Ba'al, and presiding deity at Carthage) in the 1920s, the assumption has been that the earliest city was in the immediate vicinity. This assumption seemed to be strengthened by the fact that the sanctuary was situated immediately beside the city's two inland harbours. Moreover, an excavation in the sanctuary in the 1940s produced the very earliest evidence of settlement at Carthage, dating to the last quarter of the eighth century BC – the dating being provided by an imported Greek vessel (a proto-Corinthian *skyphos*) found with a group of pottery in a context interpreted as belonging to the first stage of the sanctuary. Thus, a picture could be formed of the harbours as the primary focus of settlement and the city's expansion northwards through the centuries. This seemed to be reflected by the northwards progression of Carthage's cemeteries through time (these were presumably located at the edge of the built-up area, although there may have been a less rigid separation of built-up areas and burial grounds than was the case, for example, in Roman cities).

There were oddities about this picture, in that the earliest Punic cemeteries, dating to the seventh and sixth centuries BC, were still a substantial way north of the harbours and it was difficult to imagine all the intervening space being filled up with city, especially since positive evidence for such a city was conspicuous by its absence. One scholar drew the conclusion that earliest Carthage was not here at all, but on a hill now occupied by the village of Sidi bou Said, several kilometres further north.

These oddities were compounded when excavations by the American and British teams in the 1970s showed that the harbours were man-made creations of the third century BC and produced no evidence for human habitation at all in the harbour area before the mid fourth century BC. At the same time, with digging now happening at various points throughout Carthage, still no evidence was being revealed for the city before the fifth and fourth centuries (except for the addition of new sixth-century tombs to the known cemetery on the Byrsa Hill).

The first positive discovery came from the German excavations on the coast a kilometre north of the harbours. Here the urbanisation of the area dated back to the fifth century BC: prior to that much of the site was a beach. Among the beach sands were water-rolled sherds of the seventh and sixth centuries, hinting that this may have been close to the original city. Soon afterwards a rescue excavation about 500 metres inland where a swimming pool was being built produced stratified seventh- and sixth-century levels with pottery and, as is often the way, this was followed rapidly by other discoveries, so that we now know of five different places where these early occupation levels have been found (excluding the cemeteries and the Tophet Sanctuary). The most recent find was by the British team observing the sewerage excavations – an illustration of how valuable this type of 'salvage archaeology' can be.

None of the excavations described was on a sufficient scale to reveal

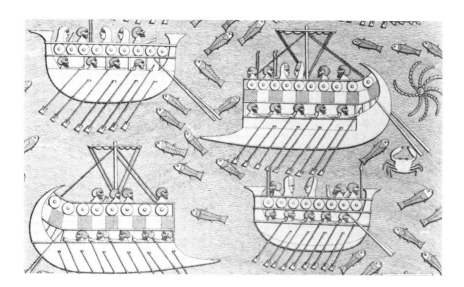

10.2 Phoenician ships

adequate traces of buildings; however, on one of the sites there was evidence of metalworking. All the evidence put together places the nucleus of seventh- to sixth-century Carthage a kilometre north of the harbours. It extended from the coast inland to the slopes of the Byrsa Hill, the city's highpoint, 400 metres away (with a cemetery on the hill itself) and has been traced southwards for *c.* 500 metres from the cemetery at Douimès. The Tophet sanctuary thus appears to have lain outside the main nucleus. It is reasonable to assume, therefore, that there is an earlier version of the harbour or an earlier anchorage awaiting discovery in the area and it may be that there was a harbour settlement discrete from the main urban nucleus.

If the central issue with Archaic (seventh- to sixth-century BC) Carthage has been simply to find it, study of the later Punic city (fifth- to second-century) has been concerned with the more complex issues of the nature and rate of urbanisation, the character and functions of the city's buildings and wider aspects of Carthage's economic and social life and its setting. The first half of the fifth century BC can be taken as a dividing line, for it was then that the massive city wall was built which (with later additions) was to confront the invading Roman forces three centuries later. The line of this has been established on the sea front over several hundred metres, the main excavation being on the German site. Here it was five metres wide, constructed of huge sandstone boulders facing stones packed in clay. This exposure was near a gate on the sea front and a later (third- to second-century) extension to the wall had been made around the gateway. Elsewhere along the line of the wall evidence for rectangular towers has been revealed, partly by the action of the sea. Associated with the construction of the wall on the German site was the laying out of streets and start of a building sequence, which culminated in the second century in substantial courtyard houses having internal porticoes with spacious rooms laid out around them. The fifth-century city wall is revealing about the wider character of Carthage at this time. Whether it enclosed just the city or a wider area, the wall must rank as one of the major pieces of urban fortification in the ancient world, and both the need for defence and the massive outlay of resources to achieve it shows that Carthage had come of age as a city and political power. Second-century descriptions are given of a wall which surrounded the entire Carthage peninsula over a length of 34 kilometres (according to Livy epitome) enclosing both the densely built city and an area of suburbs containing wealthy villas and gardens (known as Megara). Such a wall would have been equal to any of the great works of urban fortification that we know of from antiquity – the long walls joining Athens with the Piraeus harbour, or the walls of Syracuse. More work will be needed to determine whether the course of the recently discovered wall matches that description.

The centralised power of a great state is as vividly displayed in Carthage's two man-made harbours. As noted these were constructed late in the life of the Punic city, probably in the third century BC. They were excavated in a naturally flat coastal area. The subsoil is sand or clayey sand, so it was not difficult to remove, but the scale of the operation makes it impressive: an estimated 125,000 cubic metres was dug out for the rectangular or merchant harbour and a further 120,000 cubic metres for the circular or naval harbour. We may guess that a man-made hill some ten metres high, situated close to the rectangular harbour, consists largely of the soil from these excavations, though that still has to be confirmed.

The discovery of the late date of the man-made harbours raises the question of where Carthage's harbours were before that. Excavations in the harbour area have shown that in the early fourth century BC there was an earlier, probably man-made, channel some 16 metres wide running across the harbour area. The size of this channel suggests that it may have been suitable for shipping and we know from study of the associated molluscs that it was linked with the sea, but we have yet to learn whether it ended in an inland basin or, indeed, if it functioned as part of a harbour system. We can at present only guess that prior to that, the initial harbour of Carthage was a natural inlet of the sea, perhaps where the present sheltered Bay of Kram is situated, or possibly even in a corner of the (then larger) Lake of Tunis. These are geomorphological rather than archaeological questions, since their resolution turns on a detailed understanding of the sequence of coastal change in these areas. Appropriately, the excavation of the late Punic harbour is now being followed up by a geoarchaeological study, involving the systematic sampling of the coastal sediments (from cores obtained by drilling) to unravel the processes of change and date their rate of progress.

Evidence for Carthage's wider environment has been retrieved from

10.3 The Punic quay wall on the Îlot de l'Amirauté. The top two courses are of Roman date. The top of the 2-m scale is approximately at the ancient water level

the harbour area in the form of pollen and macroscopic plant remains. The deposits in the fourth-century BC channel and also in the final fill of the harbour dating to the sixth and seventh centuries AD were the most fruitful – literally so in the first case since the seeds of a range of edible fruits were recovered, both those which are common today such as grapes, figs and peaches and also the more exotic lotus (*Zisyphus lotus*) of the Lotus-eaters. Homer and Herodotus both recount how those who tasted the lotus lost all desire to leave the country where they had tasted it: one can only suppose that many of the archaeologists working at Carthage must have tasted it (but nobody told us). This deposit of fruit remains highlights an aspect of Carthaginian civilisation which particularly impressed the Romans – their agriculture. The only book they translated into Latin after destroying the city and dispersing (or destroying) its library was a series of agricultural treatises by the Carthaginian writer, Mago. Punic horticulture in particular featured in a famous historical incident when the elder Cato – the relentless enemy of Carthage, who used to end his speeches with the famous injunction *Delenda est Carthago* (Carthage must be destroyed) – held up in the Roman Senate some fresh figs from Carthaginian territory: picked just a few days earlier and still fresh, so close was their mortal enemy. One likes to imagine that these were some of the large and juicy figs of Cap Bon, which are still such a pleasure to eat. More prosaically, the technique of grafting, which is particularly appropriate to the cultivation of fruits of the *prunus* family (plums, peaches, etc.), has often been regarded as a Roman invention: the fourth-century harbour deposit suggests the Carthaginians were already doing it.

But the highlight of excavations in the harbour was perhaps the reconstruction of the physical appearance of the naval harbour at the end of Carthage's life. There is a famous description of the two harbours, recorded by Appian, who was writing in the second century AD, but based on the eyewitness description of the Greek historian Polybius, who accompanied the Roman expedition against Carthage in the Third Punic War of 149–146 BC:

> The harbours had communication with each other, and a common entrance from the sea seventy feet wide, which could be closed with iron chains. The first port was for merchant vessels, and here were collected all kinds of ships' tackle. Within the second port was an island, and great quays were set at intervals round both the harbour and the island. These embankments were full of shipyards which had capacity for 220 vessels. In addition to them were magazines for their tackle and furniture. Two Ionic columns stood in front of each dock, giving the appearance of a continuous portico to both the harbour and the island. On the island was built the admiral's house, from which the trumpeter gave signals, the herald delivered orders, and the admiral himself overlooked everything.

The island lay near the entrance to the harbour, and rose to a considerable height, so that the admiral could observe what was going on at sea, while those who were approaching by water could not get any clear view of what took place within. Not even incoming merchants could see the docks at once, for a double wall enclosed them, and there were gates by which merchant ships could pass from the first port to the city without traversing the dockyards. Such was the appearance of Carthage at that time.

Excavation has revealed the remains of 30 ship-sheds on the island and has shown that they also existed around the outer edge of the harbour. The evidence on the island was particularly detailed: not only did the ramps survive with charred slipway timbers on their surface (charred because of the burning of the harbour area in 146 BC) but there were also tantalising hints of the ships which were once drawn up on them: copper ships' nails, charcoal (perhaps the last traces of hulls) and barnacles. The barnacles lay on the ramp surface, perhaps where the hulls had once been careened, but the nails and charcoal were mixed with general debris from the destruction of the ship-shed structures, so unfortunately there was no opportunity to reconstruct the plan of a ship. However, the dimensions of the ship-sheds themselves were informative – the width of all except for two sheds was *c.* 5.5 metres, the same dimension as the beam of a Greek trireme (as recently constructed). All of the excavated sheds were at least 37 metres long – the length of the reconstructed trireme – and the profile of three ship-shed ramps studied in more detail seemed to fit the shape of the trireme's hull. A Punic ship which might once have been housed in these ship-sheds has been excavated underwater off the coast of Marsala, Sicily, by Honor Frost.

Our understanding of two other aspects of Late Punic Carthage has greatly advanced as the result of recent excavations. One is urban planning and housing. The Carthage which fought Rome was largely a planned city in what we would regard as the Greek tradition; that is, with rectangular property plots and a partially rectilinear street plan. In fact three major streets descended from the Byrsa Hill, radiating out in a fan formation. Buildings and streets over a large part of the coastal area were on a single alignment, as revealed in the German excavations already referred to. This planning must all date to the fifth century BC and later – the date-range extends from the German site on the coast, where the city wall and streets were laid out in the fifth century BC, to the Byrsa Hill, where the French excavations have shown that the pattern of streets and buildings dates only from the start of the second century BC.

These developments show, in the first place, the continuing expansion of the city, with an especially strong surge in the early second century BC – this period also saw the construction of the ship-sheds in

10.4 Model of the ship sheds of the Ilôt de l'Amirauté seen at eye-level across the harbour

the naval harbour in their final, monumental, form. As a result, we can perhaps understand better why the Romans still perceived Carthage as a threat after the defeat of Hannibal (his last battle, Zama, took place in 202 BC): apart from anything else, one of the conditions of the treaty they then imposed, that the Punic navy should be restricted to ten ships, was flagrantly breached by the splendid harbour constructions. But the urban planning also has a more general interest, in showing how Carthage shared in the common cultural heritage of the Mediterranean. Etruscan and Greek, and later, Roman, traditions of rectilinear town planning have been identified; we now also have the example of Carthage. At this time Greek, or Hellenistic, culture was dominant throughout most of the Mediterranean, and it is evident in other spheres at Carthage. Scholars have sometimes tried to make a distinction between a specifically Greek, as opposed to Phoenician–Punic or, for that matter, Etruscan–Roman, tradition of town planning, but, especially at this late date, any such distinctions are largely artificial.

The same comments could be applied to housing at Carthage. Substantial houses with courtyards were revealed in the German excavations on the coast, and smaller buildings, still with small open courts, occupied narrow plots fronting onto the streets of the Byrsa. The layout of the houses on the German site looks similar to that of the contemporary housing on the island of Delos, which, while set in a Greek context, served an international trading community, including many Romans and, one suspects, some Carthaginians. At Delos the materials were more long-lasting and elegant – marble columns for the courtyards, superb mosaic floors and wall decorations – while at Carthage columns were of stucco-covered sandstone and floors were of coloured cement, often with stone or ceramic *tesserae* (small cubes) used for decorative effect – the

10.5 An urn with the cremated remains of an infant set in a pit cut into natural bedrock at the Tophet

first step towards mosaic. Water-storage and disposal were well-provided for, with cisterns in every house to store water collected on the flat roofs, and drains leading to soakaways in the street. Houses were also provided with small bathrooms. In other words, the domestic comforts and basic design of Carthaginian houses were equal to those of the Greek world, and at least the equal of anything in the Roman world of this time, even if artistically they did not match the best that the Greek world had to offer.

In the last aspect of Carthage to be considered we are reminded of a barrier which divided the Carthaginians from the Greeks and Romans: religion. All three shared a polytheistic religion focused on a series of divine functionaries, or deities with special attributes; for example, Zeus for the Greeks, Jupiter for the Romans, or Baal for the Phoenicians/Carthaginians was the presiding male divinity with special control over the sky; Asklepios, Aesculapius, Eshmoun was a male healing deity, and so on. The principal divinity of Carthage was a mother-goddess figure, Tanit (called by the Phoenicians Astarte), to whom Baal was consort. Where the Carthaginians differed was that their worship of Tanit involved human sacrifice. Small children, generally two to three years old, or less, were sacrificed in fulfilment of vows of piety or in order to obtain special favours of the deity. This practice horrified the Greeks and Romans – the Sicilian Greek Diodorus recounts how, when Carthage was threatened by the invading forces of Agathocles, the ruler of Syracuse, in the early fourth century BC, children from 500 of the city's leading families were sacrificed in order to appease the gods. It worked, too, since Agathocles never took Carthage.

The Sanctuary of Tanit, or Tophet as it is called (borrowing from the Old Testament the name of the place where the Phoenicians carried out similar sacrifices), is one of the best-known sites of Carthage. It was first excavated on a large scale in the 1920s by an American team associated with the University of Michigan, again in the 1940s by the French and more recently, on small scale, in the late 1970s by the American Schools of Oriental Research. The sanctuary consists of an open area, probably walled, with lines of small stone monuments or *stelae*, marking the places where the urns containing the cremated remains of sacrificed infants were buried. Its general aspect must have been similar to that of a modern graveyard, though it is important to remember that this was not a cemetery but a religious precinct.

Literally thousands of sacrifices over six centuries of Carthage's life, from the eighth to the second century BC, are recorded in the sanctuary. When the whole area was filled with *stelae*, it was buried beneath soil and clay and a new series of urns and *stelae* were added at a higher level. Here, then, is a remarkable stratigraphy, both for the chronology of the urn and *stelae* types, and also for the history of this religious practice.

10.6 2nd-century BC *stelae* or stone monuments set up in the Tophet of Carthage to record the sacrifice of infants to the goddess Tanit and her consort Ba'al. The simplified triangular figure with outstretched arms is a representation of Tanit. The Greek-style decoration (egg-and-dart and bead-and-reel) is a striking characteristic of these *stelae*, mixed with Phoenician religious symbols and dedicatory inscriptions

The recent American excavations produced especially revealing information on this last point. If we start with a generalised preconception of 'progress' in which human brutality decreases as time goes on and 'civilisation' increases, we would be exactly wrong in the case of this precinct. In the earliest levels, dating to the seventh and sixth centuries BC, the sacrifices in the urns were of human infants in two-thirds of cases excavated by the Americans and of animals, generally lamb, in the other third. In the latest levels, dating to the third to second century BC, the rate of human sacrifice had risen to 90 per cent of the total. Why should this be so? Using the evidence of the inscribed *stelae*, which also date to the third to second century BC, the American excavators point out another feature of the Carthage sacrifices: that they always appear to be of the property-owning class. The Phoenician phrase *mulk 'adam* ('sacrifice of a commoner') is never present in the inscriptions. This implies a socially upper- or middle-class context for this religious practice. If this is linked with the tradition which existed in the Phoenician world of partible inheritance, in which property is divided between heirs, a possible explanation emerges: the sacrifices may have been socially efficacious as a form of birth-control for the better-off families of Carthage, since their standing might otherwise be weakened by excessive subdivision of their property. This would also make sense of the chronology, for in early days, when such families were relatively less numerous, their concern simply to preserve their numbers would be that much greater. Obviously this explanation, advanced by the American excavators, remains hypothetical and it may even seem far-fetched: however, it does account for the different pieces of evidence and it has the merit of being a coherent and socially based explanation of a religious practice which is otherwise difficult to explain in its historical context. Behind all the vaunted horror of the more 'civilised' contemporaries of the Carthaginians, it is salutary to remember the Greek habit of exposing unwanted babies on the hillside; and institutions such as the foundling hospitals of more recent

Christian Europe remind us that the problem was not confined to ancient society. Professor Stager, the director of the American excavation, summed up the Carthage Tophet very neatly: 'In this way the elite could control their numbers in a rather systematic way while still receiving the blessings of the gods.'

The overall view of Carthage that archaeology is now providing therefore shows, in the first place, that the city shared in the mainstream of Mediterranean urban development. After a still shadowy start, when it appears to have been of a modest size, it became, perhaps in the fifth century BC, one of the metropoleis of the ancient world, rivalling such famous Greek centres as Athens, Corinth and Syracuse in its scale. From the fifth century until its destruction by the Romans in 146 BC it displayed the great works of public building and the high level of urban organisation that one associates with major ancient cities.

Architecturally and artistically, the dominating influence of the Greek world was felt in Carthage as throughout the Mediterranean. But it was only an influence: Carthaginian architecture and art retains its own character, also making references to its more oriental origins and contacts in the Phoenician world and to its native African base. The Carthaginian 'aesthetic' was not the same as the Greek. Starting from a Greek-biased viewpoint one would call the Carthaginians notably less artistic: for example, there was no Carthaginian tradition of painted pottery; the Greek and later Roman use of marble for statuary and architectural ornament had no counterpart in Carthage; Carthaginian architecture lacked the harmony and sense or proportions of the Greek, and so on. Indeed, the impression given, from the plant remains to the artificial harbours, domestic architecture and urban planning, is of technological rather than artistic sophistication. Waterproof cement, for example, was freely used in the ubiquitous cisterns and also in some external wall facings in Late Punic buildings at a date when this material, which we think of as so characteristically Roman, had barely appeared in Italy: it is tempting to speculate that agricultural technology was not the only field in which the Romans learnt from their conquest of Carthage.

Yet beside this image of modernity, there were strongly conservative strands. Tanit, the presiding deity of Carthage, was a female earth goddess, appropriate to a primitive agricultural society, and her worship involved human sacrifice, for which (in the Mediterranean) we have to look back to the Bronze Age or earlier to find parallels. The lack of a monumental religious architecture comparable to that of the Graeco–Roman world (a lack which, with further discoveries, may turn out to be relative rather than absolute; but it is certainly evident in our knowledge up to now) also perhaps suggests that Carthaginian religion retained the forms of expression of the pre-classicial world. Such religious conservatism may reflect an essential difference between Carthage's origins and those of Graeco-Roman cities. Whether in Greece or Italy, and whether a mother-city or a colony, the classical city was a new form, the expression of a new ordering of society, following the end of the Bronze Age civilisations and a period of evolution in Greece which we know as the Dark Age. This new society had devised its own forms of collective religious expression which mark a clear break with what had gone before. Carthage, on the other hand, was a colony planted by an urban culture which, in the case of Carthage's mother city, Tyre, had centuries of earlier history, or, in the case of nearby Byblos, millennia. The Phoenician cities had, moreover, had an existence as small independent polities long before the concept of the city-state even entered the Greek world, and thus it is reasonable to assume that they had evolved much earlier a set of appropriate religious practices and that these, along with the Phoenician language and script, were exported to their new foundation at Carthage.

Archaeology, then, is slowly bringing Carthage back to life. As we learn more about the Punic city and its place in the ancient Mediterranean world, we are led to subtle revisions of our view of ancient civilisation as a whole. The Greeks and Romans, who are so much more familiar to us because of the survival of their writings, were after all only part of the picture. It is salutary to remember how close Hannibal came to victory and thus how close we are to being the heirs of Graeco–Punic rather than Graeco–Roman civilisation.

Note: Some explanation of the terms 'Punic', 'Phoenician' and 'Carthaginian' may be helpful as these words are commonly used inconsistently. 'Phoenician', used geographically or culturally, has both a narrow and a broad sense. In its narrow sense it refers to the area known as Phoenicia in the ancient world – the coastal area of modern Lebanon and Syria, extending for about 350 kilometres, in which there were five famous cities (from south to north) Tyre, Sidon, Berytus (Beirut), Byblos and Aradus. These cities set up trading stations and founded colonies in the western Mediterranean and on the Atlantic coasts of Spain and Portugal, most notably Carthage, and Carthage did likewise. Thus 'Phoenician' can also be used in a wider political-geographical and cultural sense to include the west. 'Punic' is derived from the Latin Poenus, which is a variant of the Greek Phoenix (=Phoenician). In practice when the Romans were writing about the Poeni, they meant the western Phoenicians with whom they came into contact, and particularly Carthage. Thus 'Punic' is often an alternative adjective for Carthaginian, as in the Punic Wars, and it often has a chronological sense, the Punic period, meaning the period before 146 BC when Carthage was destroyed by the Romans. In the present account the normal usage is followed, with Punic meaning Carthaginian and Phoenician being used in both senses (it is hoped, unambiguously, from the context).

CHAPTER ELEVEN

A NEW LOOK AT POMPEII
ROGER LING

Pompeii is an archaeological site of unique importance and interest. Buried, along with its neighbours Herculaneum and Stabiae, by the catastrophic eruption of Mount Vesuvius in AD 79, it preserves the buildings, decorations, furnishings, wall-posters, graffiti, and even the hapless inhabitants of a small commercial and agricultural town of southern Italy at the height of the Roman Empire. Of other Mediterranean sites only the pre-Hellenic city of Santorini (Thera), destroyed in a much earlier volcanic disaster, can rival it; and here excavations are still in their infancy. Pompeii has been under excavation for over 200 years; something like three-fifths of the area within its city-walls have been exposed; and detailed study by generations of archaeologists and art-historians has given us an unrivalled knowledge of its life and society.

Pompeii's fame, however, has sown the seeds of a new and more permanent ruin. The ashes and clinkers which rained from the volcano in the fateful hot August days 1900 years ago enshrined the city in a kind of time-capsule which preserved it for posterity; but the greed and curiosity of the modern world have turned it into a quarry for works of art and artefacts, and offered it as a prey to the forces of destruction from which it lay protected for so long.

Much of the blame for this situation lies with the early explorers of the city. Even before excavations began in 1748, the site was known to tunnellers who dug their way down to search for coins, jewellery and other removable trinkets; their routes from room to room can be charted from the holes that they dug through the walls to avoid the deep accumulations of volcanic debris in open spaces such as courtyards and gardens. Some of these tunnellers met a similar fate to their ancient predecessors, asphyxiated by noxious gases; but the majority escaped, laden with spoils. The beginning of excavations merely turned the unofficial despoliation into legalised plunder. Agents working for the Bourbon kings of Naples and Sicily removed bronzes, sculptures, mosaics and wall-paintings to the royal palace at Portici, frequently at the expense of destruction to the fabric of the houses. Many of the works recovered were, admittedly, preserved for posterity – either in the Naples National Museum which developed from the royal collection, or in other European collections which benefited from the generosity of the Bourbons – but the archaeological context of the discoveries was broken up, frequently without record, and Pompeii itself was left to become a romantic ruin, the goal of watercolour painters and Grand Tourists.

The unification of Italy in 1860 brought a greater awareness of the archaeological potential of the site and of the state's responsibility to protect and preserve it. Under the direction of Giuseppe Fiorelli, excavations became systematic, bulletins were published on a regular basis, and the practice of cutting interesting details out of painted wall-decorations, leaving the rest to their fate, was stopped. These basic policies have been continued in the twentieth century, there being an even greater emphasis upon preserving the integrity of the monument, with all its information about the life-style of the ancient inhabitants. Small objects, such as iron tools and pottery, have been left in the houses; and the houses themselves have been reconstructed, re-erecting fallen ancient masonry and supplying modern roofs, in order to give the visitor an understanding of how they originally appeared. The inter-war excavations at Herculaneum provided a marvellous illustration of the value of this approach, since the peculiar conditions of that city's burial favoured the survival, albeit in carbonised form, of such organic materials as timber, grain, rope and foodstuffs.

But the practice of making Pompeii into a kind of vast open-air museum has itself accentuated and accelerated the processes of destruction. The natural forces are an ever-present threat. Brambles, ivy and the ubiquitous acacia tree, which can grow to the height of a man in a matter of months, continue to flourish, undermining the walls and sinking their roots into the mortar which holds the masonry together; and, since chemical means of controlling the undergrowth are harmful both to the ecological environment and to the actual structures, it is necessary to clear the site by hand – an operation which is prohibitively expensive and so is carried out as seldom as possible. Weathering is a further problem. Torrential downpours, fluctuations in temperature, winter frosts – all wreak havoc on unprotected walls and especially on the wall-paintings, some of which have faded beyond recognition or collapsed altogether. Even the modern reconstructions of the early part of the present century have begun to give way; in particular, the weight of concrete beams restored in place of wooden ones upon the ancient walls, and the incompatibility of modern and ancient mortars, have led to deterioration.

Maintaining and consolidating the fabric of the ancient city ought, in fact, to be no less a continuous commitment than painting the Forth Bridge; but, in spite of special grants both from the Italian government and from the European Community, the very scale of the work means that it inevitably becomes an *ad hoc* response to intermittent crises.

11.1 Map of Pompeii

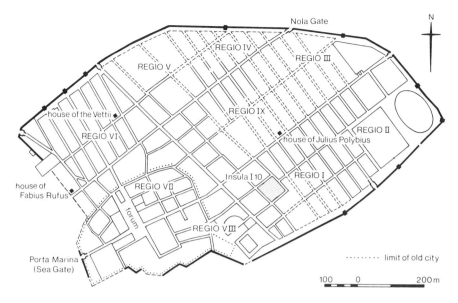

Matters were made ten times worse by the disastrous earthquake of November 1980. Although there were few dramatic effects in Pompeii (unlike in Stabiae, where a villa excavated in the 1950s was extensively damaged), much insidious damage was done: structures were weakened, cracks appeared in walls that were previously sound, water seeped in where none had entered before. The forest of wooden props and barriers which sprang up in the streets after the earthquake has performed a very real function in protecting tourists from the long-term risk of falling masonry. It is also, however, a visible reminder of the size and difficulty of the conservation problem: even after six years certain quarters of the city remain unsafe and closed to the public.

To the threat posed by natural forces is added the threat presented by man. The pressure of modern tourism brings its own difficulties – the wear and tear of thousands of feet, the damage inflicted by graffiti and other forms of vandalism, the depredations of souvenir-hunters who think nothing of slipping a fragment of sculpture into their bags. More serious still are the professional thieves. In 1976, a raid on the small site museum resulted in the removal of a large haul of small objects, such as gems; in 1977, a house excavated in the late 1860s and early 1870s was stripped of most of its saleable wall-paintings; in 1978, thieves broke into one of the city's main showpieces, the House of the Vettii, and took five bronze statues from the garden. In the last instance the spoils were eventually recovered some years later on the art-market in Cologne, but small, less well-known pieces are easily smuggled out of the country and sold by unscrupulous dealers to unquestioning collectors, never to be traced again.

The immediate effect is the impoverishment of Pompeii as an archaeological monument; objects are made more inaccessible, being transferred from houses to safe store-rooms. Even the site museum has now been turned into a deposit, while the House of the Vettii is denuded of most of its portable art-works, thus spoiling a unique display of ancient bourgeois taste. As a concomitant of the increased security problem, it has obviously been necessary to step up the policing of the site; at night the ruins are patrolled by 60 or 70 men, while dogs are stationed in high-risk areas such as the Villa of the Mysteries. This works further to the detriment of the site, because much-needed resources are diverted away from conservation and investigation.

To make the scenario seem still more depressing, very few of the excavated buildings of Pompeii were properly recorded, let alone published, before the process of deterioration began. This was especially true, of course, of the remains excavated before 1860, where there is now very little left to be salvaged from the wreckage. It was also true of houses excavated in the 1860s and 1870s; when the small house known as I 3,25 was stripped of its paintings in 1977, the authorities had very few photographs to help the police in their enquiries. Even in the present century, with a few shining exceptions, the excavations have been inadequately recorded and superficially published. Worst of all, the extensive excavations carried out in the 1950s in Regions I and II by Amedeo Maiuri, one of Pompeii's most distinguished archaeologists, were never published; and apparently the surviving documentation consists of no more than a patchy coverage of photographs and type-written lists of finds stored in the local *direzione*. Maiuri is long since dead, and the onus of publication has fallen on people who played no part in the excavations and thus have to piece together the results from imperfect evidence.

Despite this state of affairs, major excavations continued to take place in the 1960s and 1970s. The split-level House of M. Fabius Rufus, terraced over the city's western walls, and the imposing House of G. Julius Polybius, on its main commercial thoroughfare, were the object of thorough programmes of recovery, in which excavation and restoration proceeded in close step. At the same time, various investigators probed problems of the earlier development of Pompeii.

It was against this background that Professor Fausto Zevi, who was appointed Archaeological Superintendent of the Provinces of Naples and Caserta in 1977, took the courageous step of imposing a moratorium upon new excavations. Though nearly two-fifths of the area within the city-walls remained buried, he took the view that there was no pressing reason to open up more of a site which lay under farmland and was protected by antiquities legislation; it made better sense to concentrate resources upon specific threats from building and road development in the surrounding region. Within the city it was more important to carry out programmes of conservation, consolidation, and documentation.

This policy has been largely maintained to the present day under

11.2 After-effects of the earthquake of November 1980. A balcony restored in the 1930s, with concrete beams simulating the ancient timber, is supported by wooden props to prevent it from collapsing

11.3 Plan of Insula I 10 indicating some of the possible early property boundaries

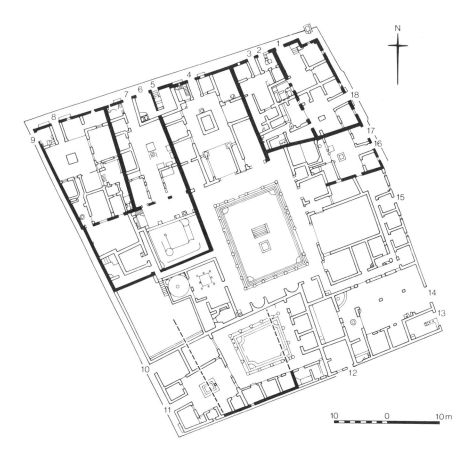

Zevi's successors, M. Giuseppina Cerulli-Irelli and Baldassare Conticello. The only major exceptions to the rule have been an excavation outside the Nola Gate to expose the last unexcavated stretch of the city-walls, which led to the discovery of a number of tombs and of the skeletons of 15 fugitives from the eruption; a trench to lay electric cables from the Porta Marina to new store-rooms and workshops to the east of the Forum, which revealed important evidence of the earlier history of the city; and, more recently, in connection with the construction of new Superintendency buildings, the exposure of the area outside the city-walls next to the Porta Marina ('Sea Gate'), which has resulted in the discovery not only of houses and gardens terraced down the hillside overlooking the sea but also of a new bath-building (the Suburban Baths). Only in the last year, with improved financing as a result of a grant from the European community, has there been further systematic excavation of houses within the city; but this work, whose aim is the completion of Maiuri's excavations in Region II, is once more conceived as part of a programme of consolidation and systematisation.

The emphasis of the last ten years has therefore been upon recording and analysis. This has been carried out in various ways and by various institutions. The Central Institute for Cataloguing and Documentation in Rome has undertaken a series of photographic campaigns to record the wall-paintings and mosaics of the city together with brief descriptions which are stored in a data bank; a series of catalogues is currently being published. A further campaign of photography, launched by the Superintendency with the aid of units from the Italian army, recorded the state of all the structures after the 1980 earthquake. A team from the University of Milan has undertaken an in-depth analysis of one of the city-blocks in Region VI; and students from Perugia have begun work on another. In addition, the Superintendency generously encouraged the participation of foreign teams. Since 1973 a German team has been engaged in recording the wall-paintings of various houses by a system of photogrammetry (accurate surveying by means of photography), with a view to publishing a series of monographs; the first volume, on the House of the Prince of Naples, appeared in 1984. More recently an Australian group has worked in collaboration with the Germans, increasing the number of houses under study to 12. A Franco-Italian team with similar methods and priorities has meanwhile begun a campaign in the Villa San Marco at Stabiae, which was badly damaged in the 1980 earthquake.

As part of the international effort a British campaign has been taking place in Pompeii I 10, the *insula* (city-block) of the Menander. Begun in 1978, with a generous grant from Imperial Tobacco Ltd., part of the proceeds of the exhibition 'Pompeii AD 79' held at the Royal Academy of Arts in 1976–7, this project was conceived by the late Dr J.B. Ward-Perkins in response to a suggestion from Professor Zevi and has now been in progress for nine years. Its object is nothing less than the complete recording and analysis of the architecture and decorations of the whole city-block.

The *insula* of the Menander is one of a number of large and slightly irregular blocks lying between the old city which goes back to the sixth or seventh centuries BC and the regular rectangular grid which occupies the eastern part of the final walled area, the 'new city'. It is certainly intermediate in date between the two, and its form is perhaps dictated by surburban development outside the old city before its enlargement to incorporate the spaces to the north and east. The present circuit of city-walls was laid out at least as early as the fourth century and possibly as early as the sixth, but there is no evidence that any of the existing structures in I 10 goes back much beyond 200 BC. The lay-out of the eastern quarter may be as late as 80 BC.

In its final form, the *insula* was dominated by one great house and its dependencies: the so-called House of the Menander. This house, which is one of the tourist show-pieces of the city, consists of three main sections. Entered from the north (doorway 4) is the monumental 'display' part of the house, consisting of the canonical Pompeian sequence

11.4 Structural techniques in the Insula of the Menander. The actual construction is of mortared rubble, and the visible fabric is merely a facing. At the right, brickwork with panels of *opus incertum* (irregular rubble); at the left, *opus listatum* (alternating courses of bricks and stone blocks). The nature of the joint between the two techniques shows that the *opus listatum* is later than the brickwork. The lintel is a modern concrete replacement for ancient wood

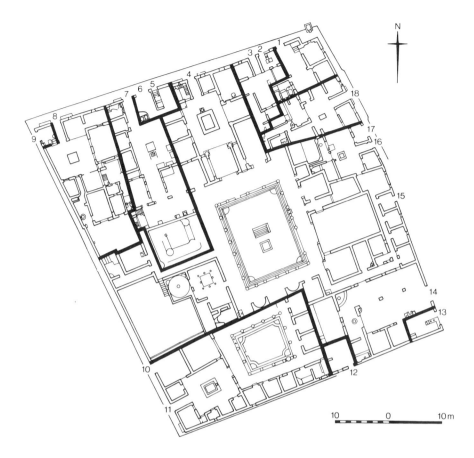

11.5 Plan of Insula I 10 with final property boundaries

of an entrance-passage (*fauces*), a hall with central opening to the sky (*atrium*), a large room for the reception of the owner's clients (*tablinum*), and a colonnaded garden (peristyle); from these, and specifically round the *atrium* and peristyle, open the bedrooms, store-rooms, living-rooms and reception-rooms used by the owner and his immediate family. To the west of the peristyle, beyond a small bath-suite which was in process of alteration at the time of the eruption, an L-shaped corridor gives access to a kitchen area and vegetable-garden. To the southeast, approached from the peristyle by another L-shaped corridor and taking up the whole of this quarter of the *insula*, is a working-establishment incorporating a yard, a stable, store-rooms and servants' rooms. The remaining three corners of the *insula* are occupied by minor houses: the House of the Lovers (entrance 11) at the southwest, the House of the Cabinet-Maker (entrance 7) and another small atrium-house (entrance 8) at the north-west, and three rather irregular houses (entrances 18, 1 and 3) at the northeast. A small workshop complex straddles the adjacent angles of the House of the Menander and the House of the Cabinet-Maker (entrance 6; entrance 5 leads to an upstairs flat).

Underlying this final lay-out there are traces of a complex historical development, the most notable of which are the remains of an early house found nearly 1.70 metres below the floor of the great reception-room opening on to the Menander peristyle (room 18). Evidently the houses of the *insula* originally followed the slope of the land, which here runs down from north to south; but at some stage, or rather in a series of stages, the Menander's owner terraced his peristyle and the adjoining rooms over the earlier buildings so as to secure a more or less level platform for the main part of his house. The House of the Lovers stayed at the original level, with floors about 2 metres below the floor of the Menander.

It is one of the principal objectives of the British project to plot and interpret the phases in the history of the *insula*. The full story is highly complicated, and to resolve many of the problems would require excavation, which is not allowed under the terms of the existing agreement with the Superintendency; but much can be achieved by patient analysis of the visible structures and decorations. It is known, for example, that certain building techniques found in the *insula* are characteristic of particular periods in the history of Pompeii, and similarly that certain building materials do not appear before certain times. Datable pottery

11.6a Shop-doorway (entrance 9) in the Insula of the Menander. The function of the shop, which was created from a room at the corner of the neighbouring house, is unknown; but the circular emblem visible above it was some form of shop-sign. The label with the region and insula number is modern
11.6b Side-street on the east side of the Insula of the Menander. Stepping-stones enabled pedestrians to cross the road without soiling their feet in the mire that would have accumulated there

embedded in the mortar of the walls will provide an upper limit for the date of their construction. Anomalies in plan will offer suggestive hints about early configurations, and abutment joints will indicate where one wall has been added against another. Further criteria add greater precision. The installation of a street-fountain at the northeast corner and the resulting changes in the building behind it can be dated to the period when the city received its first supply of running water at the end of the first century BC. A number of makeshift repairs can be linked with damage caused by the disastrous earthquake which struck Pompeii in AD 62. Finally, the styles of the decorated pavements and more especially of the wall-paintings, whose general chronology is well established, enable us to ascertain the latest possible date by which a room could have taken its present form.

By this means it has proved possible to chart the development of the *insula* and to get a glimpse of the complicated ebb and flow of property-boundaries which took place over the years. It emerges, for instance, that there were originally probably only two properties at the northeast corner, both entered from the north and extending backwards to a common building-line about 20 metres from the façade; only later were the rear parts hived off to form a separate house entered from the east. Similarly, at the northwest corner, the House of the Cabinet-Maker and its neighbour terminated about 20 metres from the street-front, and a separate property ran cross-wise behind them, in the position occupied by their present gardens. House 16, behind houses 1 and 3, was originally an independent property, but later became a dependency of the House of the Menander (after first being nibbled away at the rear to provide rooms opening off the Menander peristyle). The House of the Lovers was a comparatively late addition to the *insula*, replacing an earlier house which was entered from the south.

So we could go on. But what does the structural analysis tell us about the development of this quarter of the city and about its social life?

There are four main conclusions which have sociological interest. Firstly, the addition of upper storeys is a relatively late development; none is certainly datable before about 50 BC and most belong to the last generation in the life of the city. By AD 79, however, virtually every property had an upper floor over large parts of it. In the House of the Lovers even the peristyle colonnade received an upper storey, something which is extremely rare at Pompeii. In the House of the Menander, whose wealthy owner was otherwise able to maintain the grand scale of the rooms round his *atrium* and peristyle (the great reception-room 18 was well over 7 metres high, and the rooms to the east of the *atrium* at least 5 metres), the rooms to the west of the *atrium* were lowered to accommodate an independent upstairs flat entered directly by a stairway from the street (entrance 5). Evidently by the middle of the first century AD pressures upon living space were forcing proprietors or

their tenants to build upwards. For the Menander upstairs flat, however, the motivation may have been largely commercial; the rent paid by the tenants would have been a useful supplement to the house-owner's income.

Secondly, there was an increasing tendency during the last century of the *insula*'s existence to open workshops, shops and bars along the street-fronts, often at the expense of the front rooms of houses; a good example is the two-roomed complex, perhaps a fullery, which was constructed in the adjacent corners of the Houses of the Menander and of the Cabinet-Maker (entrance 6). This tendency testifies not so much (as is frequently claimed) to the increasing strength of the small commercial classes in the city; commercial premises had long been thickly concentrated in other regions, notably in the old quarter and in the main streets of Region VI. It is due, rather, to increased traffic on the streets round our *insula* and to the need to service the increased population in this quarter of the city. As for the social functioning of the shops and workshops, some (the shop at entrance 17, and the presumed workshop at entrance 10) were linked to the houses behind them, and so were presumably operated by the householder, perhaps through a trusted slave or freedman. Others (9, 13), having originally been so

11.7 Peristyle of the House of the Lovers (1st century BC, with the upper storey added about a century later). The parapet round the garden contained a sunken channel which would have been planted with flowers

157

linked, were eventually closed off from the rest of the house, though they may still have remained under the same ownership, being operated by a freedman or perhaps rented out to a tenant. It is worth noting, however, that the trend towards the creation of shops was not entirely one-way, for at least two which had been open earlier were closed before the eruption. At the northeast corner, for example, the occupant of house 1, having been obliged to cede about 1.5 metres of his frontage to make space for a street-fountain, cashed in on the situation by opening a shop in his front room to sell wares to the water-carriers; later, however, perhaps in consequence of earthquake-damage in 62, the shop was blocked off once more to make a living-room.

Thirdly, there was a trend in the larger houses to expand backwards to obtain a garden and, where space allowed, to shift the residential focus of the house from the *atrium* to this garden. Thus houses 7 and 8 both acquired gardens at the expense of a pre-existing property to the south, then built dining-rooms with wide south-facing doorways to take advantage of the new amenity. In more spectacular fashion the gradual expansion of the House of the Menander provided the owner with a number of finely decorated rooms round the peristyle, while the rooms opening from the *atrium* were converted to store-rooms, service-rooms and slave-bedrooms. In the House of the Lovers, constructed from scratch about 50 BC, the initial lay-out already included a peristyle with eight rooms opening from it.

Fourthly, the property-boundaries within the *insula* show a remarkable degree of fluidity. We have already referred to some of the changes: the creation of house 18 out of the rear halves of houses 1 and 3, the destruction of an early house in the southeast quarter of the *insula* to make way for an enlargement of the House of the Menander, and the destruction of another early house to provide space for the House of the Lovers. What is especially interesting is the way in which odd rooms changed hands across contiguous boundaries: note, for example, how house 3 retained two or three rooms which jutted into the rear of house 18, and how the rooms off the east side of the Menander peristyle projected step-like into house 16. A similar jigsaw-like interlocking can be seen elsewhere, for example between houses 7 and 8 and the Menander kitchen-quarter. The House of the Menander even at one stage took over the whole of the House of the Cabinet-Maker, only to relinquish it later.

A full understanding of all these changes is of course impossible in the absence of specific information as to who owned what. It is not impossible that the proprietors of the House of the Menander, always the largest house, and apparently the one least trammelled by the claims of conflicting properties, owned the whole *insula*, or a large part of it; they could then, if they so wished, take over other houses when the leases expired. At the very least they had the financial resources to buy up other properties when they came on the market.

All this gives a glimpse of the kind of information obtainable from a detailed structural analysis of *insula* I 10. We may conclude by making a few remarks on the economic basis of the life of its inhabitants.

The wealth of the owner of the House of the Menander, self-evident from the scale of the house, from the luxury of its decorations, and from the hoard of 118 items of silver plate found stored in a cellar, placed him in the first rank of Pompeii's citizens; that its source was probably agriculture is suggested by the stable-yard area at the rear of the property, with its impressive number of slave-rooms and store-rooms, with its upstairs loading-bays overlooking the yard, and with finds which included the remnants of two carts, numerous storage jars, and an assortment of iron farm-tools. This was evidently the headquarters of an estate somewhere outside the city. We may guess that one of its chief forms of production was wine-growing, which was a source of wealth for many of Pompeii's leading families (wine-jars stamped with the names of Pompeian vineyards have been found in the south of France). It has been suggested that Q. Poppaeus Eros, whose skeleton was found on a bed in the room next to entrance 16, was the manager of the farming operation. This is rather doubtful, because the position of the bedroom and the modesty of its decoration suggest a doorkeeper rather than an important employee; but the name, which is revealed by the dead man's signet, indicates that he is a freedman of a certain Q. Poppaeus (on liberation he would have taken his master's family name while retaining his old name Eros as a surname). Q. Poppaeus may therefore have been the Menander's last owner. The Poppaei were an important clan in the Vesuvius region, and one branch of the family produced Nero's second empress Poppaea Sabina.

About the other houses we have limited information. The House of the Cabinet-Maker is so named from the discovery of wood-working tools, colouring equipment and the remains of bone appliqués for cabinets – clear indications of the anonymous craftsman's trade. The neighbouring house (8) yielded 53 lead loom-weights, and it is possible, though not certain, that weaving was being carried out there on a commercial basis. From the House of the Lovers, alas, there is no firm evidence for the proprietor's occupation, because most of the loose objects in the house were removed by plunderers before the exca-vations. The workshop 5 was perhaps a fullery, as implied by the remains of a couple of tanks at one corner. The shops 2 and 13 were certainly bars, being equipped with the characteristic counters contain-ing jars for food and drink. The upstairs flat 5 has been identified as a brothel on the strength of erotic graffiti inscribed on the walls of the stairway.

One of the important general features to emerge from this survey is the way in which the different classes rubbed shoulders in the city. A member of Pompeii's landed gentry, Q. Poppaeus, counted among his immediate neighbours small craftsmen, inn-keepers and a fuller; while an upstairs flat over part of his own property may, if the above-mentioned inference is correct, have been used by prostitutes. It is the opportunity of observing this remarkable social mixture that gives Pompeii its unique interest and makes the study of the available evidence for social patterns so rewarding. It is all the more regrettable that, for all the evidence that has been retrieved, much has been lost or has remained neglected over the 240 years since excavations began.

CHAPTER TWELVE
WINE FOR THE BARBARIANS
BARRY CUNLIFFE

Writing of the Gauls at the end of the first century BC the Greek historian Diodorus Siculus gives us an entertaining thumb-nail sketch: 'They are exceedingly fond of wine and sate themselves with the unmixed wine imported by merchants; their desire makes them drink it greedily and when they become drunk they fall into a stupor or into a maniacal disposition.' Diodorus goes on to tell us that the Italian merchants, with their usual desire for quick profit, look on the Gallic love of wine as their private source of wealth. The merchants 'transport the wine by boat on the navigable rivers and by wagon through the plains and receive in return for it an incredibly high price: for a single amphora of wine they receive a slave – a servant in exchange for a drink'. Elsewhere Diodorus adds further local colour by telling us something of the appearance of the Gauls:

> Some shave off the beard, while others cultivate a short beard; the nobles shave the cheeks but let the moustache grow freely so that it covers the mouth. And so when they are eating the moustache becomes entangled in the food and when they are drinking the drink passes as it were through a sort of strainer.

These endearing characteristics, and many others, were what was being communicated to the Roman audience about their warlike barbarian neighbours at the moment when the Roman state was poised to engulf them.

Moments of contact like this can provide rare insights into the social and economic systems at work in the past. In Gaul in the first century BC and early first century AD the impact of Rome on mature Celtic society is a particularly fruitful area of study, for not only do we have an array of contemporary texts like those quoted above but we also have a rapidly increasing body of archaeological evidence to control, enliven and expand the picture.

The port of Massilia (Marseilles), founded by Greek colonists *c.* 600 BC, firmly established the interest of the classical world in the Mediterranean coastal zone of Gaul, and within a few centuries daughter colonies had sprung up all around the coast from the River Ebro in Spain to the Maritime Alps on the borders of France and Italy. These maritime cities served two purposes: they provided ports of call for merchant ships using coastal waters and they served as contact points with the barbarian hinterland. Through them Greek imports could pass northwards to the barbarians in exchange for a variety of raw materials and slaves. For a brief period (*c.* 530–480 BC) this trade was brisk and Massilia, commanding the Rhône route to the north, played a significant role in it, but the Celtic migrations of the fifth century seriously disrupted these well-established networks.

At the end of the third century Rome was drawn into the affairs of the Greek cities of Gaul and Spain during the Second Punic War (218–202 BC). Southern Gaul provided the land route by which the Roman armies marched to the Spanish battlefront and the Carthaginian army, led by Hannibal, moved into the north of Italy to threaten Rome itself. By the end of the war the Roman leadership would have become all too aware of the vital importance of the route, not only to the security of Italy but in supplying the now-considerable military presence in Iberia where Rome was fast establishing provincial control.

From 200 BC, then, we find the Roman presence in the coastal strip becoming consolidated. The Greek cities were still free allies but they looked more and more to Rome for protection against the warlike hill tribes of the hinterland. On several occasions Roman armies had to be deployed to protect the cities and to keep the land routes open. In 154 BC, for example, envoys from Massilia appealed to Rome to beat back the Ligurian tribes who were threatening the cities of Nicaea (Nice) and Antipolis (Antibes). The problem was so serious that the Roman expeditionary force had to remain in the area throughout the winter.

Matters finally came to a head in 125 BC. This time the inhabitants of Massilia itself came under threat from the Saluvii, their northern neighbours. Successive Roman forces were sent and battles were fought deep into the hinterland, up the valley of the Rhône. By 121 BC, Roman control had been established over a very considerable territory, but now, instead of returning home, Rome stayed and within a few years southern Gaul was brought under Roman administrative control as the Province of Gallia Transalpina – the area we now know as Provence.

Military considerations must have featured large in Rome's decision to annex southern Gaul but it would be wrong to think that this was the sole consideration. Long-established contact with the area would have impressed upon the Roman mind its very considerable commercial possibilities. The land was comparatively fertile, at least in supporting a Mediterranean economy of olives, vines, and corn. (Generations of Roman quartermasters would have learnt this in their task of acquiring supplies for the Spanish campaigns.) More to the point, southern Gaul commanded two vital routes, a northern route via the Rhône valley to the river systems of western central Europe and a western route, via the

Carcassonne Gap, to the River Garonne and the Atlantic seaways. It is no surprise, therefore, that the new province thrust deep along these two routes, north, along the Rhône to the vicinity of Vienne and west to Toulouse. One of the first major acts of the Roman authorities in about 118 BC was to establish a citizen colony at Narbo (Narbonne) at the mouth of the Aude through which the trade between the Mediterranean and the western route could be channelled.

Beyond the limits of the province central France was populated by Celtic peoples generally known to the Romans as Gauls. To the west lay the Aquitani, an indigenous people lightly influenced by Celtic culture, while to the north, roughly between the rivers Seine and Rhine, were the Belgae – considered by Caesar, in the middle of the first century, to have been a hybrid group, basically Celtic but with some Germanic inter-breeding. It was the Celtic tribes of the centre, descended from the migratory Celts three centuries before, with whom the Romans came into immediate contact.

'The whole race', wrote Strabo, 'is war mad, high spirited and quick to battle, but otherwise straightforward and not of evil character'. He goes on to say:

> To the frankness and high-spiritedness of their temperament must be added the traits of childish boastfulness and love of decoration. They wear ornaments of gold, torcs on their necks, and bracelets on their arms and wrists, while people of high rank wear dyed garments besprinkled with gold. It is this vanity which makes them unbearable in victory and so completely downcast in defeat.

Until the period of Roman contact the Celts seem to have been organised in tribes comprising a number of chiefdoms. The paramount chief served as king and the elite maintained their prestige by deeds of valour and by displays of lavish consumption. The feast was the central ceremony by which social order was displayed and reaffirmed, as is attested by Athenaeus, writing in the first century AD.

> When a large number eat together they sit around in a circle with the most influential man in the centre . . . whether he surpass the others in warlike skill, or nobility of family, or wealth. Beside him sits the host, and next on either side the others in order of distinction. Their shieldmen stand behind them while their spearsmen are seated in a circle on the opposite side of the feast in common like their lords.

The passage is fascinating for the impression it gives of formality, but these occasions could quickly degenerate into violence.

> The Celts sometimes engage in single combat at dinner. Assembling in arms they engage in mock battle . . . but sometimes wounds are inflicted

and the irritation caused may even lead to the slaying of the opponent unless the bystanders hold them back.

Athenaeus goes on to give a tantalising insight into the causes of the aggression: '. . . in former times when the hindquarters were served up, the bravest hero took the thigh piece, and if another man claimed it they stood up and fought in single combat to the death.' Clearly, the feast was an occasion circumscribed by ritual. Each man was treated according to his status and if anyone objected the issue was settled there and then by a fight to the death if necessary.

It was at feasts of this kind that young men eager for prowess would plan raids into neighbouring territories and encourage others to follow: the larger their following the greater their prestige, and the better their chances of acquiring worthwhile booty to distribute. By Caesar's time the size of personal entourage that a man could call up, including followers, clients and family, was often a decisive factor in the quest for absolute power. Rivalry between powerful factions, therefore, kept Celtic society fragmented and weak.

In the 60 years or so between the subjugation of Transalpina and the campaigns of Julius Caesar, who began his conquest of the rest of Gaul in 58 BC, the Celtic tribes close to the province had learnt a lot from Rome – not least that alliance with Rome meant power in their intertribal conflicts. They had come to appreciate, too, that their divisive social systems were a distinct disadvantage when dealing with Roman envoys. By Caesar's time significant changes can be discerned in the socio-political structure of several of the border tribes, in particular the Aedui and Helvetii. The old concept of kingship was now ousted and the power of the entourage carefully curtailed. Tribes were ruled by annually elected magistrates and to aspire to kingship was a crime punishable by death. But for all these changes the Celts were still flamboyant barbarians, quick-witted, quick-tempered and hungry for the Mediterranean luxuries that gave them prestige.

Before exploring the relationship between Roman and barbarian we must pause to consider, all too briefly, what was happening to the Roman economy at this time. Rome's wars of conquest in the third and second centuries BC had totally upset the old order. Men had left the Italian countryside, where their families had for generations eked out a meagre existence, to serve for a term in the army, and had been reluctant to return afterwards, preferring instead to gravitate to the towns and in particular to Rome. The inevitable result was that vast tracts of countryside previously farmed as small holdings or family establishments were bought up by the wealthy and turned into huge estates. Land confiscated by the state for one reason or another was also acquired and further consolidations occurred. In the second century BC it was not unusual for a wealthy aristocrat living in Rome to own a

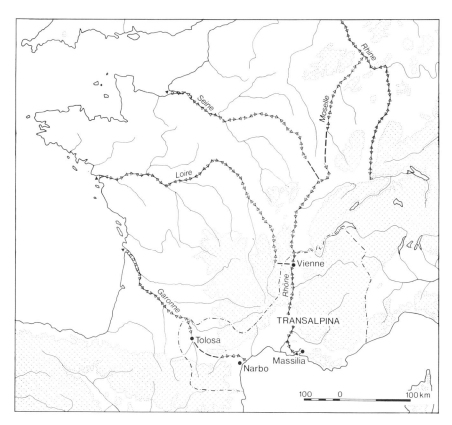

number of large estates scattered in various parts of the Italian peninsula.

Investment in land was a natural course for the aristocracy to take. It could be profitable but, more to the point, since involvement in commerce was frowned upon (though by no means prohibited), it was the principal way in which the rich could grow richer. One problem, however, was labour. Free labour was in comparatively short supply but could be hired in from neighbouring owner-occupied farms when pressure of seasonal work required it. For the most part, however, the large estates relied very heavily on a permanent slave-labour force overseen by a farm manager. Contemporary textbooks on agriculture abound with good advice on how to control the slaves to get the maximum amount of work out of them. Slaves, however, had a comparatively short life-span. It was necessary therefore to maintain a constant supply if the agrarian economy of Italy was to be kept in good order. To give some idea of the scale of the problem, on the island of Delos where a slave market was regularly held, it was not unusual for 10,000 slaves to change hands in a single day's trading! Many of these would have been put up for sale by pirates operating along the southern coasts of Asia Minor but elsewhere, and particularly after Pompey had destroyed the pirates, barbarian territories beyond the frontiers were the normal source of supply – augmented of course, during the wars of conquest, by native captives.

The Italian estates produced a variety of commodities for the home market. Those close enough to Rome concentrated on fresh fruit and vegetables while those further away grew corn, if they could, together with olives and vines. Most farms were mixed but a great many of them produced wine which was comparatively easy and cheap to make. The total yield is difficult to estimate but it is quite clear that by the first century BC many of the Italian estates were generating surpluses which their owners were intent on getting rid of in the rapidly expanding overseas markets.

Having sketched in the Italian background we can now return to the newly won province of Gallia Transalpina and to Diodorus' statement, with which we began: 'for a single amphora of wine they receive a slave'. Here is direct evidence of an exchange rate, one of the first we have for barbarian Europe. If we accept it at its face value it is extortionate. The Celt was getting a very bad deal. If he had taken his slave to a Roman slave market he might have expected to get 6 or 7 amphorae. But what we are seeing here is not so much a market transaction as gift exchange. A Celt receiving a valuable gift like an amphora of wine would reciprocate with an even more valuable gift such as a slave. If he failed to do so he would lose prestige.

In all probability the Celts into whose country Roman entrepreneurs penetrated were grossly exploited, as is usually the case in such situations. There was even a court case in which Cicero defended the governor Fonteius against accusations of corruption. From Cicero's speech we learn how a tax was charged at every town in southern Gaul through which consignments of wine passed, thus increasing its price with the journey. This was of no consequence, said Cicero, because the wine was destined to be sold to barbarians!

The Celts' insatiable appetite for wine is mentioned several times by classical writers. It impressed them, as did the barbarians' habit of drinking the wine undiluted! But, as Diodorus said, it was a godsend to the Roman merchants who saw this as a way of making rapid profits. It was also enormously beneficial to the estate owners of northern Italy since it provided a nearby market for them to dump their surplus wine and to acquire, in return, profitable slaves.

In recent years archaeological research in France and Britain has filled out the picture of the Roman wine trade in fascinating detail. A particularly vivid demonstration of the influence of the Romans has come from the study of pottery found in well-stratified settlement excavations in the Vaunage, just west of Nîmes. By working out the changes in percentage of different types over time it is possible to show two distinct trends: the dramatic increase in the percentage of Italian wine amphorae and the corresponding decrease in the percentage of local Massiliot amphorae (the Italian amphorae almost totally replacing the Massiliot by *c.* 120 BC), and from about 120 BC a very dramatic rise in the number of amphorae compared with other pottery on the site. The implications are clear enough – during the second century BC imported Italian wine ousted local wine and after the Roman conquest the overall consumption of wine greatly increased.

Interesting confirmation comes from a totally different source, the study of wrecks off the southern coast of France. If we assume, as it is surely safe to do, that the number of wrecks of a particular date are in direct proportion to the intensity of shipping at that date, then it is possible, simply by counting wrecks, to show when the shipping lanes were busiest. The evidence points clearly to a peak in the first century BC – the moment when trade with barbarian Gaul was being opened up.

It is comparatively easy, by studying the form and fabric of amphorae, to suggest roughly where and when they were made. The type of particular interest in the present context is called a Dressel 1 type (named after its classifier). There are two main subtypes: 1A and 1B. Precise dating is difficult, but since some 1A types were present at Carthage when it was destroyed in 146 BC the type must have originated before that date, and on various evidence it is thought to have gone out of common use soon after 50 BC. The 1B type, though beginning in the first half of the first century BC, only became common after the middle of the century and declined quickly in the early first century AD. Therefore as a rough and ready guide 1A amphorae generally date to before Caesar's campaigns in France while the 1B type is usually later. Fabric analysis has shown that both types were made at several locations in western Italy. Their presence is therefore an indication of trade with Italy.

Recent work by a number of French and British archaeologists has shown that both types of Dressel amphorae are widely distributed in France but their distribution is by no means even. There are colossal concentrations at Old Toulouse and at Chalon-sur-Saône, suggesting that both sites, both close to the boundary of the Roman Province – one on the western route, the other on the northern – were the places where the Italian wine was decanted into native barrels or leather containers for further trans-shipment to the native courts. But not all of the wine was dealt with in this manner, since several of the native *oppida* within easy reach of the frontier have produced quantities of amphorae – places like the capital of the Aedui at Bibracte (Mt Beuvray, near Autun). These important centres may well have been served by Roman traders bringing the amphorae in unopened. From here they would have been taken to the courts of the nobility for consumption at the feasts.

A further aspect of the distribution is the comparatively dense scatter along the Narbonne–Toulouse–Bordeaux route, up the Atlantic coast

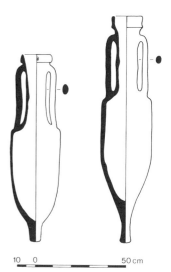

10 0   50 cm

12.2 Amphorae (wine jars) of the first century BC made in eastern Italy. In these containers wine was imported to the barbarian Celts in Gaul and southern Britain. The smaller vessel (Dressel type 1A) was common in the early 1st century BC, the larger one (Dressel type 1B) was widely used in the late 1st century BC

12.3 Hengistbury Head was one of the main ports of southern Britain engaging in overseas trade in the early 1st century BC. It was in easy reach of the Continent, and the rivers gave access to the densely settled areas of Wessex

of France, where several wrecks have been found, and at certain concentrations in Brittany, particularly around the Baie de Quiberon (near Vannes), around Quimper and at the promontory site of Saint Servin, in the estuary of the River Rance, near St Malo. The clear implication of this distribution is that loads of Italian wine were being carried across France by cart and river boat to the vicinity of Bordeaux where they were trans-shipped to sea-going vessels to be sailed northwards around the Bay of Biscay for the main ports and *oppida* of Armorica (Brittany). Since the Armorican massif is rich in metals, particularly silver and tin, it may fairly be assumed that these were some of the commodities that the Roman entrepreneurs were intent on acquiring. Some further credence is given to this idea by a brief reference to Publius Crassus, who, we are told by Strabo, tracked the Phoenician merchants in the Atlantic until he had discovered their routes to the metal-rich areas of the northwest. Thereupon he made the information widely available to his fellow Romans.

In 1971, David Peacock published a discussion of the Dressel 1 amphorae found in Britain, emphasising the comparatively large numbers of type 1A from a rather enigmatic site on Hengistbury Head, flanking Christchurch Harbour on the borders of Hampshire and Dorset. The site had been extensively trial-trenched in 1911–12 by J.P. Bushe-Fox and the results published soon afterwards; although there were some later excavations, it had been rather overlooked since then. In the light of the old discoveries, and of Peacock's reassessment of the amphorae, we developed a new research programme which began with a detailed restudy of all the material and proceeded, in 1979, to the first of a series of new excavations. Work is still proceeding but a brief summary of the results to date can be given.

Hengistbury is a headland lying between the open waters of the Solent and the well-protected, nearly land-locked, harbour of Christchurch. The harbour is really a large brackish-water lake into which the two principal rivers of Wessex, the Avon and the Stour, flow, the great volume of water now finding its way to the sea through a narrow channel called the Run – a name reflecting the hectic speed of flow. To prehistoric sailors and merchants Hengistbury had much to offer: it lay midway between two distinctive headlands at Ballard Point in Dorset and the Isle of Wight and was therefore comparatively easy to navigate towards; it had a safe well-protected harbour; and the two rivers leading deep into the heart of Wiltshire and Dorset provided easy access to the productive hinterland.

The site had been occupied on and off from *c.* 10,000 BC and in the early part of the Iron Age (roughly the eighth to sixth centuries BC) a fairly extensive settlement existed along the harbour shore, protected from the off-sea weather by the mass of the headland to the south. For the next 400 years occupation was sparse until some time about

100 BC, when the character of the site completely changed.

Midway along the northern shore is an area of marshland known as Rushy Piece, lying between two projecting ridges of gravel. It was potentially extremely interesting because here we stood a chance of finding waterlogged archaeological levels stratified within the silts and peats of the marsh. Not only was there the likelihood of survival of organic rubbish but it was also possible that here we might find evidence of sea-level fluctuation and of environmental change.

Our hopes were well rewarded. Deep in the marsh we found evidence to show that about 100 BC the site had lain in an intertidal zone of mudflats and that this had been dramatically modified by man. Some of the mud was dug away to create a deep water channel and at the inland end a sloping hard of gravel was laid, presumably so that ships could easily be beached. The gravel had been dug from the gravel promontory on either side.

Even more interesting were the well-preserved organic deposits found in the bottoms of contemporary ditches. Analysis of the debris has identified several beetles of the kind that infest stored food, together with a range of seeds amongst which the seeds of fig stand out as an imported exotic. There is no way that those figs could have reached

12.5 A pot of a kind made in north-west France and imported into Hengistbury in the early first century BC. Presumably they contained a commodity such as honey or pâté which the Britons wanted

12.6 Bead probably made in the Mediterranean and imported to Hengistbury by merchants eager to trade with the natives

Hengistbury other than on boats coming from the Mediterranean.

Against this must be seen the pottery and industrial debris found in contemporary layers on other parts of the site. As one might expect, Dressel 1 amphorae, particularly the 1A type, are comparatively common, but so too is a range of fine pottery made in Armorica and easily recognisable not only from its form but also from the distinctive mineral inclusions in its fabric. Together the amphorae and Armorican wares leave little doubt that Hengistbury was a major port, receiving cargoes of Italian wine sent northwards from the Garonne as well as cargoes of pots, presumably containing something desirable, loaded at the Armorican ports. How this trade was organised it is difficult to say. It could be that Garonne ships made the journey direct to Hengistbury, stopping off in Armorica en route to offload some amphorae and take on additional cargo; alternatively, they may have sailed only to the Armorican ports, leaving the final leg of the route to local Breton sailors who were more used to the treacherous waters of the Channel. What is clear is that in the first 50 years or so of the first century BC, Hengistbury Head was the place where Mediterranean luxuries were offloaded to be distributed to the courts of the British Celtic elite. We are unlikely ever to know the full range of the exotic imports. Italian wine, Mediterranean figs, Breton luxury foods in distinctive pots, have already been mentioned. In addition we have found chunks of imported glass, both purple and yellow, from some source, possibly in southern Gaul. There must have been much more besides – other foods, perhaps olives, fabrics, fine metalwork. The only direct evidence is the handle of a silver cup probably made in Gaul, but further excavation may well produce new finds.

The evidence for linking Britain ultimately to the Mediterranean in the first century BC is, then, extensive and indisputable. It is best understood in the context of Roman entrepreneurs penetrating and manipulating the long-established Atlantic trading routes for their own profit, much as Publius Crassus had intended when he explored these waters. But what commodities desirable to the Romans were extracted from Britain? In the early years of the first century AD the Greek geographer Strabo listed them as metals, hides, corn, slaves and hunting dogs. Against this checklist we can assess the archaeological data from the relevant levels at Hengistbury.

Evidence for metalworking is extensive – iron ore was extracted from the headland itself and smelted in the settlement. But more impressive is the evidence for the importation of metals and metal ores from further afield. A hoard of scrap gold was found in the earlier excavations, together with the hearths where silver was extracted from silver-rich lead which was probably brought in from the Mendips. Elsewhere in the excavation there is ample evidence of bronzeworking and one large block of copper ore was identified as having come from Callington on

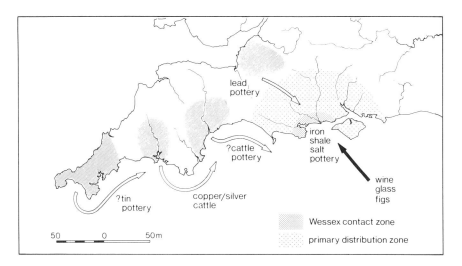

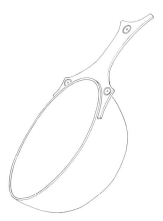 (map labels: lead / pottery; ?cattle / pottery; iron / shale / salt / pottery; wine / glass / figs; ?tin / pottery; copper/silver / cattle; Wessex contact zone; primary distribution zone; 50 0 50m)

12.7 At Hengistbury a wide range of goods were exchanged. Metals and other commodities came from the south west. Corn and possibly cattle and slaves were brought in from central Wessex while Mediterranean luxuries reached the port along the busy Atlantic seaways

the borders of Devon and Cornwall. Analysis of some of the recently found crucibles suggests that copper and tin ores were being smelted at the same time to make bronze. Taken together, the evidence shows that considerable quantities of metals were being brought to the site from all the major metal-producing areas of southwestern Britain, presumably to be exchanged for the Mediterranean luxury goods.

Two other pieces of evidence are of potential interest. A study of the cereal grains and weed seeds preserved at the site shows that in the first century BC corn was being brought in, some of it grown in non-local environments like the chalk downs. Here, then, is evidence to suggest that grain was collected and stockpiled for export. The animal bones, too, are interesting. Though not well preserved, it has been possible to assess the relative proportions of the different species on the basis of their teeth. What stands out is the unusually high percentage of cattle teeth. This is unlike normal finds in southern Britain from this period, and suggests the deliberate selection of cattle. Could it be that the teeth represent beasts driven from all over Wessex to Hengistbury, where they were killed and their hides salted for export? Broken salt containers were quite common on the site at this time. The suggestion is tenuous but might be supported (or rejected) when a larger sample of bones is available for analysis.

Finally, what of the slaves and hunting dogs mentioned by Strabo? For neither is there any evidence, nor could we reasonably expect it.

Standing back from the detail, Hengistbury emerges as a port-of-trade ideally situated to link the productive landscape of southern Britain to the maritime routes leading to the western Mediterranean and ultimately to Rome. The impact of trade on the native economy must have been considerable, for not only was a totally new range of

12.8 Handle of a silver cup of a kind in use in France in the 1st century BC. One of the items carried to Hengistbury for trade

171

luxury commodities made suddenly available to the elite of central southern Britain, but slaves became a marketable product, virtually overnight. The disruptive effects of all this on native society cannot yet be assessed in any detail, but there can be little doubt that these were significant factors in the process which led to the widespread upheaval, most obviously manifest in the abandonment of long-occupied hillforts, some time about or soon after 100 BC. The situation must, in many ways, have been analogous to the disruption caused by the initial European contact with West Africa and the slave trade which rapidly developed from it in the seventeenth and eighteenth centuries.

All the time that large areas of Gaul remained free the Atlantic route to Armorica and Britain provided one of the most convenient routes for the Roman entrepreneurs to manipulate. But all this changed in 58 BC, when Julius Caesar began the first stage of his conquest of Gaul. Within less than a decade Gaul up to the Rhine was under direct Roman control and, although it took a further 40 years for the vast territory to become fully integrated into the Roman Empire, new and more direct routes across the country to the Channel coast developed facilitating contact with still-barbarian Britain along a much wider front.

Not surprisingly, Atlantic trade began to decline, though it by no means ceased altogether. Dressel 1B amphorae are found in Armorica and at Hengistbury but in much smaller numbers than the earlier 1A forms. Clearly the direct flow of Italian wine to the West was drying up. This was to some extent compensated for by Spanish wine from Catalonia, imported in distinctive amphorae, but the quantity was never great. By now, however, the ports of eastern Britain had taken over and a few decades later Britain, too, became part of the Roman Empire, thus ensuring a plentiful supply of wine for all. After a few decades of Romanisation most Britons would have agreed with the anonymous Roman who scratched a graffito: 'Wine, women and baths corrupt our bodies – but these things make life itself.'

EPILOGUE

BARRY CUNLIFFE

The Graeco-Roman system, which had emerged by the eighth century BC, lasted for 1300 years, spreading from its Aegean origin to engulf the entire Mediterranean region and much of mainland Europe besides. By the beginning of the third century AD, however, it was in decline, and within 200 years the entire edifice had shattered, leaving a much modified fragment of itself, recently rooted at Constantinople, to continue to grow in almost hot-house isolation. This offshoot gave rise to the remarkable Byzantine civilisation, which survived until the fifteenth century, a very late and extenuated growth, oriental in aspect and very different from its sturdy central Mediterranean stock.

While Byzantium continued, Roman culture in Europe, North Africa and the Near East crumbled beneath the onslaught of innumerable barbarian inroads. The core had grown rotten: the political superstructure was incapable of supporting the edifice and the economic underpinning was beginning to fail. Against the increasing pressure from the barbarian hordes the empire simply gave way and fell in upon itself. It was all over in 50 years. Just as the Minoan–Mycenaean civilisation of the Aegean collapsed in the thirteenth century BC, so the Graeco–Roman civilisation of the Mediterranean fell in the fifth century AD. Both were followed by roughly two centuries of turbulent migration which archaeologists and historians refer to as Dark Ages.

Once the folk movements had died down new groupings began to crystallise out and, inevitably, new trading systems were established which linked them in a network of reciprocity and obligation. Small kingdoms, like that of Charlemagne, soon became states and so there arose, from the remnants of one civilisation, fertilised with new genes and new ideas, a wholly new civilisation – that of western Europe – different from its predecessor and yet deriving much of its substance from what had gone before.

In this book we have, quite deliberately, restricted our canvas to Europe in order to present a coherent theme in reasonable detail. The approach could well have been applied to many other regions of the world and wherever we had gone, to India, China or Middle America, we would have found many of the same general themes recurring – the rise of centres of innovation, the development of peripheries bound to

173

them in networks of exchange, the decay of the core, and the emergence of new innovatory foci – quite often in what had previously been a peripheral zone. Broad themes pervade but to state them so blandly is to belie the fascinating complexity of human behaviour.

It is the task of the archaeologist to sift through the detritus of the past and to create order from the chaos of other men's rubbish. In doing so he recognises patterns and changes, and from these, painstaking step by painstaking step, the picture of past societies is built up. Only then can we begin to see our own brief lives in a proper perspective.

```
┌─────────────────────────────────────────┐
│  ┌───────────────────────────────────┐  │
│  │                                   │  │
│  │                                   │  │
│  │        WHAT TO SEE                │  │
│  │                                   │  │
│  │                                   │  │
│  │                                   │  │
│  └───────────────────────────────────┘  │
└─────────────────────────────────────────┘
```

WHAT TO SEE

ISLAND ORIGINS: THE EARLY PREHISTORIC CYCLADES

It is in the nature of things that few of the sites mentioned here offer much of interest, after excavation, beyond their often very beautiful landscape settings. The three most completely excavated prehistoric sites in the Cyclades – Ayia Irini on Keos, Phylakopi on Melos, and Akrotiri on Santorini – are well worth a visit, although almost all of their standing visible remains belong to the Middle or Late Bronze Ages, rather than the earlier periods discussed in this chapter. Less accessible sites such as Kastri Chalandriani on Syros provide a memorable trip for the more adventurous and well-informed visitor. Most of the islands, however, have small museums, usually located in the main town, with important (if not always well displayed) collections of prehistoric finds. Daily ferryboats, and in some cases planes, serve all the larger islands during the summer season, and travel to the minor ones can generally be arranged in local caïques.

The finest and most representative collections of Neolithic and Early Bronze Age material are to be seen at the National Archaeological Museum in Athens and at the Archaeological Museum in Iraklion on Crete. An exciting new addition, however, is the Nicholas P. Goulandris Museum of Cycladic and Ancient Greek Art in the Kolonaki district of Athens, opened in a splendid new building in January 1986, whose primary focus is the art of the Early Bronze Age Cyclades. Outside Greece, many international museums – notably the British Museum in London, the Louvre in Paris, and the Metropolitan Museum of Art in New York – have significant prehistoric material from the Greek islands in their collections; the Badisches Landesmuseum at Karlsruhe in West Germany also has remarkable holdings. In Britain, the Ashmolean Museum in Oxford and the Fitzwilliam Museum in Cambridge contain small, but interesting, groups of finds.

CRETE: THE MINOANS AND THEIR GODS

The sites described in this chapter, apart from Akrotiri on the Cycladic island of Thera, are all located on Crete. They are best visited with P. Cameron, *Blue Guide: Crete* (4th ed., A. and C. Black, London, W.W. Norton, New York, 1986). Nearly all the objects discussed are in the

Archaeological Museum, Herakleion, Crete. The goddess statuette from Myrtos is in the Archaeological Museum, Aghios Nikolaos, Crete; some of the cult scenes engraved on gold rings, which have survived as impressions on burnt clay, are in the Archaeological Museum, Khania, Crete. There is a splendid and splendidly exhibited collection of Minoan antiquities in the Ashmolean Museum, Oxford, and other collections in the British Museum, London, the Museum of Fine Arts, Boston, the Metropolitan Museum, New York, and the University of Pennsylvania Museum, Philadelphia.

NEOLITHIC LAKE VILLAGES OF FRANCE

Since the sites are now submerged beneath the lakes there is little to be seen in the way of standing monuments. A modern reconstruction of a lake village has been built on the edge of Lake Constance at Unterhuldingen (West Germany). However, the site of Charavines arranges an annual open day for visitors. Those wishing to find out further information about this should write to:

> The Director
> Centre de Documentation de la Préhistoire Alpine
> 2, Rue Très Cloîtres
> 38000 GRENOBLE

The material from Clairvaux and the surrounding area can be seen at the museum at Lons-le-Saunier. The museum is open 10–12 a.m. and 2–5 p.m. except Tuesdays and public holidays. The address is:

> Musée de Lons-le-Saunier
> 25, Rue Richebourg
> 39000 LONS-LE-SAUNIER

A more general museum always worthy of a visit when in France is the National Antiquities Museum at St.-Germain-en-Laye on the outskirts of Paris. The address is:

> Musée des Antiquités Nationales
> 78100 Saint-Germain-en-Laye
> Paris

The museum is open from 9 a.m. to 5 p.m. except Tuesdays. It contains a magnificent collection of artefacts and reconstructions of the archaeology of all periods in France.

WARRIORS AND TRADERS:
BRONZE AGE CHIEFDOMS IN EUROPE

The Mycenaean sites of Pylos and Mycenae in Greece are visited by thousands of tourists each year, and are easily accessible. The less spectacular remains of Bronze Age fortified sites in central Europe are reached with greater difficulty and are unprepared for tourists. However, the old towns of Nitra and Košice in Slovakia – the southern province of Czechoslovakia – are well worth a visit as regional archaeological centres, and the northwards route through the Špis goes through outstanding scenery. The great museums for the bronze and gold hoards of the lowlands are the Hungarian National Museum in Budapest, the Deri Museum at Debrecen, both in Hungary, and the Regional Museum at Cluj and the National Museum at Bucharest in Romania. The British Museum and the Ashmolean Museum at Oxford contain examples of the decorated bronzework.

LEFKANDI AND THE GREEK DARK AGE

A small selection of the finds from the settlement and cemeteries is displayed in the Eretria Museum on the Greek island of Euboea, and it is proposed to exhibit the material from the Heroon burials in the National Museum in Athens. The Heroon building is at present not visible but there are plans for its consolidation and restoration.

THE SILVER MINES OF ATHENS

There is a wealth of classical art – marbles, bronzes, terracottas, and vases – much of it produced in Athens or under Athenian influence, to be seen in the great museums such as the National Archaeological Museum at Athens, the Louvre in Paris, the British Museum in London, the Metropolitan in New York, and in other comparable collections. But these and other museums contain very little directly derived from or related to the Laurion silver mines, apart from the Athenian coins in their numismatic collections. A visit to the area of southeastern Attica to view the remains on the ground is therefore essential. There by bus or car, visit on the coast: Thorikos (theatre, houses, washeries, galleries) at 2 kilometres north of Laurion itself; Puntazeza (smeltery site on the northern headland of the bay) at 4 kilometres south of Laurion, off the main road to Sounion; and ever-popular Sounion (temples on the headland, trireme-sheds below). Inland ascend by bus or car by paved road from Laurion to Kamariza (5 kilometres), then turn south to Hagia Triada church (3 kilometres) where an ancient washery lies open alongside the church and a large area of washeries and cisterns may be seen, half a kilometre southeast, down a branch from the paved road; by the unpaved track directly south from the church, visit washery compounds at Soureza (1 kilometre) and Agrileza (1 kilometre further). This route also passes through abandoned workings of modern times, so that one can see remains of the industrial archaeology of 2000 years ago and of the last 100 years, almost side by side.

KING PHILIP OF MACEDON

Visitors should begin with the display in the Archaeological Museum of

Thessaloniki, splendidly laid out and including the gold caskets from the tomb, the textiles, ivories, gold and silver and the armour (with the spectacular and well-restored display shield) – as well as the bones of Philip himself. (Also in the museum the impressive series of gold and other objects from the earlier tombs of Sindos, which reveal something of the background context to the development of Macedonia, should not be missed.) At Vergina itself the exterior of the tomb of Philip can be seen, but not the (less interesting) interior. The general area of the Iron Age cemetery, with its vast number of low tumuli, is best seen outside the village, along the road back to the coast and the National road. Above the village is the early Hellenistic palace, presumably replacing the earlier royal residence from which Philip made his way to the theatre and his assassination. The theatre has been excavated, and, though not impressive (its seats were wooden, not stone), this can be seen, as well as the adjacent sanctuary of Eukleia. At Pella only some town houses can be visited, and the museum. Philip's palace is some distance from this and not yet accessible to the public. There are other good Macedonian tombs at Lefkadia near Naoussa, which can be seen. The most accessible Macedonian tomb is that at Pydna, under a mound by the second parking place (going north) along the National road from the Katerine junction (a torch is advisable). Outside Macedonia the most spectacular monument to Philip is the great stone lion at Chaironeia in Boiotia, commemorating his victory over the Thebans and Athenians in 338 BC.

CARTHAGE: THE PUNIC CITY

The site of Carthage is largely built over as a suburb of Tunis, but its setting is one of great beauty with superb views across the Gulf of Tunis. Package-tour arrangements – a half-day coach outing from Tunis – generally involve a quick drive past the Tophet and ancient harbours with an ill-informed commentary, followed by a stop at the Roman baths where visitors are preyed upon by sellers of fake antiquities and general tourist rubbish.

A visit is best begun on the summit of the Byrsa Hill, where there are views of both sides of the Carthage peninsula and across the Gulf, with the ancient harbours in the low-lying coastal area in the foreground. To the side of the viewing point are the Late Punic houses and streets excavated by the French and behind is the Musée de Carthage. This has the best display of Carthaginian artefacts to be seen in Tunisia (the Bardo Museum at Tunis has some items but is mainly famous for its Roman mosaics and sculpture): particularly notable are some early figurines, *stelae* from the Tophet and two superb fourth-century tombs of a priest and priestess. Apart from the Byrsa, two other areas in Carthage are worth seeing for Punic remains: the harbours and Tophet (which are close to each other) and the German excavation site on the coast adjacent to the Avenue de la République. At the Circular Harbour it is worth crossing the bridge to the former island and asking to see the models housed in a small Antiquarium. At the Tophet a number of *stelae* are set out on the modern ground surface, but those in the deep excavation are in their original positions; sometimes this site is overgrown and little is visible, but it deserves a try. At the German excavation site the most interesting things to see are the vast boulders belonging to the fifth-century city wall, in a deep excavation near the sea, a reconstructed stretch of city wall with its decorative architectural moulding, and a collection of types of Punic flooring material house in one of two small covered buildings; here there are also models of the site and of the Punic quarries on Cap Bon (where the most common type of sandstone used in Carthaginian buildings was obtained).

Visiting these sites can be done on foot (about 20 minutes' walk between each of the areas referred to) and for those without their own car, the best transport from Tunis is the suburban train, the TGM (Salammbo or Dermech stations for the harbours/Tophet; Byrsa for the Byrsa; Hannibal for the German site). A charge is made for entry to the different sites.

Apart from Carthage itself and the Bardo Museum, the site of the Punic city of Kerkouane, situated on the tip of Cap Bon, is well worth a visit. Here, uniquely in the Punic world, the remains of houses, streets and the city defences can be seen in plan without the accretions of later centuries. The most notable intact piece of Punic architecture is the tomb of a Numidian prince at Dougga (demolished by a British explorer to obtain its bilingual inscription and later rebuilt by the French) while another museum with interesting Punic artefacts is that at Sousse.

A NEW LOOK AT POMPEII

The archaeological site at Pompeii is open to the public, at the time of writing, seven days a week from 9 a.m. to one hour before sunset. It is situated about 32 kilometres southeast of Naples and is accessible either from the amphitheatre gate in the modern town of Pompeii or from the Porta Marina (sea gate) to the west, immediately adjacent to the Circumvesuviana railway station Pompei Villa dei Misteri, alternatively called Pompei Scavi (on the line to Sorrento). The latter entrance can also be reached from the Pompeii exit of the motorway from Naples to Salerno. The site of Herculaneum (Ercolano), midway between Naples and Pompeii, is also open to the public; it is situated in the modern town of Resina (Circumvesuviana railway station Ercolano). Paintings, mosaics, statuary, domestic utensils and other materials from Pompeii, including the silver treasure from the House of the Menander, are on display in the National Archaeological Museum in Naples.

WINE FOR THE BARBARIANS

The best place to begin (of course) is southern France amid the monuments, museums and landscape of Provence and Languedoc. The new museum in the Bourse, in the centre of Marseilles, has a superb exhibition explaining the early development of the city as a trading port and you can actually look out across the ancient port, now laid out as an archaeological park. Not to be missed are the displays in the museums of Antibes and Fréjus. Narbonne, once the Roman Colonia of Narbo Martius, has an excellent museum full of pottery and inscriptions reflecting on its Roman commerce and industry. If you were to follow the trade route used by the Roman entrepreneurs you could visit the museums in Toulouse and Bordeaux, thence to Brittany, to the Bay of Quiberon and the nearby museum at Vannes. Traversing (or circumnavigating) Brittany the natural port of departure for the north then, as now, is St Malo. Close by, in the estuary of the River Rance, is the headland of St Servan, once a great Gallic trading port. Its counterpart in Britain is Hengistbury Head by Christchurch Harbour, an impressive natural headland with massive Iron Age banks and ditches defending it now from the urban sprawl of Bournemouth. At present the best place to see imported wine amphorae and the cups and plates which accompanied them is in the Prehistoric Britain gallery of the British Museum.

WHAT TO READ

The theme covered by this book is vast and all we can do here is to introduce the reader to some of the more useful general books.

Three volumes dealing with the entire span of European prehistory can be particularly recommended: S. Piggott, *Ancient Europe* (Edinburgh, 1965); P. Phillips, *The Prehistory of Europe* (London, 1980); T. Champion, C. Gamble, S. Shennan and A. Whittle, *Prehistoric Europe* (London, 1984).

For the different periods of European prehistory see: A. Whittle, J.M. Coles and A.F. Harding, *The Bronze Age in Europe* (London, 1979); J. Collis, *The European Iron Age* (London, 1984); B. Cunliffe, *The Celtic World* (London, 1979). The Mediterranean has been thoroughly covered by P. Phillips, *Early Farmers of West Mediterranean Europe* (London, 1975) and D.H. Trump, *The Prehistory of the Mediterranean* (London, 1980). The question of the Neolithic and Bronze Age innovatory society in the Aegean is treated with great skill by Colin Renfrew in *The Emergence of Civilization* (London, 1972). For the later period the standard work is J. Boardman, *The Greeks Overseas* (London, enlarged edition 1980). As to the Romans the literature is vast but two books present a general view in heavily illustrated form: T. Cornell and J. Matthews, *Atlas of the Roman World* (London, 1982) and B. Cunliffe, *Rome and her Empire* (London, 1978). Having got this far you may like to follow up the individual chapters with more specialist reading.

ISLAND ORIGINS: THE EARLY PREHISTORIC CYCLADES

The most comprehensive introductions to the prehistoric Cyclades are C. Renfrew, *The Emergence of Civilisation* (London, 1972) and J. Thimme and P. Getz-Preziosi (eds.), *Art and Culture of the Cyclades* (Karlsruhe, 1977). C. Doumas' catalogue to accompany the exhibition of the N.P. Goulandris Collection, *Cycladic Art* (London, 1983), emphasises the remarkable art, but also outlines what is known of the people of the Cyclades in the Early Bronze Age and of their material culture. Summaries of the most recent work on the prehistoric Cyclades can be found in two collections of conference papers: J.L. Davis and J.F. Cherry (eds.), *Papers in Cycladic Prehistory* (Los Angeles, 1979), and

181

J.A. MacGillivray and R.L.N. Barber (eds.), *The Prehistoric Cyclades* (Edinburgh, 1984). The latest information on the colonisation of the Greek islands may be found in J.F. Cherry's paper in *Proceedings of the Prehistoric Society* 47 (1981) 41–68. M. Gorman's *Island Ecology* (London, 1979) forms a convenient introduction to biological and geographical ideas about insular populations.

CRETE: THE MINOANS AND THEIR GODS

B. Rutkowski, *Cult Places in the Aegean* (London and New Haven, 1986), is a substantial and up-to-date survey of Aegean religion, illustrated. Of older works still fundamental are Sir Arthur Evans, *The Palace of Minos at Knossos*, vols. I–IV (and Index) (London, 1921–36), A.W. Persson, *The Religion of Greece in Prehistoric Times* (Berkeley and Los Angeles, 1942) and M.P. Nilsson, *The Minoan–Mycenaean Religion and its Survival in Greek Religion* (2nd ed. London, 1950). R. Hägg and N. Marinatos, eds., *Sanctuaries and Cults in the Aegean Bronze Age* (Stockholm, 1981) is the publication of a recent conference in Athens, with an exciting and richly illustrated series of papers giving up to date information and discussion of many recently excavated Minoan and Aegean religious sites. G. Gesell, *Town, Palace and House Cult in Minoan Crete* (Göteborg, 1985) is a new, thorough and fully illustrated presentation of a major class of Minoan shrines and their contents. Some other publications have recently provided rich and sometimes controversial evidence of religion, from three sites in Crete, from Akrotiri in Thera and from Phylakopi on the island of Melos. The two last are N. Marinatos, *Art and Religion in Thera* (Athens, 1984), richly illustrated in colour, and C. Renfrew and others, *The Archaeology of Cult: The Sanctuary at Phylakopi* (British School at Athens, London, 1985), with a far-ranging discussion of the Phylakopi sanctuary within a wider religious perspective. From Crete come N. Platon, *Zakros: The Discovery of a lost Palace of ancient Crete* (New York, 1971), with beautiful colour illustrations of the wealth of objects from the shrine treasury of the palace; J. and E. Sakellarakis, 'Drama of Death in a Minoan Temple,' *National Geographic* 159 no. 2 (February 1981), 204–222, with remarkable evidence for human sacrifice; P. Warren, *Archaeological Reports for 1980–81*, 27 (1981), 73–92 (British School at Athens, London), and in *Archaeology* 37 no. 4 (1984), 48–55, where the remains of mutilated and apparently sacrificed Minoan children are presented and discussed, together with a series of ritual vessels.

NEOLITHIC LAKE VILLAGES OF FRANCE

Inevitably, most of the literature published on the lake villages is in French. For those who can read French the best general account is Pierre Pétrequin's *Gens de l'eau; gens de la terre* (Paris, 1984). A good general account of Charavines can be found in the French popular magazine *Histoire et archéologie* No. 64, 1982 under the title 'La vie au néolithique: Charavines un village au bord d'un lac il y a 5,000 ans.' This is written by the excavator, Aimé Bocquet, and contains good colour photographs and reconstructions of the village. English accounts of the French Neolithic for most areas of France can be found in *Ancient France 6000–2000 BC*, edited by Christopher Scarre (Edinburgh, 1985). A good general account of the contemporary situation in Switzerland can be found in the Ancient Peoples and Places volume, *Switzerland from earliest times to the Roman conquest* by Marc-R Sauter (London, 1976).

WARRIORS AND TRADERS:

BRONZE AGE CHIEFDOMS IN CENTRAL EUROPE

There is no up to date summary of all the aspects covered in this chapter. A major illustrated monograph is M. Gimbutas, *Bronze Age Cultures in Eastern and Central Europe* (Mouton, 1965), though many of its views are now outdated. For the Mycenaean world a recently reissued book of the same vintage is W. Taylour, *The Mycenaeans* (London, 1984). In the same series as the last, R.F. Hoddinott, *The Thracians* (London, 1981) includes an account of Bronze Age developments. A.F. Harding's *The Mycenaeans and Europe* (London, 1984) offers a minimalist view of Mycenaean contacts with Europe; the contrary view is expressed in a long article by J. Vladar in *Slovenská Archeologia* for 1973 ('Osteuropäische und mediterräne Einflüsse im Gebiet der Slowakei während der Bronzezeit'). K. Kristiansen gives a stimulating account of the contacts between Denmark and the Carpathian Basin in the Bronze Age in an article entitled 'Economic models for Bronze Age Scandinavia' in B.A.R. *Int. Ser.* 96 (*Economic Archaeology*, edited by A. Sheridan and G. Bailey). A more extended account of some of my own arguments is given in A.G. Sherratt, *Drinking and Driving: Bronze Age Status Symbols* (University of Edinburgh Occasional Papers in Archaeology, 1987). A fold-out chart of the new radiocarbon chronology is available from the Ashmolean Museum, Oxford, under the title *Ancient Times*.

LEFKANDI AND THE GREEK DARK AGE

An outline account of the Bronze Age settlement on Xeropolis is given in *Excavations at Lefkandi, Euboea 1964–66*, edited by M.R. Popham and L.H. Sackett and published for the British School at Athens (London, 1968), while the excavation and finds from the Iron Age levels and the cemeteries are fully published and illustrated in *Lefkandi I: The Iron Age Settlements and Cemetaria Plate and Text Volumes*, edited by M.R. Popham, L.H. Sackett and P.G. Themelis (London, 1979–80). The same authors, joined by E. Touloupa, describe the subsequent dig in 'Further Excavation of the Toumba Cemetery at Lefkandi, 1981' in

183

The Annual of the British School at Athens, vol. 77 (1982), pp. 213–248 and describe the finding of the Heroon in 'The Hero of Lefkandi', *Antiquity* LVI (1982), pp. 169–174. A later account, in Greek, in the *Journal of Euboean Studies* (1984–5), pp. 253–269, 'Excavations at Lefkandi, Euboea 1981–4' (in Greek) by P.G. Kalligas, offers some differing interpretations of the Heroon building and of the nature of the settlement.

Two excellent surveys of the Early Iron Age have been given by A.M. Snodgrass, *The Dark Age of Greece* (Edinburgh, 1971) and by V.R.d'A. Desborough, *The Greek Dark Age* (London, 1972), both taking account of the Lefkandi excavations.

THE SILVER MINES OF ATHENS

There is no lack of books in English on the social and political history of Athens: e.g. R. Flacelière, *Daily Life in Greece in the time of Pericles* (London, 1965); J.C. Stobart, *The Glory That Was Greece* (London, 1962); C.M. Bowra, *Periclean Athens* (London, 1971); Rex Warner, *Men of Athens* (London, 1972); T.B.L. Webster, *Athenian Culture and Society* (London, 1973); J.A.C.T. *The World of Athens* (Cambridge, 1984).

The topography and monuments of the city are also well covered, to cite only I.T. Hill, *The Ancient City of Athens* (London, 1953); Angelo Procopiou, *Athens, City of the Gods* (London, 1964); R.J. Hopper, *The Acropolis* (London, 1971); J. Travlos, *The Topographical Dictionary of Ancient Athens* (New York, 1971); and R.E. Wycherley, *The Stones of Athens* (Princeton, 1978). However, there is no book in English specifically about the silver mines of Athens; some discussion of technical aspects is found in J.F. Healy, *Mining and Metallurgy in the Greek and Roman World* (London, 1978) and of historical and organisational aspects in R.J. Hopper, *Trade and Industry in Classical Greece* (London, 1979). The best recent full-scale account is Constatin E. Conophagos, *Le Laurium antique et la technique grecque de la production de l'argent* (Athens, 1980), which includes a brief description of the Soureza excavations, appears also in a Greek version; it replaces Ed. Ardaillon, *Les Mines du Laurium dans l'antiquité* (Paris, 1897), which is still the classic account of the knowledge gained in the nineteenth century about the silver mines.

The publications of the Belgian Archaeological Mission in Greece discuss mining activities at the town site of Thorikos: see H.F. Mussche, *Thorikos: a Guide to the Excavations* (Brussels, 1974) or the updated German version, *Thorikos, Fuhrung durch die Ausgrabungen* (Gent-Nurnberg, 1978), and also individual articles in the volumes of interim reports entitled *Thorikos*, e.g. Paule Spitaels, 'The Early Helladic Period in Mine no. 3 (Theatre Sector)' in the latest volume, *Thorikos* VIII (Gent, 1984). Thorikos VII 1970/71 (Gent, 1978), contains an article discussing the photogrammetic survey of the theatre, and one on a house site in the Industrial Quarter, while *Thorikos* VIII 1972/76 (Gent, 1984) has reports on two Bronze Age tombs on the summit, one of the Geometric period cemeteries, and the mine gallery near the theatre. Recent articles in English by J. Ellis Jones on various aspects of the Athenian mines are: 'The Laurion Silver Mines: a Review of Recent Researches and Results' in *Greece and Rome* (second series) vol. 29 (1982), pp. 169–183; 'Ancient Athenian Silver Mines, dressing floors and smelting sites' in *Historical Metallurgy* (Journal of the Historical Metallurgy Society), vol. 18 (1984), pp. 65–81; and 'Laurion: Agrileza, 1977–1983: Excavations at a Silver Mine Site' in *Archaeological Reports* of the Hellenic Society and British School at Athens, no. 31 for 1984–85 (London, 1985), pp. 106–123.

KING PHILIP OF MACEDON

There is a good, well-illustrated and comprehensive popular account of the discoveries at Vergina by the excavator: Manolis Andronikos, *Vergina: The Royal Tombs* (Athens, 1984) in both Greek and English versions. Accounts of early archaeological discoveries at Vergina by Leon Heurey and Henri Daumet are given in their work, *Mission Archéologique de Macedoine* (Paris, 1876). The fullest historical account of Philip and his times is in N.G.L. Hammond and G.T. Griffith, *A History of Macedonia, volume II* (Oxford, 1979). The section on Philip (by Griffith) is serious and scholarly but very readable and exciting. (Volume I, by Hammond, describes the geography and earlier history of Macedonia.) Some account of Macedonian tombs and their architecture is in A.W. Lawrence, *Greek Architecture* (4th ed., London, 1983, pp. 270–275). A brief account and a plan of excavations at Pella have been published in *Archaeological Reports* for 1984–5, p. 44.

CARTHAGE: THE PUNIC CITY

The best introduction to the Phoenicians and Carthage is D.B. Harden, *The Phoenicians* (London, 1971). There is no book in English about the archaeology of Punic Carthage. S. Tlatli, *La Carthage Punique* (Paris, 1978) is the most up to date, written by a former director of the Institut National d'Archéologie et d'Arts at Tunis and displaying the author's combined expertise as a geograher and ancient historian. G.C. and C. Picard, *The Life and Death of Carthage* (London, 1968, translated from the French) and B.H. Warmington, *Carthage* (London, 1960), make references to archaeological evidence but are mainly narrative historical accounts and are now out of date, having been written before the UNESCO Save Carthage project. The chapters by L.E. Stager on the Tophet and S. Lancel on Late Punic town planning and domestic architecture in J.G. Pedley (ed.), *New Light on Ancient Carthage*

(Michigan, 1980) provide excellent up-to-date accounts of these aspects of Carthaginian archaeology. Evidence for the harbours is summarised in H. Hurst and L.E. Stager, 'A metropolitan landscape: the Late Punic Port of Carthage', *World Archaeology*, IX (1978), pp. 334–346, and the reconstruction of the naval harbour is discussed in H. Hurst, 'Excavations at Carthage 1977–8: Fourth Interim Report', *Antiquaries Journal*, LIX (1979), pp. 19–49. The important German excavations are described in F. Rakob, 'Deutsche Ausgrabungen in Karthago, Die Punischen Befunde', *Mitteilungen des Deutschen Archaeologischen Instituts, Romische Abteilung*, Band 91 (1984). Annual summaries of work at Carthage in the UNESCO campaign are published in CEDAC Bulletins 1–7 (obtainable from INAA, Musée de Carthage, Carthage).

A NEW LOOK AT POMPEII

The best general book on the buried cities is T. Kraus and L. von Matt, *Pompeii and Herculaneum: the Living Cities of the Dead* (New York, 1975). Also valuable are the various editions of the exhibition catalogue *Pompeii 79* (London, 1976; Boston, 1978) edited by J.B. Ward-Perkins and A. Claridge. Brief popular surveys are M. Grant, *Cities of Vesuvius: Pompeii and Herculaneum* (London, 1971); A. De Franciscis, *The Buried Cities: Pompeii and Herculaneum* (London, 1978); and R. Seaford, *Pompeii* (London, 1978). Still an important synopsis, though excluding the twentieth-century excavations, is A. Mau, *Pompeii, its Life and Art* (trans. F.W. Kelsey, 2nd edn., New York, 1902). Specifically on the British work in the Insula of the Menander: see articles by the present writer in *Current Archaeology* VII (1982–84), pp. 55–61, and *Antiquaries Journal* LXII (1983), pp. 34–57.

WINE FOR THE BARBARIANS

The only general book to include the theme covered in this chapter is Barry Cunliffe, *Greeks, Romans and the Barbarian West* (London, 1987). For a study of Italian wine we now have a masterly work by André Tchernia, *Le Vin de l'Italie Romaine* (École Française de Rome, 1986) which must be the starting point. A volume of essays edited by P. Garnsey, K. Hopkins and C.R. Whittaker, *Trade in the Ancient Economy* (London, 1983), contains much that is relevant to the theme. The literature on shipwrecks is considerable but André Tchernia's 'The Roman wreck of La Madrague de Giens' in *Progress in Underwater Science* 3, pp. 19–24, is a useful introduction. Several useful papers, especially those by Patrick Galliou and David Peacock, are to be found in a volume edited by Sarah Macready and Hugh Thompson entitled *Cross-Channel Trade between Gaul and Britain in the Pre-Roman Iron Age* (London: Society of Antiquaries, 1984). Two useful (but very detailed) discussions of the distribution of Roman wine amphorae in

France are: Patrick Galliou, *Corpus des amphores découvertes dans l'ouest de la France* (Brest: Archéologie en Bretagne, Brest 1982) and Andrew Fitzpatrick, 'The Distribution of Dressel 1 amphorae in North-West Europe,' in *Oxford Journal of Archaeology* 4:3 (1985), pp. 305–40. The port of Hengistbury Head is reviewed in Barry Cunliffe, *Hengistbury Head* (London, 1978) and the results of the recent excavations are given in detail in the same author's *Hengistbury Head, Dorset. Volume 1: The prehistoric and Roman settlement, 3500 BC–AD 500* (Oxford University Committee for Archaeology, 1987).

CONTRIBUTORS

John Cherry is University Lecturer in Classical Archaeology at the University of Cambridge and Fellow of Fitzwilliam College, where he also directs studies in Archaeology and Anthropology, and in Classics. He has undertaken fieldwork in Greece, Italy, Yugoslavia, England and the USA. His main general research interests are the prehistoric archaeology of the Aegean, especially the development of Minoan civilisation, the archaeology of islands, archaeological field surveys, and computers and archaeology.

Barry Cunliffe is Professor in European Archaeology at the University of Oxford where he is currently Professor in Charge of the Institute of Archaeology. He has excavated widely in Britain, at Fishbourne, Danebury, Bath and Hengistbury. His research interests include the relationships between classical and barbarian societies and urbanisation. He enjoys broadcasting and writing books on archaeology for the general public.

John Ellis Jones is a Senior Lecturer in Classics and the Curator of the Museum of Welsh Antiquities at the University College of North Wales in Bangor. He was a Student of the British School at Athens in 1954–55 and has assisted at many British excavations in Greece, at Emborio on Chios and at Knossos in Crete, and at Belgian excavations at Thorikos in Attica. He has also directed excavations at classical house sites in Attica in the 1960s and more recently (1977–83) at a mining site in the Laurion area.

John Howell read Prehistoric Archaeology with Stuart Piggott at the University of Edinburgh before undertaking his doctorate at St John's College, Oxford. He is an Honorary Research Fellow at the University of Liverpool. He is now employed as a tax consultant but still writes and researches on the early agriculture of western and eastern Europe, in both of which areas he has broadcast for BBC Radio 4 in the Origins series.

Henry Hurst is a lecturer in Classical Archaeology at the University of

Cambridge. His main research interest is urban archaeology, both in Britain and the ancient Mediterranean. He directed the British excavation at Carthage and is currently excavating in the Roman Forum at Rome.

Roger Ling is a Reader in the University of Manchester. He has excavated on Roman and medieval sites in Britain and Italy, has conducted survey work in Turkey, and has been field director of the British research project at Pompeii for the past ten years.

Mervyn Popham was Macmillan Student and Assistant Director at the British School of Archaeology at Athens and then Associate Professor at the University of Cincinnati before coming to Oxford as Lecturer in Aegean Archaeology and Fellow of Linacre College. He has directed and co-directed excavations at Knossos and Palaikastro in Crete as well as at Lefkandi in Euboea. His special interests are late Minoan pottery and the Dark Ages.

Andrew Sherratt is in charge of the prehistoric European collections in the Ashmolean Museum and teaches archaeology in the University of Oxford. He is particularly interested in the relationships between European and Near Eastern cultures in early times, and he has carried out fieldwork in Hungary.

Richard Tomlinson is Professor of Ancient History and Archaeology at the University of Birmingham, and editor of the Annual of the British School at Athens. His research interests are in Classical Architecture, particularly of the Hellenistic period, where he has made special studies of vaulting techniques. He has conducted excavations at the Sanctuary of Hera, at Perachora.

Peter Warren is Professor of Ancient History and Classical Archaeology at the University of Bristol and a former Chairman of the British School at Athens. His research field is Aegean Prehistory, in particular the Minoan civilisation of Crete. He has directed excavations in the island at Myrtos, Debla and Knossos.

INDEX

PICTURE CREDITS

940 ORI
Origins

✓